# DEMOCRATIC PARTICIPATION AND CIVIL SOCIETY IN THE EUROPEAN UNION

Manchester University Press

**EUROPE IN CHANGE** SERIES EDITORS: THOMAS CHRISTIANSEN AND EMIL KIRCHNER

Dawid Friedrich

# DEMOCRATIC PARTICIPATION AND CIVIL SOCIETY IN THE EUROPEAN UNION

**MANCHESTER UNIVERSITY PRESS**
Manchester and New York

*distributed in the United States exclusively*
*by Palgrave Macmillan*

The right of Dawid Friedrich to be identified as the author of this work has been asserted by him in accordance with the Copyright, Designs and Patents Act 1988.

Published by Manchester University Press
Oxford Road, Manchester M13 9NR, UK
and Room 400, 175 Fifth Avenue, New York, NY 10010, USA
www.manchesteruniversitypress.co.uk

Distributed in the United States exclusively by
Palgrave Macmillan, 175 Fifth Avenue, New York,
NY 10010, USA

Distributed in Canada exclusively by
UBC Press, University of British Columbia, 2029 West Mall,
Vancouver, BC, Canada V6T 1Z2

British Library Cataloguing-in-Publication Data
A catalogue record for this book is available from the British Library

Library of Congress Cataloging-in-Publication Data applied for

ISBN      978 0 7190 8354 9 hardback

First published 2011

The publisher has no responsibility for the persistence or accuracy of URLs for any external or third-party internet websites referred to in this book, and does not guarantee that any content on such websites is, or will remain, accurate or appropriate.

Typeset
by Action Publishing Technology Ltd
Printed in Great Britain
by CPI Antony Rowe Ltd, Chippenham, Wiltshire

# CONTENTS

# *Figures and Tables*

## Figures

## Tables

| | |
|---|---|
| BDI | *Bundesverband Deutscher Industrie* (German Association of Industries) |
| CBI | Confederation of British Industry |
| CCME | Churches' Commission for Migrants in Europe |
| CEEP | *Centre européen des entreprises à participation publique et des entreprises d'intérêt économique général* (European Centre of Enterprises with Public participation and of Enterprises of General Economic Interest) |
| CEFIC | European Chemical Industry Council |
| CFI | Court of First Instance |
| CoFR | Charter of Fundamental Rights |
| CONECCS | Consultation, the European Commission and Civil Society |
| CoR | Committee of the Regions |
| CSO | Civil society organisation |
| DG | Directorate-General |
| EC | European Community |
| ECAS | European Citizens Action Service |
| ECIC | European Chemical Industry Council |
| ECJ | European Court of Justice |
| ECRE | European Council on Refugees and Exiles |
| EEB | European Environmental Bureau |
| EESC | European Economic and Social Committee |
| EFTA | European Free Trade Association |
| EIRR | European Industrial Relations Review |
| EMCEF | European Mine, Chemical and Energy Workers' Federation |
| ENAR | European Network Against Racism |
| EP | European Parliament |
| ETI | European Transparency Initiative |
| ETUC | European Trade Union Confederation |
| EWC | European Works Councils |
| FECC | European Association of Chemical Distributors |
| FoE | Friends of the Earth |
| ILGA | International Lesbian and Gay Association |
| ILPA | Immigration Law Practitioners' Association |
| ILR | International Labour Review |
| IPM | Interactive Policy-Making |

| | |
|---|---|
| JHA | Justice and Home Affairs |
| MEP | Member of the European Parliament |
| MPG | Migration Policy Group |
| NGO | Non-governmental organisation |
| OECD | Organisation for Economic Cooperation and Development |
| QMV | Qualified-majority voting |
| REACH | Regulation on the Registration, Evaluation, Authorisation and Restriction of Chemicals |
| RIPs | REACH Implementation Projects |
| SEA | Single European Act |
| SEMDOC | Statewatch European Monitoring and Documentation Centre on Justice and Home Affairs in the EU |
| SME | Small- and Medium-sized Enterprise |
| SPORT | Strategic Partnerships on REACH Testing |
| TCN | Third-country national |
| TEC | Treaty of the European Communities (Nice Version) |
| UEAPME | *Union européenne de l'artisanat et des petites et moyennes enterprises* (European Association of Craft, Small- and Medium-sized Enterprises) |
| UNECE | United Nations Economic Commission for Europe |
| UNHCR | United Nations High Commissioner for Refugees |
| UNICE | *Union des confédérations de l'industries et des employeurs d'Europe* (Union of Industrial and Employers' Confederations of Europe), renamed BusinessEurope |
| VCI | *Verband Chemischer Industrie* (Association of German Chemical Industry) |
| WTO | World Trade Organization |
| WWF | World Wide Fund for Nature |

# *A*CKNOWLEDGEMENTS

Without the support of many wonderful and helpful people, this book would not have been accomplished. This project began as my Ph.D. dissertation at the Bremen International Graduate School of Social Sciences (BIGSSS) at the University of Bremen. Thus, thanks are very much due to my supervisors, Patrizia Nanz and Markus Jachtenfuchs. They both left their profound marks on this project through the discussions with them and through their own work on the European Union, Civil Society and legitimate governance beyond the nation-state. My material base was secured by a generous scholarship of the Hans-Boeckler Foundation.

Although it is often said that the time of writing a book is a time of loneliness, this was not the case with me. I owe this, in great part, to the infrastructure of BIGSSS, which succeeded in bringing together a number of young, bright and friendly people, several of whom became close friends. I also benefited from the people and the resources of the Collaborative Research Centre 597 'Transformations of the State', particularly from Jens Steffek and Claudia Kissling, and wish to thank the close company that I received when finishing the project at the Institute for Intercultural and International Studies (InIIS), University of Bremen. Last, but not least, my colleagues at the Centre for the Study of Democracy, at the Leuphana University of Lüneburg, greatly facilitated my settling into a new environment so that I could finish this manuscript.

After some years of working on one topic, there is a great danger of becoming short-sighted with regard to one's own errors and inconsistencies. Thus, external scrutiny is essential to avoid the all too obvious mistakes. I am particularly indebted to the members of my book-completion working group, Kerstin Blome, Ralf Bendrath, Kristina Hahn and Silke Weinlich. I profited enormously from their expertise, thorough reading, and precise criticism of the individual chapters of this book as well as from their collegial understanding of the difficulties of getting it done. Furthermore, three friends and colleagues of mine were so kind as to spend a considerable amount of time reading the monograph as a whole. This invaluable effort by Christian Möllmann, Thomas Richter and Christian Völkel offered me crucial input for the overall coherence, strengths and weaknesses of the work. Also extremely beneficial to the overall work were the precise and constructive comments made by many colleagues both on conference papers and on the individual chapters of the book. My special thanks go particularly to Nadja Meisterhans, as well as to Robin Celikates, Nicole Deitelhoff, Matthias Freise, Sandra Kröger, Thomas Pfister, Carlo Ruzza, Stijn Smismans and Jens Steffek. My Teutonic English was significantly improved by Chris Engert and I thank him for his efforts. I apologise to all whom I have forgotten to name personally. Clearly, all the remaining inadequacies of this book are my responsibility alone.

I do not have the appropriate words to express my indebtedness to the encouragement of my family. More than others, it was Katinka's company, and, since her birth, also Maresa's, which made the years of writing this book a valuable experience full of joy and adventure.

Dawid Friedrich
Lüneburg, May 2010

For Katinka

*'Light is the only thing that can sweeten our political atmosphere ... light that will open to view the innermost chambers of government'*

(Woodrow Wilson 1884)*

*Cited in Curtin 1996: 96.

# 1

# Introduction: participation and democracy in the postnational age

## The basic question: democratisation through the participation of organised civil society?

The modern democratic state is a remarkable example of the immense power which an intimate relation between a normative ideal and specific institutional practices possesses. Within the territorial boundaries of the modern nation state, unprecedented social and political congruence have emerged, resulting in significant achievements of security and prosperity, at least in the OECD world. But this 'national constellation' (Habermas 1998) is faltering, and, with it, so is the proximity of democracy and the state. Processes of de-nationalisation and de-parliamentarisation (Zürn 2000) challenge the democratic state from inside and outside. Territorial representative politics have, at least partially, lost their sovereign grip on many policy areas as diverse as global trade, global warming and even global security. A number of transnational and supranational decision-making arenas have emerged, in which states are no longer the sole actors, if, indeed, they ever were, but are accompanied by a multiplicity of public, semi-public, economic and civil society actors.

In the wake of these transformations of the state, democracy is losing its institutional centre. We are both witnessing, and partaking in, the transformation of the national age towards the postnational age, whose future form of rule-making is contested. Will this future be democratic? How is democracy possible in a globalising context? What institutions are necessary in order to maintain the democratic ideal of self-determination? It is this set of questions that has inspired this volume. It is written in the conviction that it is worthwhile striving for the continuation of democracy despite the significant theoretical and practical challenges posed by the postnational age. I believe, with Jürgen Habermas *et al.* (1961), that there is no excuse for giving up the ever-ongoing struggle for the identity of the rulers and the ruled, democracy's core idea, because of practical difficulties of implementation. Though the future shape of political organisation cannot be foreseen, it is, nevertheless, both possible and important to discuss and reflect upon the direction that postnational institutions should, and, indeed, might, take in order to uphold the idea of democracy.

In this book, I will not propose an encompassing normative model of European or global democracy as such. The concern is not one of 'how can we save democracy or popular sovereignty in a globalising world [but rather] what kind of political institutions ... do we need' (Peters 2005: 116) in order to render policy-making processes beyond the nation state more democratic. Bernhard Peters' reminder (2004a: 3) that democracy 'is often used in two different senses' is helpful in this context. Democracy can either refer to the entirety of a political order, or it can refer to the procedures and processes of policy-making and decision-making within a given political order. This book refers to the latter conception and thus contributes to 'a debate that attempts to map the direction, speed, and character of change' (Greven 2005: 261) that democratic practices and institutions might take.

In particular, this book is interested in both the prospects of, and the contribution of, one of the core democratic practices, namely, political partic-ipation, to the actual future of democracy in one specific institutional setting which has often been called the laboratory for global politics (Olsen 2003; Pollack 2005; Zürn and Checkel 2005), to wit, the European Union (EU).[1]

According to the normative background assumption of this study – Robert Dahl would call it its 'shadow theory' (Dahl 1989: 3) – democracy is unthinkable without participatory practices. Political participation is the key mechanism that connects the people with the places in which the decisions of direct concern to them are made. It is through the participatory activities of people in public affairs that life is brought into the philosophical idea of self-determination. The democratic character of politics depends on the extent to which those affected by particular policy-decisions are equally able to establish, to contribute to, to influence or to hinder, the decisions and/or the implementation of public affairs. However, this background assumption is sufficiently flexible to be able to avoid conceptual and practical over-deter-mination: like democracy, participation, participatory practices and the nature of participatory agents all change over time, too, and vary in different institutional contexts. This book maps such recent developments in the practice of participation in the specific institutional setting of the EU.

The EU represents the most ambitious attempt to re-integrate the political and the social spaces in a political system beyond the nation state. Yet the lively scholarly debate about what is called the EU's democratic deficit bears witness to the fact that, to date, the new political system has not (yet) found an appropriate institutional answer that convincingly either replaces, or at least complements, the institutions of the democratic state (see, among others, Follesdal and Hix 2006; Jensen 2009; Kohler-Koch and Rittberger 2007a; Offe and Preuss 2006). It is even disputed as to whether the EU really suffers from a democratic deficit (Majone 1998, 1999; Moravcsik 2002, 2004, 2008). The recent downsizing of the Constitutional Treaty to the Treaty of

Lisbon has made it increasingly clear that we will not witness the emergence of a single State of Europe. Nevertheless, since supranational law, at least that from the supranational polity of the European Union, even exerts direct effect on the individual, there are good reasons to adhere to the democratic aspiration in order to find ways of individual participation in policy processes that extend beyond the nation state. European integration affects every citizen of its Member States to such an extent that the European policy-making processes require an independent element of democratic legitimacy that cannot be upheld by intergovernmental diplomacy alone. And it is the role that participation *might* play in doing so which is elaborated in this book.

But what *is* political participation, who are the participants, and why is it so hard to identify institutional solutions that are both practically feasible and normatively convincing for political participation in the EU?

The father of the term 'participatory democracy' (Hilmer 2010: 45; Mansbridge 2003: 177) stated that participation is a communicative action which 'involves preliminary deliberation' (Kaufman 1969a: 192) in both formal and informal arenas. Thus, participation encompasses societal self-regulatory efforts as well as the interactions of citizens with the political institutions, but it excludes violent protest as it lacks the readiness to become engaged in some form of communicative interaction in public affairs. By underlining the interactive character of participation, Kaufmann conceptualises participation as a two-way process. Participation includes activities from below, i.e. from the citizens and other actors of civil society, and from above, i.e. from the political institutions that have to support and to engage participation. Without this reciprocal connotation, participation would be reduced to mere consultation.

With regard to the participants, intuitively, as well as according to prominent conceptions in democratic theory, individuals are perceived as the natural participatory agents in public affairs (see, among others, Barber 2003; Fung and Wright 2003b; Greven 2007; Kaufman 1969a; Pateman 1970). According to the conventional conviction, democracy is only alive if individuals actively participate in the organisation of their society. The authority of the people is exercised through participation in elections, above all in national elections. Thus, this conventional intuition is based upon the intimate relations between the nation state and democracy, which, to date, has been re-invigorated by strong advocates, such as the German Constitutional Court in its ruling on the Treaty of Lisbon.[2]

However, this conventional normative intuition is challenged. The complexities and spatial extensions of Europeanising, yet alone globalising, politics heavily restrict the capacity of the individual to participate. Even the narrower conception of participation as voting, which successfully adapted democracy to the large-scale territories of modern nation states, loses its practical and normative singularity as the main participatory activity through which democracy can be realised.

This can be witnessed in the case of the EU, where, despite significant increases in the powers of the European Parliament (EP) (Hix, Noury and Roland 2007; Rittberger 2006), the debate on the EU's democratic deficit has not lost its power. On the contrary, many observers seem convinced that it is urgent for us to identify political actors, other than individuals, who could uphold the participatory core of democratic practice. Attention has particularly been paid to the democratic potential of the participation of non-state collective actors, usually called civil society organisations (CSOs). The assumption is the following: an increase in the participation of organised civil society could boost the democratisation of policy processes beyond the nation state, and hence could contribute to the future of democracy beyond the nation state (see, among others, Armstrong 2002; De Schutter 2002; Freise 2008; Friedrich 2008; Greenwood 2007; Knodt and Finke 2005; Rossteutscher 2005; Ruzza and Della Sala 2007; Smismans 2004, 2006; Steffek, Kissling and Nanz 2007).

In this book, I elaborate upon this proposal to broaden the concept of political participation towards organised civil society, and offer a better understanding of the proposal's normative grounds, its empirical reality and its institutional consequences. I specify both the promises and the limits of placing the democratic burden of participation upon the shoulders of collective, rather than upon individual, actors. I reconstruct this prominent assumption, juxtapose it with original empirical research and develop an institutional perspective for a democratically valuable form of collective participation. In so doing, I contribute to a clearer view of whether civil society participation is a normatively appropriate development of participatory democracy, whether it should instead be conceived as a second-best alternative in institutional contexts which are too remote for individual participation, or whether it is even damaging key democratic values. Even for those in favour of individual participation, an estimate of the limits and the strengths of this alternative is valuable for reflections upon both the need and the role of individual participation in the postnational age.

The remainder of this introductory chapter sets out the study's normative and empirical contexts, and introduces the organisation of this book. The following section elaborates on the changes which the concept of participation has undergone throughout the history of democracy. In particular, explanation is given regarding how to understand the shift of focus from the participation of the individual to the participation of civil society organisations. Then, the empirical context of this book is introduced, namely, the European Union, and the recent discussions on democracy and participatory governance in the EU are outlined. As Political Science rarely integrates normative and empirical research, as this book does, some comments on the specific research approach of the book follow. I argue that it is the institutional perspective that bridges the rift between the normative and empirical accounts of democracy, so that this study pursues a triad of a theory-driven empirical investigation of the *normative* potential, *empirical* practices and *institutional* implications of democratic participatory governance beyond the nation state. The introduction concludes by presenting the organisation of the book and summarising each chapter.

## Democratic participation revisited? From individual participation to the participation of collective actors

Political participation is closely connected to democracy. Consequently, as democracy has undergone both conceptual and practical changes, it is unsurprising that both the significance and the configuration of participation have also changed. This section demonstrates that the modern democratic state favours a thin conception of participation, unlike the thick understanding of direct participation in the early days of democracy. In the looming postnational age, even this thin conception seems to be at risk. However, recent years have seen a revival of participatory discourse in democratic theory – but this revival has a new focus on collective, rather than individual, actors.

### The changing roles of participation

The proliferation of democracy as the nominal form of government in most countries of the world has undoubtedly been one of the most significant political developments of the twentieth century.[3] Even in many of the countries which cannot be described as democratic, democracy is often on the lips of the rulers and/or in the people's minds as a desirable aim. Ironically, in the moment of its apparent triumph as the globally most accepted, if not universally or coherently implemented, ideal for organising political authority,[4] history reveals once more the contingency of democracy's future. The quantitative increase of democracies worldwide appears to be paralleled by a growing normative modesty. The pure democratic ideal of self-determination through the participation of the people is forced onto the defensive against an understanding of democracy merely 'as a universal franchise with institutionalised opposition' (Warren 2002: 678).

This is not the first time in history that democratic ideas and practices have been challenged and forced to undergo significant changes in order to be sustained (see, among others, Buchstein and Jörke 2003). So far, at least, the idea of self-determination, of democracy, has demonstrated extraordinary resilience to historical challenges, due to its remarkable adaptability. In his influential work *Democracy and its Critics*, Robert Dahl (1989) shows, in some detail, how democracy is interwoven with historical developments that have changed democratic practices and have thus influenced varying conceptualisations of both democracy and participation. He distinguishes two transformations of democracy as a reaction to, and an interaction with, the historical context; consequentially, he identifies conceptions of both the forms and the significance of participation. Dahl argues that, as a result of the different transformations, contemporary democratic thought builds on a heritage of partially inconsistent theoretical and practical assumptions.

The first democratic transformation[5] signifies the first coherent practical experiment with the idea of democracy. This took place in the city-states of ancient Greece, the *polis*, above all in Athens, approximately 2,500 years ago. Small in territorial terms and manageable in the numbers of citizens, the city-states of ancient Greece provided the grounds for an experiment of public authority, in which the 'citizens were at one and the same time subjects of political authority and the creators of public rules and regulations' (Held 1995: 6). The city-states are excellent examples of how democratic practices responded to, and depended upon, the correspondence of a concrete socio-historic situation with the normative ideal of democracy at that particular time. A political system evolved that provided citizens with both the rights and the resources to govern themselves, instead of being governed by only a few.[6]

The role of the citizen was extensive in that he[7] had the right, and the duty, to attend public meetings, and, furthermore, to become engaged in the implementation and administration of public affairs. This right to direct participation was guaranteed by political equality among citizens and by the rule of law, ingredients which are still central to democracy to this very day, and they provide the reason why *polis*-democracy serves as a starting point for many contemporary democrats.[8]

In this ideal understanding, participatory democracy is characterised as the direct involvement of citizens in the making, deciding and implementation of policies. The direct participation of equal citizens was the ideal and main democratic mechanism in assembly-democracy, and the small-scale political systems of the polis offered a good match of spatial (small territory) and social (small number) conditions for realising this ideal. In theoretical terms, *polis*-democracy thus appears as an almost perfect institutionalisation of democracy's core idea of equal self-determination. Consequently, for a long time, it was believed that only small-scale systems with a few thousand people could be seen as being capable of democracy.

Changes in the socio-historical context as well as new normative concerns characterise the second transformation of democracy. Historically, it was the growing inter-dependencies among city-states, and, above all, the gradual emergence of nation states, which increased both the number of people and the expanse of territory to such an extent that the rule of the people in the institutions of a direct participatory democracy lost its practical meaningfulness. Furthermore, the rising prevalence of the territorial state as the main form of centralising coercive power and for organising public affairs stimulated (liberal) political theorists to reflect upon how to strike a balance between the liberty of the individual and the centralised power of the state. Both developments triggered the search for new democratic mechanisms that extend beyond direct participation. In the constitutionalisation process of the USA, the normative and the concrete historical dimensions coincided, and the *Federalist Papers* (Hamilton, Madison and Jay 2003) remain, to this day, significant testimonies of how to justify democracy normatively in large-scale territorial states.

A solution to both the normative and the historical challenge was found in the establishment of representative democracy. It is, in particular, the development of representative government and the emerging belief that the combination of representativity with democracy is normatively justifiable that characterises the second democratic transformation. Representative democracies are voting-based systems in which, for the limited time-span of an election cycle, political authority is delegated to the elected representatives through the voting act that followed the basic rule of political equality, namely, one person, one vote.[9] Normatively, this cyclical danger of losing the power to rule ensures that the rulers abstain from abusing their power, and forces them to act in accordance with the common good. Thus, electoral competition, the independent and equal voting act, and the responsiveness of the rulers to the demands and needs of the people have – since then – been perceived as the most convincing democratic mechanisms for large-scale political systems, displacing citizens' direct participation.

From this liberal perspective, the role of the state is to aggregate the interests of its citizens and to translate them into reasonable and effective policies. From a pragmatic perspective, the shift away from direct participation, to voting as the central mechanism, reconciles democracy with the substantial growth of political systems, both territorially and in terms of numbers. It promises to be a practically feasible and normatively justified path towards democracy, as it is significantly more socially inclusive than the restricted citizen model of Athenian democracy. 'To this extent,' Dahl concludes, 'the capacity of citizens to govern themselves was greatly enhanced' (Dahl 1989: 30). As Warren (2002: 698) observes, 'Smaller is not always better with regard to democracy'. Nevertheless, the role of the citizen in terms of his or her individual participatory capacity diminished from constant and direct participation to occasional participation in voting.

### The challenges to participation

Today, we are – arguably – faced with a third transformation of democracy. Democracy, so the challenge goes, has to cope with an emerging postnational constellation that is characterised by the disintegration of three components, namely the territorial state, the nation, and the national economy (see Habermas 1998: 94). The temporary congruence of these components during the modern age facilitated the emergence of the institutions of national modern liberal democracy, in which an institutional centre within a clearly confined territory became both the ultimate arena and the target of political participation.

Policy-making in the postnational age is characterised by a disconnection of the social and spatial congruence that pervasively characterised the national age (Zürn 2000).[10] These changes are in danger of profoundly disconnecting the policy-making processes from the people, and of allowing the participatory activities of the people to disappear. In the postnational age, a multiplicity of decision-making *loci* at sub-national, national, regional and global level are emerging (among many, see Held 1995; Leibfried and Zürn 2006; Zürn 1998), hereby reacting to the increased (awareness of) inter-dependencies. The postnational age not only *extends* social and spatial boundaries, as was the case in the second transformation, but also *transcends* them. This renders the third transformation of democracy not only a quantitative, but also a qualitative, challenge to the conceptualisation and institutionalisation of democracy. Each of these boundaries consists of different elements whose concrete shape and balance vary according to the concrete historical moment, thus affecting any concretisation of democratic ideas and practices.

With regard to the issue of spatial congruence, the large-scale, territorial nation state is today in a comparable situation to the medieval small-scale city-state at the turn to the age of nation states.[11] Participation is, firstly, challenged at the level of the nation state, for the citizens' capacity for self-rule is further diminished beyond that which had already happened in the second transformation. The unprecedented degree of international (not just economic) inter-dependencies of states again challenges national boundaries:

> Territorial boundaries demarcate the basis on which individuals are included in and excluded from participation in decisions affecting their lives (however limited the participation might be), but the outcomes of theses decisions often 'stretch' beyond national frontiers. (Held 1995: 18)

This diminishes the participatory opportunities of citizens, and it does so in an uneven way, as the citizens of most countries of the globe are deeply affected by the decisions taken by a few powerful states.

Furthermore, participation in the postnational age is also challenged at global level. An important feature of modern globalisation is that states, themselves, gain company[12] within the international system. Instead of states being monistic actors in an anarchic international system, as the realist school of International Relations argues, the global system is now crowded with a diverse multitude of public and private actors, such as International Organisations, Non-Governmental Organisations and Multi-National Corporations, and structures, such as International Regimes or codes of conduct. These new structures and actors influence and interact with nation states so that 'state sovereignty is no longer conceived as indivisible but shared with international agencies' (McGrew 1997: 12).

The actors in the contemporary structure of the international system engage in significant activities of global governance which are not coupled with forms of democratic practices in a way that is normatively more than purely functionally justified.[13] The European Union is the only polity above the nation state that has gone a remarkably long way in its attempt to reply – in territorial terms – to the challenges of international inter-dependency and de-nationalisation, to use Zürn's (1998) terminology. But even the EU is seen by some as a 'regulatory state' (Majone 1999), which emphasises its functional – rather than its territorial – character. In the foreseeable future, the EU will not become a European state, and thus the simple transfer of representative democratic practices from national to EU level seems neither possible nor desirable. The EU has not (yet) found a convincing answer to the democratic challenge of governance above the nation state, as the extensive and controversial debate on its democratic deficit shows.

With regard to the issue of social congruence, the addressees of participatory rights have become unclear. Social boundaries refer to the problem of inclusion and exclusion. Each system of authority needs rules regarding upon whom it can (legitimately) exercise power. This is particularly central to democracies, as it affects the central democratic idea, namely, the rule of the people over themselves. Each institutionalisation of democracy has to find answers to the questions of who to accept as citizens, whether to grant them participatory rights, and whom to deny rights, which, in modern societies, go beyond basic human rights. Today, the definition of citizenship and its eligibility criteria are still highly controversial and sensitive subjects in every nation state, as are the measures to regulate legal and illegal migration. In the postnational age, as I will demonstrate in the case study on the EU's Directive on Family Re-unification (Chapter 5), the monopoly of nation states to decide upon inclusion has started to become diluted.

The transcendence of territorial boundaries also adds to the growing complexity and plurality of both the needs and the demands of a population. This is problematical for every democratic society because the latter requires a certain degree of integration and mutual recognition as a pre-requisite for collective decisions. Thus, processes of inclusion and exclusion in democratic societies always need politics of identity and difference as a means to stimulate integration, mutual recognition and respect (see Benhabib 1996b). Even if there were something akin to the original homogenous *demos*, the nation state would no longer be in a position (if it ever was) to select its inhabitants according to requirements of homogeneity.

Furthermore, the relationship between the social sphere and the state becomes unclear. A nation state can either restrain itself by only minimally regulating the life of its citizens in order to guarantee security and personal autonomy, or it can intrude more extensively into the social sphere, and thus seek to influence and to shape the lives of its individuals. The emergence of centralised representative governments in the nation states was accompanied by an expansion of the responsibilities of the state. This is clearly visible in the development of the modern welfare state, which transformed the former rule-setting state into an interventionist state (Leibfried and Zürn 2006).

Today, the expansion and transcendence of social boundaries undermine such sovereign statehood, without replacing it, for instance, at EU level. For some, this does not pose an overly important democratic problem since governance beyond the nation state restricts itself to regulation (Majone 1999), or points to the inability of a postnational polity, such as the EU, to become truly democratic (Scharpf 2002). Others, however, regard the increase in diversity as a chance both to learn and to establish structures of experimental governance with genuine democratic legitimacy and a signifi-cant role for collective actors as the bearers of societal self-organisation (Sabel and Zeitlin 2006).

These accounts suggest that we are currently within a third democratic transformation, in which political theorists, scientists and practitioners are struggling to find new institutions that are democratically justifiable. The ability of citizens to have a participatory influence and to control the decisions which affected them is diminishing. Thus, it is nothing less than the very core of democracy that is, arguably, at stake here. While ancient direct participatory democracy, ideally, guaranteed congruence between the rule-givers and the rule-takers, and where representative government was perceived as the appropriate democratic solution for nation states, the socio-economic changes of today severely undermine the close linkage between citizens as governors and citizens as governed, which is so central to the continuation of any model of democracy.

Thus, in order for the age of democracy to continue, democrats need to find democratic mechanisms which not only transcend national frontiers, but which are also sensitive to the additional actors of policy-making and their democratic vices and virtues. Consequently, there is a need for democratic mechanisms that respond to the challenges to both the territorial and the social boundaries. Both kinds of boundaries differentiate and transcend simultaneously. Permeable territorial boundaries provide spaces to private actors when they are not immediately, or even deliberately not, fully occupied by new forms of state-like public authority.

If one sums up the extensive literature, one can say that contemporary societies are too differentiated and complex to be steered and regulated centrally. Parliaments and central governments both lose *and* share legislative and policy-making competencies with both public and private actors, and an increasing amount of political issues are delegated to non-majoritarian, regu-latory agencies. This diffusion of governance forms and practices goes from the global to the national level, down to the regional and local level. So, the talk about a third transformation of democracy has been triggered, but there are different views about the viability of the idea of democracy in a world that is de-nationalising.

## The re-discovery of participation

This narrative of the transformations of democracy is also a story about the changing forms and objectives of participation, because it is the central mechanism that renders the self-government of the people operational. To some extent, it is a story about cutting back the pure democratic ideal of self-determination to that of co-determination, and even this more slender version of democratic participation has recently been challenged in the newly emerging systems of multi-level governance. Consequently, now that the third transformation of democracy even endangers the existing forms of representative government with electoral participation, the question comes to the fore as to 'whether, in fact, the democratic ideals of equal participation in the self-government have become so unrealistic in contemporary societies as to be irrelevant' (Warren 2002: 679), or, to put it differently, whether participation has become the mere 'ballast to the concept of democracy' (Buchstein and Jörke 2003: 474)?

This worrying question is countered by voices that are optimistic about the possibility of maintaining democratic forms of public policy-making even in contexts of blurring territorial and social boundaries. According to them, the new landscape for democratic practices not only endangers the existing forms of democratic participation, but also 'offer[s] new opportunities to cultivate capacities for self-rule and generate multiple spaces within which self-rule can develop. Yet, these same developments tend to undermine formal democratic institutions' (Warren 2002: 686) of representative government. The concept of political participation becomes re-invigorated at the very moment in which representative democracy as the major institutional invention of the national constellation is severely under pressure. Participation re-enters the political and scholarly stage as a potentially suitable device for the 'appropriate institutional remedies' (Fung 2006: 670) to the existing democratic deficits, either complementing, or even replacing, the familiar institutional designs of democratic representation.

Calls for a new democracy mix between the representative and the participatory elements of democracy, in particular, show a demand to complement citizens' 'electoral rights with new kinds of participatory patterns' (Magnette 2003: 151) at local, regional and global levels of governance (see, for example, Fung 2003; Fung and Wright 2003b; Heinelt 2003; Heinelt *et al.* 2002; Hilmer 2010; Steffek and Kissling 2007). But there is no consensus about what this democracy mix could, or should, look like. What seems clear, however, is that it will vary in different political systems at different points in time, and that there is need for a constant re-balancing between representative and participatory practices. The shape of this mix evades a normative *a priori* determination, but requires knowledge of the concrete institutional context in which the mix is to exert its influence.

For the national and, in particular, the local, level, there are normatively saturated proposals on how to organise this mix of representation and participation. Archon Fung (2006; Fung and Wright 2003b), for instance, present a number of proposals for enhancing individual participation in situations in which democratic deficiencies of electoral participation in representative systems are identified. These proposals, however, share the difficulty of being transposed to a level beyond the nation state, not least because there is no functioning system of representative government at regional and global level, the democratic fallacies of which could be repaired by participatory means. Nadia Urbinati and Mark Warren (2008) also try to overcome the traditional dichotomy of (electoral) representation and participation, but, once again, this succeeds only in the context of established representative institutions. How participation could, or should, be implemented beyond the nation state, let alone with regard to civil society organisations and other forms of 'self-authorised representatives' (Urbinati and Warren 2008: 403ff), remains unresolved.

Even more unsatisfactory are the solutions for enhanced individual participation beyond elections in a non-national context, which are put forward from the political realm of the EU itself. In fact, the inclusion of individual citizens is somewhat treated as an orphan in the public debates. Moreover, with a view to institutional efforts, more attention was given to the participation of collective actors. Only the shock of the French and Dutch 'no' to the proposed Constitutional Treaty in 2005 triggered some activity. Under the guidance of the Communication Commissioner, Margot Wallström, *Plan D for Democracy, Dialogue and Discussion* was invented to address the citizens of Europe more directly. However, what was promoted as 'Six experiments in participatory democracy at EU level'[14] has turned out to be predominantly a means of political education in order to make the EU better known, instead of being observably connected to European policy-making. In fact, on Mrs Wallström's webpage, the following sentence seems to capture these (paternalistic) efforts well:

> Communicating Europe – what it means to listen to the general public and equip them with the information they need to know.

The democratic *problématique* of political arenas beyond the nation state is, thus, the absence of convincing ideas on how to transpose the model of electoral representation onto the new levels of political action. The scale of the postnational decision-making arenas exceeds the capacity of electoral representation. This suggests that the current challenges should be distinguished from being merely a second transformation of democracy writ large, as Dahl suggests (Dahl 1994: 27), and that it necessitates other forms of participation and representation. With regard to participation, it has been particularly proposed that the participation of civil society organisations in policy-making processes beyond the state possesses normative democratic qualities which are independent from the existence of a representative system of government.

In this debate, the concept of participation underwent a two-fold transition: first of all, the focus changed from the participation of individual citizens to the participation of collective actors. Secondly, the recent discussions of democratic participatory governance often purport a rather top-down perspective (see, similarly, Bevir 2006), whereas the traditional conception of participatory democracy pertains a bottom-up perspective. These shifts, whose theoretical implications are further elaborated in Chapter 2, are important, and should be kept in mind throughout this book. The normative expectations connected to the participation of the individual as the central means of the democratic ideal of self-rule might not be easily transposed to collective actors. It is therefore necessary to weigh the potential democratic gains of participatory governance against the possible democratic pathologies cautiously.

Today, the potential of grass-roots organisations and social movements, such as the alter-global movements, to enhance a democratic society seems to be, by and large, undisputed. Yet, the actual contribution of these CSOs with regard to open, transparent and accessible policy-making practices in political institutions beyond the nation state, i.e., their democratising potential, still requires conceptual and empirical clarification – particularly because these participatory practices are often supported, if not induced, by bureaucratic actors from above, such as the European Commission.

By focusing on the participation of collective, rather than individual, citizens from normative, empirical and institutional perspectives, I will be able to contribute to a realistic estimation concerning both the factual democratising values and the limits to their participation in policy processes beyond the nation state. It might turn out that the establishment of democratic policy-making requires more attention for the direct participation of citizens even in policy processes beyond the nation state than the current discourse on civil society participation suggests.

### Participatory governance in the European Union

The focus on the participation of civil society organisations has gained particular strength in the context of the EU, both from political and from scholarly perspectives. A democratic framing of participation appeared to be providing normative relevance to the all-present concept of governance. This coming-together of the two concepts in the EU discourse on governance and democracy is introduced in this section.

When the Member States of the European Communities decided to take a considerable step forward in European integration by presenting the Treaty establishing a European Union (Treaty of Maastricht 1993), it was felt by some Member States that it was time to give their people a greater say in accepting this new treaty. Referendums on the Treaty of Maastricht were held in Denmark, France and Ireland and caused significant disturbances, due to the Danish 'no',[15] and to the referendum which was almost lost in France. Suddenly, it was felt by both the Member State governments and the European institutions that the assumed permissive consensus of the European public for deeper integration had lost its power and a lively political and academic debate about the EU's democratic deficit began (see for example Kohler-Koch and Rittberger 2007b).

The European institutions made some efforts to increase democratic legitimacy by, first of all, strengthening the representative elements within the EU system. Indeed, in the meantime, the European Parliament has gained considerable power[16] and qualified-majority voting (QMV) has almost become the default decision-making mode in the Council.[17] Secondly, a debate about good governance and participation emerged – partly stimulated by, and partly being the stimulator of, the academic debate – and possibly accelerated by the feeling that the increasing competences of the European Parliament had not eased the legitimacy crisis. This debate peaked for the first time with the publication of the Commission's White Paper on European Governance in 2001 (European Commission 2001a), and several accompanying communications of the Commission (see Chapter 4), which tried to (re-)shape the system of European participatory governance, and then resulted in Article I-47 on the Participatory Democracy of the failed constitution for Europe.

This move towards participatory democracy as a possible remedy of the EU's perceived democratic deficit can be understood as a reaction to the crisis of representative democracy in its parliamentarian shape, as described above. The advocates of European democracy started to seek alternative democratic institutions and agents, which promised to contribute to the democratisation of the European governance system. Indeed, the EU polity's complex, polycentric multi-level system challenges both democratic models and practices, which are familiar from the context of the nation state. At the same time, this complexity opens up new avenues for participatory activities by making use of the shift from hierarchical government to co-operative and less hierarchical forms of governance. Governance promises greater opportunities for the involvement – and thus self-governance – of citizens, both individually and collectively. In addition, the inclusion of stakeholders and the self-organisation capacities of both individual and collective actors seemed promising for the enhancement of the effectiveness and efficiency of policies.[18]

Thus, it came as little surprise that, during the 1990s, the terms 'participation' and 'governance' became the buzzwords of the governance turn in EU Studies (Kohler-Koch and Rittberger 2007b) from both an efficiency, and a democratic legitimacy, perspective (Armstrong 2002; De Schutter 2002). More recently, these terms have become combined to form the term 'participatory governance' (Grote and Gbikpi 2002; Heinelt 2003: 115ff; Heinelt *et al.* 2002), in order to capture analytically the systematic inclusion of different non-state collective actors in political processes. All in all, a pragmatic approach to European democracy prevails in this literature, focusing on the incremental democratising reforms of (new) governance arrangements, rather than on huge democratic leaps forward (see, among others, Jachtenfuchs 1997; Schmitter 2000, 2002).

In terms of the appropriate agents for these new participatory arrangements, civil society organisations became the new focus (Ruzza 2004; Smismans 2003). In this debate, civil society often remains rather vaguely defined, largely referring to the space between the state and the individual. Thus, the already existing, predominantly analytical research strand on lobbying and interest representation in the EU (see, among others, Clays *et al.* 1998; Eising and Kohler-Koch 2005; Greenwood 1997, 2003; Greenwood, Knodt and Quittkat 2011; Wallace and Young 1997)[19] has become enriched by publications on the normative turn in EU Studies (Bellamy and Castiglione 2003; Chryssochoou 2000). The existence of the analytical literature *corpus* shows that the issue of participation in CSOs – in its broad definition, thus capturing interest representation – is less new than the enthusiastic discourse on participatory governance might suggest. In fact, the existence of Europe-wide active CSOs has seen significant growth rates over the last thirty years,[20] and the EU had also already made provisions for the participation of non-state actors before the recent discourse on participatory governance emerged (see sections below).

This literature tells us that a growing number of hugely diverse private actors are present in Brussels, having developed from mere 'listening-posts and liaison groups' (Butt Philip 1985: 2) to actors actively trying to shape and gain stakes in the EU's policy-making processes. The European Commission and the European Parliament, in particular, have long been widely regarded as being very open and receptive to the concerns of stakeholders (Butt Philip 1985: 21). However, empirical research on participatory governance that explicitly builds on democratic theory has only been begun relatively recently (Friedrich 2007; Friedrich and Nanz 2007; Smismans 2004, 2005c, 2006), and often in the context of social policies and new modes of governance (De la Porte and Nanz 2004; De la Porte and Pochet 2005; Friedrich 2006; Smismans 2005b).

In this normatively oriented literature, the institutional perspective on participation and interest representation that is tied to democratic theory is still under-developed. The literature goes some way to tell us about the participatory pattern in specific EU policy areas and governance arrangements, and it even cautiously judges them against some normative standards. However, despite some criticism of the empirical results from a normative perspective, it neglects to ask whether the institutional setting in which these participatory activities take place is appropriate for participatory governance to become democratic and, eventually, to enhance the overall democratic quality of EU policy-making.

## The research approach: normative reflection, empirical analysis and institutional perspectives

### Normative theory and empirical research

In order to understand the nature of this study and the triad of normative reflections–empirical research–institutional perspective, one needs to take account of the fact that social scientific research on democratic participation is a thorny undertaking because it is difficult to integrate normative reasoning with empirical research. The 1960s and 1970s had already seen a debate in (the English-speaking) Political Science about the difference of normative and empirical approaches to democracy, a discussion which continues to obscure research on democracy within International Relations and European Studies. Even then, scholars mutually accused each other of failing to consider the differences between normatively and empirically motivated research (see, among others, Dahl 1966; Schonfeld 1975; Skinner 1973). In most recent publications, similar arguments re-occur (see the review essays by Mutz 2008 and Thompson 2008), and the present study is both a plea for and an attempt at such an integrated research approach. Thinking about the feasibility of democratic participatory practices in the European context always requires us to be attentive to the normative ideal as well as to the empirical reality.

But what makes research on democratic participation such a difficult undertaking? One can reasonably claim that both underlying concepts – democracy and participation – are intrinsically so ambiguous as to impede any conceptual consensus. One could specify that they necessarily entail propositions about both the *ought* and the *is*, i.e. they include normative and empirical elements. But since there is neither a unitary normative, nor an empirical, theory of democratic participation,[21] a consensus for each side cannot be achieved. Most important for the existing conceptual disarray, however, is the fact that democracy is situated at the intersection of both these dimensions. It is almost impossible to disentangle the enmeshment of the democratic ideal from the institutional practice, and it is equally hard to specify the relation of normative reasoning and empirical observations.

Although this conceptual double nature certainly hampers a conceptual consensus about democratic participation, I will argue in this study that this conceptual pluralism is not necessarily a weakness, and that it also constitutes a strength by proving that democratic participation is relevant for political thought and practice to this day. Democratic participation, understood as a communicative social practice based upon normative grounds, needs both dimensions in order to survive, renew itself and adapt to changing contexts. This demands considerable efforts for conceptual clarity in research on democratic participation (similarly, Thompson 2008).

Increased scholarly accuracy and transparency appear to be needed. Political theorists need to strengthen their efforts to make their conceptual ideas palpable for concrete contexts, and empirical research needs explicit reference to the underlying normative model of democracy, which inspires the elaboration of assessment criteria and possible institutional proposals. A failure to provide the reader with this information would result in misconceptions, lack of precision and accuracy, and ontological and epistemological shallowness.

Lamenting such a lack of normative transparency in much empirical research, Robert Dahl speaks about the existence of 'shadow theories' of democracy (1989). This is not to say that every empirical researcher needs to become a philosopher. On the contrary, more often than not some theoretical considerations would suffice. In any case, good empirical research on democratic participation essentially requires awareness of the normative background of the concepts applied.[22] This speaks against the empirical theories of democracy that do not even consider participation to be an important independent variable, but merely focus on rationality, output and efficiency (Buchstein and Jörke 2003).

Ideal theory needs to be sensitive to its institutionalised implications, and empirical research constantly has to re-ensure that it does not deviate too far from the *spirit* of ideal theory. Social scientific research needs to be reflexive about both the level and the scope of its arguments, and also has to be conscious of its normative and empirical implications. One needs to be very careful when making inferences that cross the different levels. There are four traps that researchers easily fall into if they engage with these ambiguous concepts (similar aspects are purported by Fraser 2007: 226):

- empirical realities are too easily labelled as the realisation of normative ideals;
- empirical realities are too easily found to be inefficient in the light of normative ideals;
- normative ideals are too easily refuted by means of empirical observations; and
- normative ideals are too readily supported by empirical realities.

It is no accident that defining and assessing democracy is notoriously difficult. Normative theory is therefore fruitfully used as a critical foil (Deitelhoff 2006; Meisterhans 2007) if its ideal reflections are confronted with real practices in a concrete institutional setting. Integrating normative theory and empirical analysis into one research project thus exerts critical potential if institutionally embedded political practices are rationally reconstructed,[23] i.e. if the normative underpinnings written into social practices are made explicit through empirical analysis, and if institutional proposals are formulated in the spirit of normative theory with some sense of pragmatism in the light of the empirical analysis.

### The research approach

The nature of this study's interest, i.e. its basis upon the intersection of normative and empirical research, has consequences for my research approach, which transcends the distinction between the confirmatory and the explorative tradition of social research (Gerring 2001, Chapter 10). Research that combines normative reasoning with empirical analysis is epistemologically distinct from analytical research that seeks to test specific democracy theory approaches. It is particularly the significance of theory that distinguishes these research approaches.

Analytical research uses theory either as a framework from which evaluative criteria can be extracted and applied in empirical research, or uses it as a hypotheses-generating tool which can then be assessed. Following such understandings of theory, research could elaborate specific thresholds for the fulfilment of the criteria of participation, in the end producing participatory scores. Such a research approach would imply a quasi-quantitative research strategy that cannot be applied in a research context that uses a normative language. There, it is about interpreting, rather than measuring, empirical observations. In this study, normative theory establishes a conception of reality against which empirical processes can be critically reconstructed. This research is about reflecting on the normative characteristics of the empirical reality which is reconstructed and interpreted in the light of these normative conditions. Empirical evidence is used in an exploratory manner in order to consider the extent to which the *ought* has found entrance into the *is*.

The normative-theoretical dimension of this study consequently implies a deductive approach: conditions are deduced from ideal theory in order to guide the empirical analysis, following a confirmatory logic. Yet from a theoretical perspective, the different approaches of democratic theory cannot be proved right or wrong through empirical evidence. Normative theories cannot be falsified because they do not presume to be explanatory; no empirical evidence has the power to show that the ideal of democracy is wrong. What *can* be done empirically is to identify empirical evidence that potentially makes plausible the expectations about the democratic value of participation in European policy-making. The critical potential of normative theory is evoked if its insights are bound back to a concrete case which becomes reconstructed in the light of theoretically deduced conditions.

Overall, this book applies a research strategy of plausibilisation (Deitelhoff 2006, Chapter 1). The empirical presence of the participatory pattern in EU policy-making processes is reconstructed in the light of the normative ideals. It is about the empirical identification of elements in the real world which possess attributes that are normatively valuable and open for institutional enhancement in the direction of the theoretical ideals. This research approach, which bases the empirical analysis upon explicated normative conditions, which ultimately lead to an institutional perspective, is the appropriate research strategy for realising the transition from normative theory to empirical research.

## The organisation of the book

The triadic characteristic of studying democratic participatory governance suggests splitting the basic research interest into three themes, each of which will be dealt with in one of the three parts of this study, respectively.

The normative-conceptual Part I attempts to come to terms with the Janus-faced character of the key term, participation. Having introduced the recent rediscovery of participation, in Chapter 2 I dig deeper into the concept of democratic political participation. I will elaborate on the democratic credentials of participation from a democratic theory perspective, portraying the shift from the participation of individuals towards collective actors. I show that participation possesses both an instrumental and a normative dimension (see, among others, Scharpf 1970; Schultze 2002). The former emphasises the decisiveness of participation within existing democratic structures, whereas the latter highlights that, if properly implemented, participation adds to the democratisation of not yet democratic practices of policy-making.

Having introduced the democratic virtues of individual participation, the chapter then discusses three actual approaches that deal with the participation of collective actors, namely pluralism, associative democracy and deliberative democracy. It will be shown that they share the normative belief in the centrality of political equality, but that they deviate in the institutional conclusions for the participation of collective actors in order to achieve political equality among them.

In preparation for the study's empirical research, in Chapter 3 these theoretical considerations on the democratic participation of collective actors are made operable in an evaluative intent. The foregoing discussion is employed to develop an analytical framework for judging the democratic potential of collective actor participation in policy-making processes beyond the nation state, focusing on the extent to which equal participation is achieved. The participatory equality of collective actors is made operable by distinguishing four evaluative conditions of participatory governance: I argue that the participatory practices of CSOs are only democratising policy-making processes if the latter are transparent, provide access to the processes in an inclusive manner, and, ultimately, show responsiveness to the concerns of the participants. This chapter concludes by presenting my approach of how to translate these evaluative conditions methodologically into empirical research.

The book's empirical Part II focuses on the European Union as an example of the postnational constellation in its most advanced form. I will, in

Chapter 4, analyse the European participatory regime both in its formal and in its operational form, applying the above-elaborated four evaluative aspects of democratic participation. I show that the formal participatory provisions of the EU have been expanded throughout European integration, but also that an interesting duality occurred: in the 1970s, strong participatory rights for a limited set of actors were introduced, but, since then, an expansion of actors has been accompanied by a contraction and a softening of participatory rights.

With regard to the operational form of the EU's participatory regime, in Chapter 5 I will exemplarily analyse the processes of European migration and EU environmental policies with regard to how the participation of civil society organisations contributes to the democratic quality of EU policy-making processes. I demonstrate that the participatory practices of CSOs have become an integral element of the EU's policy-making practices, which lack transparency and foster asymmetrical access to policy-making processes, thus violating the democratic key principle of political equality.

Finally, the book's institutional Part III reconsiders the theoretical discussions in a procedural intent. Chapter 6 brings together the conceptual reflections and the empirical insights from the previous chapters. In a first step, the empirical insights are put together in the light of the normative conditions spelled out earlier. In characterising the EU's participatory regime, both in its formal and its operational shape, several democratic pathologies are identified. It will be demonstrated that the participatory regime of the EU fails, in particular, in all four evaluative conditions for political equality. Upon the basis of this identified *status quo*, I will conceptualise a model of regulated deliberative participation that aims to tackle this major deficiency concerning political equality, and outlines the possible future for an organised civil society in Europe.

Regulated deliberative participation proposes a procedural frame for empowering and guaranteeing all the participants of a policy process both the legal right and the duty to give and take reasons. The model thus institutionalises a discursive arrangement based upon rights. It strives to tackle the problem of political (rather than material) inequality by proposing procedures in which these inequalities are not translated into political power. Assuming that these procedures succeed in establishing rules for reciprocal justification, a situation would emerge which would encourage self-containment and discourage domination, because everybody would be obliged to contextualise their arguments, i.e. not to disregard the existence of other positions and their specific reasoned demands. The model is grounded both in the normative reasoning of Part I and in the empirical findings of Part II, so as to be both normatively meaningful and practically feasible.

I will propose the institutionalisation of deliberative participation in a two-stage model, and show where the empirical findings offer starting points for its realisation. In particular, some developments in the area of environmental policy, such as the Århus-Convention on access to information, public participation in decision-making and access to justice in environmental matters (United Nations Economic Commission for Europe 1998), are promising starting-points for enhancing the democratic quality of participation. They might serve as a model for the EU's overall participatory regime.

This proposal for a regulated model of deliberative participation does not pretend to cover all the issues of participation and democracy in a globalising world. However, it adds to the clarification of some aspects in the discussion on democracy and participation, and shows pragmatic, but normatively informed, paths towards a democratic institutional design. The safeguarding functions of legally enforceable rights to participation attempt to ensure democratic interest representation, instead of its lobbying-like variant. In the concluding section, Chapter 7, I will reflect on the limits of the proposed model of deliberative participation and on some of the wider implications of my findings for the future of democracy in a globalising context.

## Notes

1   Clearly, one can only speak about the EU subsequent to the Treaty of Maastricht (1993); before that, accuracy would demand us to speak of the EC. For convenience, I will only speak of the EU throughout the study.
2   BVerfG, 2 BvE 2/08 (30.6.2009), available at:    (www.bundesverfassungsgericht .de/entscheidungen/es20090630_2bve000208en.html?Suchbegriff=Lissabon+Vertrag (accessed 19 February 2010).
3   According to the Freedom House Report 'Freedom in the World 2007', 123 countries of the 192 countries which are UN members are electoral democracies; see http://freedomhouse.org/template.cfm?page=368&year=2007 (accessed 19 February 2010).
4   Carter and Stokes (2002: 16) point to the fact that similar announcements about the triumph of democracy were already made after the First and Second World Wars, respectively.
5   There also exist other categorisations. Warren (2001), for instance, counts only two transformations (including a currently ongoing one), arguing that Dahl's first transformation was the emergence of democracy, rather than its transformation.
6   However, the idea of democracy was severely criticised by many philosophers of that time. Neither Plato nor Aristotle, for instance, praised democratic systems in their philosophies.
7   At that time, women did not have citizenship rights.
8   One should bear in mind that only a minority of the total inhabitants of the Athens of ancient Greece possessed full political participation rights; women, slaves, and migrants did not hold (full) citizenship rights. Thus, the high congruence of political reality and theory came at high exclusionary cost.
9   Originally, this OPOV-formula read 'one man, one vote'.
10   A note of caution against a too strong conception of such congruence is necessary from a critical perspective. The inherent assumption of this conception seems to be a fairly homogenous *demos* within nation states, an assumption which underestimates the significant internal socioeconomic cleavages within nation states. To some extent,

the incongruence of the postnational age makes these differences more distinctly visible, rather than causing them.

11   In his influential article about the insolvable tension between system effectiveness and citizen participation, Robert Dahl (1994) stresses the comparability of the second to the third transformation. The Greek city-state, he says, 'was made obsolete by the emergence of the large scale nation-state' (*ibid.*: 25), and the currently ongoing third transformation is 'something like the second transformation writ large on a world scale' (*ibid.*: 27). 'Like the second transformation, then, the third is associated with a great increase in the scale of the political system' (*ibid.*: 28).

12   'Der Staat bekommt Gesellschaft' – this nice phrasing is used by Stephan Leibfried, the Speaker of the Special Research Centre Sfb 597 (University of Bremen) on Transformations of the State, in order to describe one of the major developments within the international system and major challenges to the nation state.

13   The search for functional solutions at intergovernmental level, which triggered the establishment of International Organisations and International Regimes is common. Michael Zürn (2000), for instance, argues that International Organisations are not *per se* undemocratic, nor do they endanger the democratic quality of nation states, because they increase citizens' capabilities to deal with issues beyond the nation state.

14   http://ec.europa.eu/commission_barroso/wallstrom/communicating/conference/dialogue/six-pan-european-projects/index_en.htm (accessed 8 September 2008).

15   This referendum saw a high turnout of 83.1%, of which a slim majority of 50.7% voted 'no' and 49.3% 'yes'. Only one year after the failure, the Danish government held a second referendum on the treaty, which took place on 18 May 1993. Turnout was high (86.5.%) and positive votes held the majority with 56.7% to 43.3%.

16   For the importance of the parliamentarian dimension for EU democracy, see Rittberger (2006).

17   Qualified-majority voting is a representative element of politics in that it overcomes unanimity, which is known from traditional international negotiations; however, within the Council a culture of unanimity dominates (Hix 2005, Chapter 3).

18   In fact, the inclusion of individual citizens is rather treated as an orphan in the public debates. Also, with a view at institutional efforts, more attention was given to the participation of collective actors. The exception, as introduced already above, is Margot Wallström's *Plan D for Democracy, Dialogue and Discussion*.

19   In his 2003 volume, Justin Greenwood nicely puts together the key interests of the analytical literature on interest representation: '… the study of interest representation in the EU can help explain how public policies emerge, how they are framed and processed, why they take the character they do, and how they might contribute to our understanding of the course of European integration' (Greenwood 2003: 1). It is evident that the present study does not add to these questions, but undertakes a normative interpretation of similar processes, instead.

20   Following the Treaty of Rome (1957), the first European peak associations, particularly in the economic sphere, began to form, such as the Union of Industrial and Employers' Confederations of Europe (known by its acronym UNICE after the French name – Union des confédérations de l'industries et des employeurs d'Europe; UNICE changed its name to BusinessEurope in spring 2007) in 1958, often encouraged by the European Commission (see for example Butt Philip 1985: 9ff). The social partners were only established in 1973. Since the late 1980s–early 1990s, interest groups have mushroomed in Brussels; it is not possible to identify unambiguous numbers of such groups, as Greenwood shows by presenting the differences of numbers put forward by a variety of authors (Greenwood 2003: 8ff). One can, nevertheless, maintain that the growth rates at European level are in line with those at international level, which saw an expansion of internationally active NGOs particu-

larly from the late 1970s (Martens 2002). With a focus only on European federations, Kohler-Koch (1992: 18) sees the peak of foundations surrounding the Treaty of Rome in the late 1950s–early 1960s, but an explosion in numbers of lobby groups in the aftermath of the Single European Act (1987) (ibid.: 36). For a historical account of the evolution of federations at European level, see also Middlemas (1995, Chapter 10).

21   This is also true for a general theory of democracy. Habermas (1996b), for instance, distinguishes, most prominently, three normative models of democracy (republican, liberal and deliberative); for overviews about normative and empirical models, see, amongst others, Held (2006) and Schmidt (2000).

22   The same is true for other double-natured concepts prominently used within Political Science and which are also at the centre of this work, namely, participation or legitimacy, which are 'opaque and elusive concept[s] on the border between empirical and normative social sciences' (Nanz 2001: 14; 2006). The terminological difficulty of these concepts stems from their application within a semantic field that connects apparently contradictory concepts (see also Kratochwil 2006). Although it is less deeply rooted in political philosophy, the concept of governance also carries certain normative baggage, concerning, amongst other things, the delineation of the public and the private or the role of the state. However, the governance literature fails even more often than the democracy literature to offer reflections on the shadow theories behind its key concept.

23   A critical discussion of Habermas' writings about rational reconstruction as methodological approach is provided by Pedersen (2009).

# PART I

Civil society and democratic participation – the theoretical perspective

# 2

# Contemporary theories of democracy and participation

This chapter turns to the central democratic practice that this study focuses on, namely, political participation. It starts with preliminary conceptual clarifications and presents an overview of the different objectives and types of actors that are potentially addressed when discussing participation. The second and third sections then elaborate on the relationship between democratic theory and participation. They show that participation in the national age was predominantly concerned with the participation of the individual, whereas important parts of the discussions at the dawn of the postnational age turn to the participation of non-state collective actors. These theoretical reflections prepare the elaboration of a set of normatively meaningful, while at the same time empirically feasible, criteria (Chapter 3), which offer evaluative guidance for the book's empirical Part II.

## The conceptual field of political participation

In a broad sense, participation refers to all social activities concerned with the engaging and partaking in some form of activity with other people, be it in the cultural, the religious or the social sphere. Within the proto-typical large-scale polity of the national age, political participation encompasses societal self-organisation as well as the interactions of citizens with the institutional centre of decision-making. Political participation refers to all those activities that take place beyond the mere private realm of families, friendships and hobbies, and which aim at establishing, contributing to, influencing or hindering both the decisions and/or the implementation of public affairs.[1] It can either be formalised, for instance, in voting procedures, or take place very informally as with, for instance, civil disobedience. This continuum from formal to informal participatory practices includes diverse activities such as protesting, campaigning, writing advisory papers in an expert committee, being active in political parties, or organising a referendum, but it excludes non-legal activities, such as violent protests or rioting. Participation can take place at all levels of authority in which concerns of public interest are dealt with, i.e. the local, national, regional and global level, and is possible at all stages of the policy cycle.[2] These multiple forms of participatory activities connect the individual with the decision-making *locus* in which their concerns are collectively discussed and decided.

If the term 'democracy' is to have any meaning at all, at least some form of participation of people in politics is indispensable for any form of democracy. Unsurprisingly, however, different approaches to democracy profoundly disagree in their judgement about the necessary scope, forms and agents of democratic participation. The reason for this disagreement is simply that there is no unitary theory of democracy. Propositions about both the necessary extent and the appropriate forms of democratic participation vary according to the respective underlying conception of democracy, as do propositions about the democratic promises and limitations of participation. To complicate matters further, these disagreements already exist at national level, and the postnational challenge to democracy does not promise to make things easier. One visible reaction to these challenges in recent theoretical approaches to participatory democracy is the shift in attention from individual to collective actors. In classic democratic theory,[3] and in the 1960s and 1970s, when the concept of participatory democracy was coined, the individual person, the citizen, was naturally perceived as the bearer of political action.

In the 1960s, the term 'participatory democracy' described a research programme that wanted to counter the paternalism of the modern capitalist state by enhancing the opportunities for individuals to participate in decision-making processes in all aspects of human life. One prominent field, for instance, can be found in the discussions about democracy in the workplace (Dahl 1985; Pateman 1970). Thus, participatory democracy used to be a research programme from a people's perspective. Since this 'participatory revolution' (Blühdorn 2007), the meaning of participatory democracy has been re-interpreted, especially in the recent discourses on global and European democracy, in which the term participatory democracy predominantly concerns the public action of collective actors, mainly of organised civil society, rather than that of individuals (Greven 2007).

Despite all the disagreement in democratic theory about the specific elements of participation, there nonetheless exists the basic agreement that one can ascribe two dimensions to participation, namely an instrumental and a normative dimension (Greven 2007; Scharpf 1970; Schultze 2002). These two dimensions again demonstrate that the concept of participation is situated at the interface of normative and empirical social science. An instrumental understanding of participation is often put forward by empirical or realist approaches to democracy, whereas a normative conceptualisation is favoured by idealist approaches.[4]

Against this background, it is possible to distinguish four different types of participatory activities that are ordered alongside the normative/instrumental and individual/collective actor dimensions, respectively (see Figure 2.1). These types of activities are broad enough to capture all the forms

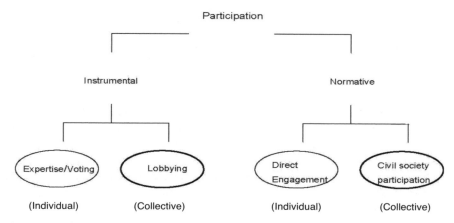

Figure 2.1  The conceptual field of political participation

of participation named above; moreover, their grouping according to a type of actor, be it individual or collective, should be understood as an ideal-type proxy, rather than as an exclusive categorisation, meaning that, in reality, the different actors engage simultaneously in different participatory activities which can be attributed to more than one of the ellipses. For instance, it is often individuals who engage in lobby activities – albeit usually on behalf of a collective actor. Furthermore, lobbyists also provide expertise, as do civil society organisations which also engage in lobby activities. Nevertheless, the figure visualises the conceptual field of this study between instrumental and normative forms of participation, and stresses once more that this study, with its focus on collective actors, is restricted to only half of the complete partici-patory picture. Later on in this chapter, I will take a closer look at how different approaches to democracy deal with collective actors in participatory arrangements, and which appropriate participatory strategies they propose for these actors.

As I elaborated in the introductory chapter, it is the central aim of this book to substantiate the claim that the participation of collective actors can be an alternative to the participation of individuals, because it contributes to the democratisation of not yet democratic policy-making practices beyond the nation state. It asks whether the participation of these actors does, indeed, result in participatory processes that fulfil the ultimate aim of political participation – self-governance by the people – or whether it establishes forms of consultative practices under the discursive umbrella of participation as a 'means of encouraging the maximum level of minimal participation' (Crouch 2004: 112), in which democratic institutions and practices are merely simulated (Blühdorn 2006) and through which the normative concept of democracy becomes affirmatively re-interpreted (Abromeit 2002: 33; Greven 2007: 238).

This question, and the concerns with regard to the normative downsizing of democracy countered, can only be answered against an understanding of the participatory democracy of individuals. Such an understanding is important because it is by no means self-evident that the transposition of the participation semantics from individual to collective actors leaves the normative underpinnings of participation unharmed. However, I will abstain from re-telling once more the history of political philosophy and of the ancestors of participatory democracy. Instead, I will present the outlines of contemporary democratic thought on participation. The following section offers a brief summary of the key arguments of different approaches to participatory democracy and critically assesses their contribution with regard to both the promises and the limits of participation for democracy. I will then discuss contemporary theories of democracy that deal with the participation of collective actors, thus entering into detail about the democratising potential of their participation.

## Democratic participation in the national age: individual actors

### The empirical approach to democratic participation

*The central arguments of the empirical approach to democracy*
Empirical, or realistic, approaches to democracy evolved particularly in American Political Science after the Second World War. They cannot be seen as a unitary body of literature or as a coherent school of democratic thought. Research on democracy within this camp is nevertheless conjoined, firstly, by a common research interest, namely the shared aspiration to describe and to explain patterns of democracy, rather than to judge its quality. Empirical approaches to democracy, in the words of Robert Dahl, 'are not attempts to prescribe how democracy ought to work but to describe how some of the political systems widely called by that name do in fact operate and to explain why they operate this way' (Dahl 1966: 298, emphasis in original; see also Held 2006: 141). This focus on description and explanation emanates, secondly, from the conviction that democracy is a method to come to collectively binding decisions, rather than a (utopian) ideal that ought to structure the whole of society, and that such a decision-making method can be analysed by empirical social science.

It was, above all, Joseph Schumpeter (1947), who stimulated empirical research on democracy. He built his theory in opposition to what he called the classic writers on democratic theory and their 'Classical Doctrine of Democracy' (Schumpeter 1947: Chapter XXII).[5] Schumpeter rejects this understanding of democracy as insufficient for defining democracy, and offers several reasons for his opinion. Some of these reasons point to important challenges to the concept of democracy, which democratic theories in a postnational age also cannot easily avoid. His key message is that he rejects philosophical justifications of democracy for spatial and practical reasons, and that he mistrusts the ability of the people to cope with the complex challenges of collective decision-making.

From his conviction that democracy is a method to reach collective decisions, it follows that Schumpeter cares most about efficient government and the means to achieve this. To what extent these means should be democratic is a secondary matter and subject to empirical research. Schumpeter does not see self-determination and self-government as the intrinsically valuable goals of a system of rule; crucial, instead, is the system's ability for problem-solving, and it is this which interests him. Thus, what Schumpeter is concerned with is the question of effective leadership. He raises serious doubts about whether a strong notion of democracy – as put forward in the classical doctrine – offers realistic avenues for achieving this goal. For Schumpeter, democracy's main task is to elect its leaders regularly, and its strength lies in the fact that they need to compete in order to be elected. Thus, a parliament should not be understood as a direct or proportional representation of the people, but as a governmental organ to which the people have delegated decision-making power. This concludes with the famous definition of democracy, which states that:

> the democratic method is that institutional arrangement for arriving at political decisions in which individuals acquire the power to decide by means of a competitive struggle for the people's vote. (*Ibid.*: 269)

Schumpeter conceives politics as a market in which, through the market mechanism of competition, citizens are regularly enabled to choose their rulers from among the competing elites. Thus, for Schumpeter and much of the subsequent empirical research on democracy, the institutionalised regular selection of the ruling personnel is what makes a political system a democracy. Elections are consequently perceived as the organisational core of democracy.[6] The model of democracy emerging from this approach was nicely dubbed as 'alterocracy' (Schonfeld 1975: 146), a label that immediately reflects the central argument that it is the alternation between ruling elites which characterises a democracy.[7]

This famous conception of democracy as a way of organising the state has come to be narrowly identified with territoriality-based, competitive elections of political leadership for legislative and executive offices, and is still very influential to this day. Many definitions of democracy mainly circulate around the mechanisms of competition and elections. It is understandable that this minimal approach to democracy was, and still is, rather attractive for empirical social scientists, because it is relatively straightforward to operationalise indicators based upon this minimal definition, as, for instance, in the Freedom House index.[8]

One of the backdrops of this concept's prominence, beyond its minimalism, is its own success. It dominates wide areas of (largely empirically oriented) Political Science to such an extent that it is often no longer spelled out. As a reader, one is often left in the dark as to whether the author uses elite competition and elections merely as an empirical proxy for a wider understanding of democracy, or whether this minimal concept itself has gathered genuine normative quality.

Moreover, it would be wrong to refer to Schumpeter if one supports a representative democracy, in which a parliament is interpreted as representing the diversity of the people. This would be outside his theory's scope, because Schumpeter does not support the idea of representation, in the ultimate understanding of the word, but, instead, speaks of the delegation of decision-making power through elections. Empirical research on democracy thus needs to be careful and very explicit about both its underlying normative ideal of democracy *and* about the extent to which the applied empirical indicators resonate with this normative concept. Often, indicators mirror the social reality rather than normative conceptions, and are thus in danger of labelling institutional arrangements and practices as democratic when, in fact, they are not. Once more, explicitness about 'one's own shadow theories' is what research on democracy requires.

*What role for participation in empirical approaches to democracy?*
Does this minimal conception of democracy leave any space for the participation of citizens? What picture is drawn of the citizen? Apparently, fear of democracy as 'the rule of the rabble' and a belief in the idea that human nature was ill-suited for democracy considerably narrow the limits of what participation can mean. In practical terms, the Schumpeterian idea of democracy as a method, dominated by a market model of competition, leads to the understanding that a system of authority is already democratic if it applies the mechanism of election as the key procedure by which the citizens delegate the power for collective decision-making to a clearly defined group of people. In this vein, voting is often used synonymously with participation. In fact, Schumpeter rules out any further reaching mechanisms of political participation and voice, arguing that 'the practice of bombarding them [the parliamentarians] with letters and telegrams for instance … ought to come under the same ban' (quoted in Held 2006: 150).

Effective leadership can only be realised, so the idea goes, if the governments, once elected and in power, are free to make their decisions undistorted from external influences. This approach significantly reduces the role of citizens in the public realm and confines them to the private realm. The citizen only enters the public realm at the moment of voting, while the reasoning behind his or her voting decisions, the emergence of his or her preferences and interests, are left to the private realm. Thus there is a divide between the political public sphere and the private sphere, which implies that politics works best if it functions fairly unnoticed by, and is unhampered by, the direct participation of the people.

This fairly confined space for the political participation of the individual in empirical approaches to democracy already points to some problems: although Schumpeter claims to argue in a value-free and empirical way, he makes normative statements based upon inferences from empirical observations, and disavows normative propositions on empirical grounds. For instance, his negative picture of human nature is based upon empirical observations, which are at a fundamentally different level than the ideal theory about the rationality of people in political philosophy. Nevertheless, it is upon this empirical basis that he rejects normative models of democracy.[9] Moreover, the relation between the elected representative and the voter is under-specified with regard to the possible degree of the voter's control over the self-interests of the representatives. Finally, he infers from the existence of a plurality of interests and values that a common will is impossible, and that one cannot commonly agree on public affairs, either. Thus, he not only confuses the difference between norms and values, but also confuses different levels of arguments.

As was already pointed out above, the relationship between normative and empirical social science is delicate, and the different levels of arguments must be clearly spelled out. Schumpeter's approach illustrates that a purely empirical approach, which neglects the empirical–normative double nature of democracy, is not feasible. Any attempt to bridge the gap must carefully avoid falling into one of the traps of normative and empirical research outlined in the introductory chapter.

### The democratic promises and fallacies of participation in the empirical perspective

Despite these theoretical problems, even a minimal conception of democracy, as proposed by Schumpeter, implies a number of fundamental principles for citizen participation to be regarded as democratic. The competitive model of democracy with both regular selection and the alternation of the rulers puts the participatory mechanism of elections at the centre of the political activities of the people. This mechanism has two sides: it must enable individuals to vote by endowing each citizen with certain political freedoms, such as the right to vote and freedom of information. Thus, at the level of the people as a whole, some form of political equality and a notion of political rights are indispensable, most prominently described in the formula 'one person, one vote', without necessarily extending the right to vote to universal suffrage, though.[10]

Furthermore, the election mechanism has to offer certain rights to those who aspire to become elected. Here, the freedom of association, to raise one's voice and to campaign in an undistorted way in a free press are all additional ingredients of democracy in the Schumpeterian perspective. Everybody should, in principle, be free to compete for political leadership. Elections are an iterative mechanism that is to assure the responsiveness of the government to the preferences of the people by relying on the rulers' urge to be re-elected.

For this, the would-be leader has to strive for the acceptance of the middle position of his society (Downs 1968). One can understand these basic principles as a vital ingredient of any political system that wants to be called a democracy. Thus, even the focus on elections as the sole participation mechanism relies on some form of political equality.

However, the instrumental dimension of participation remains in the foreground and participation is predominantly seen from the perspective of the political system, not of the citizen. Participation, understood as voting, has the purpose of selecting the leaders of this system and thus of ensuring its effective government. Co-determination, not to mention self-determination, is not the aim of this form of participation. This points to the limits of this understanding of political participation. Only at one (albeit regularly repeated) point in time, the election day, is full participation potentially realised. In the meantime, the agenda-setting and formulation of policies is left to the elected politicians and the state bureaucracy. There is no space for citizens to voice their concerns and feed them into the policy process continuously. It is, therefore, questionable as to whether this limited account of participation sufficiently guarantees the system's responsiveness. Moreover, the scepticism about the ability of human nature to rationalise, and the fear of the tyranny of the rabble undermine political equality. In this reading, only an elite minority is able to participate extensively, namely those who become professional politicians and seek office through electoral victory.

Empirical approaches to democracy in the tradition of Schumpeter have a thin conception of democracy and participation. Since democracy is restricted to a method of choice of leadership, participation is not meant to fulfil the further functions of connecting the citizenry with its rulers, let alone to strive for the ideal of self-government. Their scepticism about the technical feasibility of extensive participation and, more profoundly, its desirability in the face of the defects of human nature, leads, nevertheless, to crucial points which the advocates of participatory democracy have to answer.

### The normative approach to democratic participation

*The central arguments of the normative approach to democracy and the role of participation in democracy*
The Political Science literature of the 1960s and early 1970s saw a renaissance in the study of participation. This idealist literature was more outspokenly political in nature, in that it accompanied and responded to increasing demands for the active inclusion of citizens in the context of the student movement (Kaufman 1969b; Pateman 1970; Scaff 1975).[11] However, this increased popularity of the concept of participation was of relatively short endurance and the term vanished again in the late 1970s, to return only in the late 1990s in a different guise, which then referred to collective actors (see below).[12]

Like the empirical approaches discussed above, the idealist approach to democratic participation is not a coherent school of literature, either. Instead, it encompasses different authors who argue for more demanding conceptions of participation. For idealists, democracy is more than a method for arriving at collectively binding decisions, and more than the regular election (and only alleged control) of political leaders. Thus, democratic participation is more than the act of regularly going to the ballot box; instead, it expands to the function of improving decision-making and, ultimately, to democratising society as such. With this perspective, idealist theorists of participatory democracy criticise the empirically oriented research which, following Schumpeter, dominated Political Science, and which was based upon minimal conceptions of democracy (Habermas *et al.* 1961; Kaufman 1969a; Pateman 1970).

Unsurprisingly, the concept of participation as well as its theoretical foundations and practical implications are at the very centre of the idealist literature. In 1961, Jürgen Habermas *et al.* had already asked the question of whether 'participation is a value in itself' (1961), a question which is still raised today (see, for instance, Stokes 2002: 32). The authors replied that participation would be of no democratic value if it were merely understood as a contribution to the functioning of democratic processes (Habermas *et al.* 1961: 13ff). This implies that a focus on participation with a mere instrumental purpose for the political system would not pass a democratic test. Instead, the authors concluded that:

> Participation is only of democratic potential to the extent to which it politically influences the development of the formal to the material, the liberal to the social democracy, thus, if it is capable of influencing political decision-making towards enhancing the freedom of society. (*Ibid.*: 55; author's translation)

This perspective highlights the ultimate normative quality of participation: it directly adds to the fabric of a democratic society by enhancing the quality of the key normative principles of freedom and equality; moreover, it improves the democratic spirit of the citizens, which again strengthens the democratic quality of society.

This view of participation differs fundamentally from the empirical notion due to the differences within the underlying conceptions of democracy. For idealists, democracy is more than a container of liberal rights that 'protect individual citizens from arbitrary rule and oppression by government, as well as from infringements upon individual liberty from other citizens' (Stokes 2002: 28). Instead, as Habermas *et al.* stress, the nature of democracy is to increase the people's autonomy:

> Democracy strives for mankind's self-determination, and only if the latter has become real, does the former become true. Political participation will then be identical with self-determination. (Habermas *et al.* 1961: 15; author's translation)

Democracy, for idealists, is not only a decision-making procedure, but also a goal for societal development. In this reading, the concept of participation is of interest to critical theorists who aim at individual emancipation and empowerment as well as at the democratisation of the whole political system.

As stated above, it is not least the elitist tone of Schumpeterian notions of democracy that is challenged by the idealistic approach. Instead of upholding the idea of an asymmetrical relationship between the leaders and the people within a political system, idealist approaches to democratic participation stress the importance of direct citizen involvement in the making of collective decisions and policies. Participation is perceived as a democratic fundamental, a core element of democracy, because it contributes to the realisation of the idea of the congruence between law-makers and law-abiders. This means that, without the direct participation of the citizens, the ideal of self-governance would be meaningless. While the realist adopts a rather top-down perspective by focusing on the instrumental usage of participation for the political system, the idealist focuses on the possibilities for the creation of a democratic society and sees participatory activities from below as a crucial ingredient in order to reach this aim. The interests and reasoning of each and every citizen are seen as important for the advancement of a democratic political community. Thus, there is more emphasis on the public, as opposed to the private, realm, and citizen participation is understood as a vital ingredient of democracy.[13]

In particular, it is Carole Pateman's (1970) influential work on participation that systematically stresses the psychological or educative component of participation. Building on Rousseau and J.S. Mill, she develops the basic assertion of normative democrats, namely, that there is a direct inter-relationship and connection between individuals, their qualities and psychological characteristics on the one hand, and the types and structures of the political institutions on the other (Pateman 1970, Chapter 2).

If an individual participates in an environment of democratic institutions, his or her personality will be shaped accordingly; and an association requires the participation of its members in order to be shaped according to democratic principles. The more an individual participates, the more his or her qualities regarding participation evolve and the more the institutional structure supports his or her participation. As Pateman underlines, it is this 'stress on this aspect of participation and its place at the centre of their theories that marks the distinctive contribution of the theorists of participatory democracy to democratic theory as a whole' (*ibid.*: 22).

Thus, participation and a democratic society are mutually dependent on each other and the existence of the one both pre-supposes and enhances the quality of the other. This dialectic understanding of participation normatively pre-supposes the existence of political autonomy (independence and sovereignty) and the (not only political) equality of each individual in political decision-making, because 'the only policy that will be acceptable to all is the one where any benefits and burdens are equally shared; the participatory process ensures that political equality is made effective in the decision-making assembly' (*ibid.*: 23). Thus, participatory democracy does not aim to overcome, but, instead, to deepen, liberal democracy.

In Pateman's interpretation of participatory democracy, participation expands well beyond the borders of the political sphere, in the narrow sense, to all aspects of society, especially the economy. The aim is not only democratic politics, but also a democratic society. Thus, one can understand the emphasis that is especially given to the democratisation of the workplace.[14] From all this, it follows that the requirement of each political institution is that it not only strives for openness and responsiveness to the concerns of its members, but also that its very decisions are taken by the latter. Here, again, Pateman highlights the importance of emancipation and self-transformation.

*The democratic promises and fallacies of participation in the normative perspective*

It should by now have become apparent how crucial a role participation actually plays in the accomplishment of democracy in the interpretation of idealists. This importance is best summarised, once more, in the words of Pateman, who says that 'for a democratic polity to exist, it is necessary for a participatory society to exist' (Pateman 1970: 43). Unlike the realist democratic theory, here, participation is not considered in a top-down perspective, i.e. in its function of enabling the effective ruling of a political system by choosing its leadership, but it is considered from below, from the perspective of the people. It is 'the development of human powers of thought, feeling, and action' (Kaufman 1969a: 184) that is of interest, less so the functioning of the political institutions of a representative system.

Participation promises to unfold its democratic potential through its self-propelling function of stimulating the democratic character of the participating individual as well as of the democratic society as such. A participatory society is the condition for the creation and persistence of a democratic polity. Only through participation can the congruence of law-makers and law-abiders be achieved. Thus, participatory democracy is a democratic theory that centres on the core of democracy, namely self-determination and political equality. This very demanding and extensive role which participation has to play in such a conception of democracy is open to much criticism from multiple perspectives. I wish to highlight three aspects which point to certain limits of participation, and which have provoked criticism, namely, the critical character of participatory democracy, the psychological assumptions both about the educative function of participation and about human nature, and, thirdly, the proposals for an institutional design of participatory democracy.

Participatory democracy entails a promise both to criticise and to change existing undemocratic and possibly unjust institutional structures. However, as Kaufman (1969b) underlines from within participatory thinking, to participate in issues of public interest means, in principle, to accept the existing rules of the game. The participant 'can become an instrument of co-optation' (Kaufman 1969b: 211), and the institution might deliberately design participatory avenues to internalise criticism. To what extent such procedures and practices still satisfy the concept of participatory democracy is, ultimately, the subject of empirical analyses.

Empirical research from Social Science disciplines such as Social Psychology or Political Sociology unmasked the educative potential of participation on the democratic character of the participants as empirically not confirmable (for an early overview of such criticism, see Scharpf 1970). This kind of research not only expresses doubt about the feasibility of implementing widespread participation in modern mass societies, but also asks whether extensive participation, if realised, would not over-exaggerate the rational character of human beings. Even more fundamentally it questions whether participation has any effects on the democratic character of the participants at all. Jane Mansbridge, an important recent proponent of active participation, answers these critical points in the following way:

> Participation does make better citizens. I believe it, but I can't prove it. And neither can anyone else. The kinds of subtle changes in character that come about, slowly, for active, powerful participation in democratic decisions cannot easily be measured with the blunt instruments of social science. Those who have actively participated in democratic governance, however, often feel that the experience has changed them. And those who observe the active participation of others often believe that they see its long run effects on the citizens' character. (Mansbridge 1995)

Sceptics of the capability of human nature to become engaged in true and valuable political participation will probably not be convinced by such a statement. At the end of the day, it might be a question of standpoints on human nature and on the methods of social inquiry that leads scholars to support or to discard the idea of the psychological effects of participation.

The third criticism that I wish to mention is dissatisfaction with the institutional proposals that are put forward by idealist, participatory theories of democracy. Fritz Scharpf (1970, Chapter 3), for instance, stresses that participatory democrats, while being good at criticising the empirical, realistic literature of American pluralism, are weak at showing how participation could be institutionalised. In particular, he is unconvinced by proposals to democratise the workplace and industry by increasing worker participation, as proposed by Carole Pateman, amongst others.

A similar move is criticised by Scharpf as being insufficient for an institutional design because this would only establish specialised participation in very confined areas which, important as it might be, would, by its very nature, remain embedded in an existing (representative) political system and would thus fall (very) short of the critical power of participatory theories. The underlying charge against idealist theory is thus its utopian character and the gap between significant criticism and the lack of realistic practical implications.[15]

Such criticism has been prominent to this day, and poses a serious challenge to idealist theorising. However, one should not be unjust to the latter approaches by arguing that these theories only recognise full participation as being democratic, and, as a consequence, by exposing them as being totally utopian and blind to the realities of modern mass societies in modern nation states. Important as Scharpf's (1970) objections against Pateman's proposals are, one needs to be cautious with such criticism, because there is a distinction between a participatory society and participatory politics, as Pateman (2003) and Barber (2003) make clear in their work. These authors agree that there are, not least on practical grounds, good reasons for representative mechanisms in large-scale societies, but they also argue that the polity can only, at least potentially, become democratised if it is based upon a participatory society which again depends on participatory activities. If one criticises idealist thinking on participation and democracy only from the practical perspective of the political processes of decision-making, disregarding its wider societal standpoints, one remains, in the end, within the thin conception of democracy as put forward by realists such as Schumpeter, who conceive of democracy as a decision-making method for a political system, not as a form of living which structures a whole society.

### The democratic relevance of the participation of individual actors

What one can learn from the juxtaposition of these two, admittedly stylised, approaches is that, without some (minimal) form of political participation, no democracy is possible. Participation is a democratic imperative as it contributes to the constitution of a democratic society because no individual is capable of achieving his or her aims by simply remaining in the private sphere. Instead, the individual needs to take part in collective action, to strive for self-rule actively, and thus to make active use of the basic principle which the empirical and the normative approaches principally share above all others, namely, political equality.

This means that democratic politics requires a democratic society with a set of equal political rights. Without them, no democratic participation is possible, either in the empirical, or the normative, perspective. Yet, while the former separates the political sphere from the social sphere, and thus provides considerable limits to political participation, the latter emphasises the democratisation of society and, by doing so, extends the boundaries of the political sphere to all areas of collective action.

For realist approaches to democracy, the instrumental dimension of participation is important for the overall objective of each political system, namely, to provide effective policies in order to acquire system stability. This output objective is instrumentally linked to participation through the mechanism of responsiveness.[16] A political system has, to some degree, to be responsive to the needs of the people, and it must be capable of meeting them in an efficient way, otherwise it would be in danger of failure. Thus, some form of participation and interaction between the public institutions and the people is imperative. The more a political system possesses open and accessible participatory channels, the better it can react to the people's needs and take advantage of their expertise. In the case of a failure of responsiveness, the people would not accept the rule of the political system and would strive for a change in system. Possibly the most recent and impressive example of failing responsiveness has been the peaceful changes in Central and Eastern Europe after 1989. Furthermore, it is reasonable to assume that the extent of voluntary norm compliance, i.e. of social legitimacy,[17] of the citizens increases if a general feeling of ownership exists due to the opportunities to participate (Birch 1993, Chapter 6). Thus, any political system (also and especially the democratic one; see for example Habermas 1998: 117) requires at least some degree of participation.

From the perspective of the citizens, participation in the instrumental dimension is a voluntary undertaking that aims to influence and shape collective decision-making processes according to their specific interests. Thus, the major objective of participation in this sense is to achieve certain ends through measures of co-determination.[18] Such participation takes place in a political context which deems itself already democratic and demonstrates that instrumental participation can be conceived as an intrinsic element of democracy.

The normative dimension of participation is specifically put forward by idealist approaches to democracy. There, participation is a normative objective in order to democratise the whole political system and ultimately to achieve the goal of self-determination. In this perspective, the political system should enable self-determination with regard to collective decisions through the provision of opportunity structures that are conducive to equal participation, so that the people can exert control over, have an impact on, and partake in, policy-making processes. Participation becomes an end in itself in so far as an association of free and equal people strives for the self-determination of collective decisions and provides equal participatory opportunities to all citizens, so that, ideally, the public interest is served. Thus conceived, normative participation not only aims to stabilise the existing political structures, though stability is evidently also important, but also aims to contribute to the creation of these structures as such. Hence, participation directly adds to the fabric of democracy and therefore entails genuinely democratising potential. It requires the organisation of participatory procedures according to basic democratic principles: above all, political equality, political freedom and the ability of the people to control their rulers.[19]

Moreover, normative participation potentially reaches beyond the narrow confinements of the political system, and aims to render all aspects of society democratic. In the normative dimension, democracy is not only secured by a set of institutions that aim at political equality, interest aggregation and checks and balances, as liberal theory suggests. Instead, it understands participation as a communicative practice of citizens, which makes it a constitutive element of any democratic political order. Participation is an element of the democratic fabric, and thus – if institutionalised appropriately – it is a democratic good in itself, which is supposed to add to the democratisation of policy-making processes. Citizens who engage in participatory practices strive for self-determination rather than co-determination. Overall, in the normative dimension, the emphasis is on the creation of democratic legitimacy rather than social legitimacy. The normative dimension of participation is a constant reminder never to cease improving a normatively insufficient institutional environment. Instead of providing a theoretical justification of present circumstances, as the empirical perspective tends to do, the normative perspective points its finger at the weaknesses and deficiencies of the existing context. Thus, participatory democracy promises to be critical in nature.

Table 2.1 visualises the relation between the dimensions and the objectives of participation. Without doubt, such a table necessarily exaggerates and over-simplifies at the same time. One should bear in mind, however, that it deals with conceptual types, rather than empirical results. It shows that, on the one hand, participation is conducive to system stability and provides citizens with the opportunity to co-determine public decisions by enabling them to feed their interests into decision-making processes; thus, in the instrumental dimension, participation is a means for achieving certain ends. On the other hand, in the normative dimension, participation is an end in itself, in that it aims to democratise (not only) the political system and to give the citizens the opportunity to self-determine their lives.

Evidently, modern democracies need both dimensions of participation. In the words of Lawrence Scaff, the concept of instrumental participation affirms 'the continuation of "interest-group liberalism", accepts the valuable tranquillising effects of political apathy, and recommends a strengthening of legal and constitutional guarantees of individual rights' (Scaff 1975: 462). The concept in its normative dimension bears the potential to criticise the existing

Table 2.1   Dimensions and objectives of participation

| | | Dimensions of participation | |
| | | Instrumental | Normative |
| --- | --- | --- | --- |
| Level of objectives | Political system | Stability (output) | Democratisation (input) |
| | Individual citizen | Co-determination | Self-determination |

political practices, and calls for a strengthened, inclusive citizenship, as well as institutional arrangements that facilitate democratising participation. In a nutshell, the instrumental dimension emphasises the idea that participation is an exchange act, and thus an 'instrumental means for gaining power in order to increase the probability of realising private benefits' (*ibid.*: 449),[20] while the normative dimension highlights the pursuit of the public good by inclusive means of collective decision-making.

These two dimensions, which are fairly well mirrored in the distinction between the empirical and normative theories of democracy, are important for the further elaboration of this book. They illustrate that it is important to identify the *nature* of the EU's participatory practices, which I will analyse in Part II. Instrumental participation is part of an already democratic institutional context, while normative participation ultimately contributes to the strengthening of the democratic fabric of this context itself. If the empirical analysis shows that the participatory practices are dominantly instrumental in nature, rather than normative, I will be able to infer a limited democratising potential of these practices.

But why does it not suffice to consider participation solely from an instrumental angle, particularly in a context in which individual participation is difficult to achieve? Why is not a focus on output legitimacy more promising to solve democratic problems than a focus on democratic participation on the input side?[21] I want to express my conviction that a separation of output from input legitimacy would be a departure from the realm of democratic theory (see, similarly, Niesen 2006). Such a separation would under-estimate the linkage of the empirical (output) to the normative (input) dimension of democratic legitimacy. This position does not suggest under-rating the importance of the output dimension for policy-making, the functioning and/or the somewhat diffuse social legitimacy of a political system. Yet, as Jens Steffek clearly puts it, '[p]roviding material advantages for citizens surely can help to secure acceptance of rules but it will hardly create the "prestige of being considered binding"' (2003: 257, highlights in original). He convincingly argues that a general acceptance of a policy, or a political system, which can be empirically assessed, is not to be confused with legitimacy in a normative democratic sense, which also involves the compliance with rules that are contrary to one's own preferences (similarly, also, see Richter 1994: 31).

Simple acceptance does not suffice because democratic legitimacy cannot be based 'on purely idiosyncratic grounds, since here we are not dealing with the coincidence of personal preferences, but – as is common in politics – with the establishment of a rule or policy that is binding upon all' (Kratochwil 2006: 303). It would require significant efforts to justify why, at a conceptual level, output, i.e. efficiency, is connected to a normative understanding of democracy, because there is no convincing argument at hand that could offer *a priori* definitions of the public good or public interests. If one accepts this, and if one does not support expertocracy, (enlighted) autocracy or even authoritarianism, then there remains only the democratic alternative.

*Conclusion*

The lesson from the above discussion is that any study of political systems should strive to keep both the normative and the empirical aspects in mind. The two approaches are, to use the old expression, two sides of the same coin, which can only be truly grasped if both sides are taken into consideration equally. On the one hand, realists should not be so preoccupied with effective problem-solving that they forget for whom the problems are to be solved. A political system would lose its legitimacy without an inclusive, responsive and public government, and the selection of good leaders in elections would be in danger of being based upon sheer luck if the citizens were not enabled to select their leadership wisely. On the other hand, participationists would be badly advised if they denied that 'there is a place for leadership and representation' (Kaufman 1969b: 207; emphasis in original).

This is not only due to the practical reason that not everybody participates in a modern mass society, but there is also a more theoretical ground to it. One cannot, and should not, expect everybody to participate. In a liberal, democratic society, the choice of whether to participate in meetings and public action or not is left to the free will of the individual. But would such an absence be a convincing reason to deny these people the right to have their concerns also respected in collective affairs? I believe not. Every person should, as a citizen, be entitled to institutional devices that guarantee an adequate representation of his or her concerns. Universal suffrage and a parliamentarian system would seem to be institutional answers that were appropriate for a long time, but which do show weaknesses today. Thus, one needs institutions that complement electoral and representative instruments with participatory mechanisms. This thought has been brought forward best by Arnold Kaufman:

> The main justifying function of free competition for leadership are maintenance of order, protection against the tyrannical exercise of order, and fulfilment of actual human preferences without unduly sacrificing the values of efficient decision and expert opinion. The main justifying function of participation is development of man's essential powers – inducing human dignity and respect, and making men responsible by developing their powers of deliberate action.
>
> How can both sets of aims be achieved? By developing two sets of institutions which are able to coexist. This cannot be done without conflict or sacrifice. But rather than focusing exclusively on the drawbacks, the social cost of permitting a greater degree of participation must continually be weighed against the human cost of denying such extension. (Kaufman 1969a: 198)[22]

The challenge that we are facing today is that it is easy to forget about the importance of participation, given the complexity and the global scale of today's political problems. The distance between the individual person and the decision-making *loci* seems too far to be easily bridged. It is even more difficult in the postnational constellation than it already is in modern mass societies to speak about a clearly delineated people in the sense of a *demos*. It is therefore important to reflect upon how to disconnect democracy from territorially bound institutions, while, at the same time, linking it more directly to the participatory activities of the people who, through this communicative practice, establish themselves as a common political body.

This is where the participation of collective actors comes into play. The theoretical approaches discussed below will be assessed against their ability to deal with substantial diversity, their inclusion of collective actors in order to mirror this diversity, and their aptitude to address the issue of territoriality.

### Democratic participation in the postnational age: collective actors

Against the background of the dichotomous considerations on participation in the national age, I will subsequently assess three democratic theories with regard to what they normatively offer vis-à-vis the participation of collective actors. In this, my central aim will be to identify the key democratic virtues assigned to their participation in the respective theory.

Evidently, there are different types of non-state collective actors, and different theories focus on different types. I will start with a focus on interest groups as such, referring to the most prominent representative theory, namely, American pluralism, which is a realistic theory of democracy. Then, I will continue with accounts of the role of secondary associations as outlined in two different conceptions of associative democracy. The third type of actors is the recently most favoured one, namely, civil society organisations (CSOs). There is no special democratic theory that deals with the participation of CSOs, but their participatory activities are often discussed within a framework of deliberative democracy.

It is worth noting that these different theoretical accounts vary considerably in their theoretical depth. They share an interest in non-state collective actors, with regard to the applicability of the theory to this group, rather than talking to each other at the same theoretical level. Furthermore, all of them were developed in the context of the nation state, so this section closes with the identification of the crucial democratic elements that essentially need to be transposed onto the postnational level.

### *The participation of interest groups*

#### *Basic principles*
Interest (or pressure) groups – in an older guise addressed as 'factions' in American politics[23] – are essential ingredients of modern policy-making. Analysts and commentators of daily politics often refer to the influence of

different interests in their accounts of the success or failure of policy initiatives – often with an unmistakably critical undertone towards the influence of special interests. However, there is no contemporary account of democracy that can avoid coping with the given social complexity of modern societies, and pluralism. In particular, the efforts of American pluralism of the twentieth century,[24] and, above all, the (early) writings of Robert Dahl contribute to our understanding of the relationship between democracy and the participation of interest groups that we have today.[25]

Pluralist thinking can be understood as a reaction both to a Rousseauean belief in a common good of a society as well as to an elitist competition model in the tradition of Schumpeter. In contrast to Rousseau, pluralism fundamentally assumes that society is not an entity capable of a unifying *volonté générale*, but that it legitimately consists of a plurality of groups which struggle to make their particular interests visible in the political sphere. In a pluralist reading, there is no common good, but only multiple group-based interests that can be articulated. Pluralism, unlike Schumpeter, emphasises a process-dimension to politics, and argues that the ruling elites are not to be left uncontrolled in the time-spans in between election days.

Pluralism refers to the 'existence of a plurality of relatively autonomous (independent) organisations (sub-systems) within the domains of a state' (Dahl 1982: 5), an existence that is democratically desirable and to be found in all democratic countries. This plurality of diverse group interests rests, ideally, on a power-equilibrium, with the consequence that democracy does not equal majority rule, but, instead, comes to be understood as the government of minorities. Thus, in a pluralist understanding, politics is an interaction process between different existing groups of minorities. This process becomes democratic if there is, first, competition between the groups, which has, secondly, to be fair and equal, so that no minority group can be dominated by a majority, and, thirdly, the decision-making processes must be accessible to the interests of the different groups.

The notion of competition of interests shows the underlying rationalist assumption of pluralists. They believe in the pre-existence of interests and preferences, which, in the political process, need to be articulated, aggregated and channelled into the decision-making arena.[26] Pluralist politics is most prominently embedded in a system of representative democracy that is characterised by the choice of a governmental elite through regular elections and by the essential responsiveness of the government to these groups.

This brief description has already illustrated that pluralist thinking has both empirical and normative aspects,[27] which are, however, difficult to separate from each other. On the one hand, there exists the empirical observation of a plurality of interests in society, which are often organised in groups of different, only partially overlapping, interests. On the other hand, there is the normative idea that a society should be plural in its internal organisation in order to tame the government, to settle conflicts peacefully, to

secure the responsiveness of politics to the plurality of interests within
society, and ensure that a balance of power between the groups is possible.[28]
This proximity between empirical and normative arguments has led to a
vulnerability of pluralist theory, because 'as a theory of power in America and
as justification as well' (Manley 1983: 369), it cannot easily counter empirical
criticism with strong normative claims; instead, in reply to criticisms, it had
to limit its normative aspirations (see, already, Scharpf 1970, Chapter 2).

*A critical appraisal of the role of participation in pluralism*
In pluralist thinking, the role that the participation of collective actors plays
is crucial for democratic politics, whereas the political apathy of individual
citizens is not perceived as overly problematical. The success of democracy
depends largely on the ability of the different participating groups to reach a
compromise and to organise majorities (Gerstenberg 1997: 84). The fundamental mechanism by which democratic politics functions is intergroup
bargaining, in which the aim is to realise one's own aims, rather than to satisfy
a common good. Hereby, the existence of multiple groups 'provides reasonable assurance that most important problems and grievances will be
channelled to governmental arenas' (Connolly 1969a: 4).

    Key to pluralist thought is the ambition to find a normatively convincing
and empirically realistic solution for the problem of majority domination.
The participation of groups is crucial for this aim, as they nearly always
represent a minority of the whole population. In a pluralist society, each
minority group ideally has the possibility of becoming engaged in public
policy so that, in the end, it is minorities that rule, or, at least, the elected
rulers have to answer to the requests of different minorities. Similarly, societal
elites which are engaged in interest groups have to be accessible and responsive to the more silent members of their groups (Scharpf 1970).[29]
Furthermore, every person needs to have the opportunity to participate
actively in such groups if he or she feels that his or her interests are under-
represented. In the end, the democratic contribution of the participation of
collective actors is to provide opportunities to aggregate the existing societal
interests, and channel them into the process of government.

    Thus, a perhaps overly brief, almost vulgarised version of the pluralist
approach, as described above, does not aim at the development of a democratic society, but understands the existing form of pluralism as a crucial
element of a society which is already democratic. Thus, participation is
perceived as being instrumental for achieving democratic governance where
good government is an aim in itself, because what is good for the government
is good for society, since the priorities of the former stem from the latter.
However, the role of the state is somewhat passive in this view, since its
government is, or should be, composed of the existing interest groups.
Theodore Lowi (1969) called this perception the 'public philosophy of
interest-group liberalism' (indeed it is the title of his contribution), and,

according to him, it underlies much of modern politics.[30] In fact, the empirical analysis below will show that the participatory politics of the European Union is orientated towards classical pluralist thoughts.

It is – arguably – above all the descriptive force and empirical approximation to the reality of contemporary policy-making that has helped pluralist thoughts survive up to the present. Who could reasonably deny that interest groups do play a crucial role in the arena of democratic politics, and that it is perfectly in line with democratic requirements to promote legitimate interests? It is this successful message, that the instrumental participation of non-state collective actors is an essential ingredient of modern democratic structures, which has to be particularly underlined when it comes to the lessons of the pluralist approach for the present purpose. These writings point to the importance of an equilibrium of power between the participating groups, meaning that equality must be the leading principle for access to the political arena and that all groups must be included into the political processes.

However, although these normative aspects of pluralism have always been, and still are, crucial to the realisation of democratic governance, in the perception of pluralism, its normative content was somewhat lost from view. This is probably due to the close proximity of description and prescription. In its attempt to uphold both dimensions, pluralism could not help but become more cautious in its normative aspirations in order to incorporate empirical criticism. The empirical evidence provided by both pluralist research and its critics (see for example Connolly 1969b) on the structural asymmetry in the organisation and general capability to organise between socially included and excluded groups, between the *haves* and *have nots*, both point to one common conclusion: the necessity of institutional means to overcome this lack of the equal inclusion of all voices, especially focusing on the weaker and disadvantaged ones.

The pluralist assumption of a power-equilibrium between groups has been widely criticised, because business groups and other economic interests, in particular, are considered to be very strong indeed. Thus, the importance of equality not only in access to the decision-making *loci*, but also in the ability to voice oneself (and be heard), and, by this, shape the agenda of public discourse and political action, is not sufficiently respected in the (earlier) pluralist theory. It is the understanding of the economic asymmetries of groups and the role of business that have caused changes in pluralist thinking. Some even speak of Pluralism I and Pluralism II (Manley 1983).

The gist of the latter argument is that Pluralism II acknowledges that its earlier assumptions about equal opportunities of interest articulation for different groups have proved unrealistic, and that, in order to uphold the idea of equality, measures are needed to counter the asymmetries that favour business concerns. Nevertheless, it seems that the older version of pluralism, one could also call it conventional pluralism, is still the background foil of even the recent literature on interest groups and interest representation, at least in the context of the European Union.

To a certain extent, pluralism's attempt to offer an empirically rich, while, at the same time, normatively informative, theory was made at the cost of the critical potential that is inscribed into normative theory. If one accepts the social context as its stands, then one is easily blind to its hierarchies and asymmetries, as also reproduced in the competition of groups in the political arena. So, it comes down to the conclusion that democracy and democratic governance have to deal with the existence of diverse (asymmetrically distributed) collective actors, and that pluralism does not offer a satisfying solution to this problem.

Unsurprisingly, it is particularly the asymmetry of power between economic and non-economic concerns within a capitalist society that have been taken up by other approaches concerned with the participation of collective actors. Although these issues have also found entrance into the writings of later pluralist theorists, they have not received the same amount of lasting attention as the early pluralist writings.[31]

### *The participation of secondary associations*

*Basic principles*
Classical pluralism has reached its limits in reflecting the functioning of modern democracy in a capitalist market society, because its core idea, and the one that makes pluralism democratic, namely, equality in the groups' competition for influence, cannot be upheld in the face of the uneven distribution of resources and power alongside the economic cleavages in a capitalist society.[32] Accordingly, the interactions of economic actors in shaping the political structure has become a focus of scholarly discussion, and some even see the state as being dominated by the power-resources of classes (Korpi 1983).

A prominent conception in the 1970s and 1980s theorised and analysed in some detail the interaction of labour and capital with governmental politics. This neo-corporatist school of thought[33] moved beyond pluralism's emphasis on the horizontal relations of different interest groups by focusing on groups as policy-makers and policy-implementers. Thus, while pluralists focused on the interaction between the activities of interest groups and a representatively elected government, neo-corporatists stress the quasi-monopolistic character and the self-regulating function of associations and the fact that they are interlocked with governmental agencies. In doing so, neo-corporatism shows less normative ambition than pluralism, which seeks to be both an analytical approach for empirical research and a normative theory of democracy.[34] Instead, neo-corporatism offers an explanatory frame to grasp political and social relations in (some) advanced capitalist democratic states.

Nevertheless, also within the neo-corporatist frame, some normative arguments exist, which serve to tackle the important limits of pluralist thought. More concretely, the close inclusion of interest groups into a governmental framework (in industrial relations, one speaks of *tripartism*) can be interpreted as a normative position to ease the asymmetries of power and resources, and to encourage the divergent interests to converge around a more general interest (see, similarly, Mansbridge 1992).

In the early 1990s, two substantial efforts to integrate neo-corporatist and pluralist thinking into democratic theory were advanced – independently and very different from each other – under the heading of associative democracy, 'the core proposition of which is that as many social activities as possible should be devoted to self-governing voluntary associations' (Bader 2001a: 1). Both approaches start with the failure of modern capitalist, democratic nation states to deliver and extend the role of associations beyond economic actors, who, nevertheless, remain crucial.[35]

The first effort, by Joshua Cohen and Joel Rogers (1992),[36] seeks to overcome the weaknesses of pluralism by strengthening neo-corporatist mechanisms. Consequently, the authors argue for an extension of the competencies and the scope of secondary associations; these should transform into encompassing associations in order to serve the common good. As they are dedicated to a social democratic project (Cohen and Rogers 1994), they assign a strong role to an interventionist state by simultaneously providing considerable power to secondary associations. The authors' basic premise is that an egalitarian, social democracy needs an organisational base. But they stress that this base is not provided naturally, as pluralism suggests: it is also always a product of political decisions (*ibid.*: 145ff).

By introducing the notion of the artifactual nature of associations (Cohen and Rogers 1992: 395), the authors acknowledge the potential democratic fallacies of group participation, but offer a perspective that promises to cope with these fallacies. Their aim is to develop a strategy for improving the associational environment so that factionalism and threats to egalitarian democracy are minimised. The state should be the agent of this reform strategy (*ibid.*: 425ff). In a minimal conception of associative democracy, Cohen and Rogers (1994: 146) outline a strategy for coping with state failures and for attaining egalitarian democracy by offering secondary associations a formal role in governance. In a maximal conception, associative democracy would imply a significant change in the political order as well as the inclusion of 'non-traditional stakeholders' (*ibid.*: 147) into the associative frame.

The second version of associative democracy, put forward by Paul Hirst (1994), presents a picture of a regulatory state that sets the rules for the otherwise self-regulative activities of stratified associations. His conception resembles classical pluralism more than neo-corporatism in stressing the voluntaristic character of associational life (Rossteutscher 2000: 176).[37] His conception of associative democracy is much more bottom-up than that of

Cohen and Rogers. Instead of underlining the artifactual character of associations and the responsibility of the state to support the emergence of a balance between the different associations, Hirst favours a more modest role of the state. The latter should provide, above all, both rule of law and financial resources for civil society groups and associations, which establish themselves independently from below (Hirst 1994, Chapter 2). Society should be organised in functional pillars (Rossteutscher 2000: 176f), in which the main task of associations is to deliver services and to be responsible for their functional realm.

Despite considerable differences, both conceptions share the basic consideration that associative democracy is to be understood as a complement – rather than as a substitute – to representative democracy. Thus, unlike the grand theories of democracy, such as republican *versus* liberal democracy, approaches within the framework of associative democracy should be understood as competing middle range theories with different conceptions, particularly with regard to the role of the state.

*A critical appraisal of the role of participation in associative democracy*
Both approaches share the basic presumption that the state, the economy and civil society are not spheres that should (or could) be insulated from each other, but that it is necessary to bridge the different spheres and to re-arrange the governance structures among them.[38] Consequently, and despite all internal differences, it is evident that the role of the participation of collective actors is crucial in an associationalist understanding of democracy. Although the conviction that people engage in different associations is shared with pluralism, the main thrust of the argument differs, in that, through the participation and self-regulation of associations, some of the fallacies of modern pluralised and capitalist democracy can be countered. The participation of associations serves instrumental purposes by tackling the problems of state failure that occur in the complex environment of modern politics, and it also serves normative purposes by offering a means for overcoming the problem of factions.

Moreover, at normative level, associationalists are convinced that secondary associations offer individuals a platform for engagement and public participation, so that the educative aim of participatory democracy discussed above is achievable even in modern mass societies. In its modest form, associative democracy offers remedies to the existing weaknesses of democratic governance. In a more ambitious reading, one could interpret the different approaches as a plea for a re-organisation of the competences between state institutions and self-regulation. In the context of the present study, in which the focus lies in the contribution to the democratic quality of policy-making processes through the participation of non-state collective actors, the modest interpretation of associative democracy is more important.

However, the juxtaposition of the two approaches shows that the institutional conclusions to be drawn from them are, to a certain extent, contradictory. The two approaches do not share the same position with regard to the fundamental question of whether power should be organised within a hierarchical institutional setting or whether it should be organised by horizontal self-regulation. Thus, they offer different visions about which set of institutions is most suitable for enabling democratic autonomy. For instance, Hirst proposes a pillarisation of associations alongside functional borders, but he does not explain how this is supposed to overcome the problems of faction and asymmetry. In contrast, Cohen and Rogers favour the emergence of encompassing associations in order to give way to non-factionalised actions in the common interest, but whether such big associations would still be suitable places for the voluntary engagement of citizens and to what extent they would become party-like remains unclear.

Further disagreement exists about whether associations naturally exist and emerge in a bottom-up process in society, which is Hirst's position, or whether there is (additional) need for a politics of association, as Cohen and Rogers would argue. Hirst criticises the artifactual conception of associations and the strong role assigned to the state in shaping the associational landscape (Hirst 1992). Instead, he believes that the problem of inequality and asymmetry would be mitigated if the stronger associations supported the weaker ones, and if non-organisable concerns were taken up by existing associations (Hirst 1994: 36). It is difficult to see how this assumption would counter the problems of asymmetry and inequality, which I already discussed in the section on pluralism. In comparison, Cohen and Rogers' proposition to see the associational landscape in relation to, and in interaction with, the political context, seems reasonable, even if it is, perhaps, over-emphasised.[39] A political system cannot deny that its institutions and decisions influence the way in which kinds of associations emerge and how they develop.

However, one needs to take into account a prominent objection against state intrusion in the associational landscape, namely that of co-optation. From such a perspective, the choice of either co-optation or *laissez-faire* might appear to be the choice between the black death and cholera. I believe, however, that a middle position is more reasonable. State action seems necessary to support weaker associations (even Hirst speaks of financial support through taxes), but such measures need to be carefully designed in order to avoid blatant co-optation. The possible measures of counter-balance are, above all, transparency in financing and the provision of resources for the organisational infrastructure, not just for specific projects. Such state activities would – arguably – improve the inclusiveness towards diverse associations, without being able to eradicate asymmetrical deficiencies totally. I will come back to this point later. For the moment, it suffices to say that actions need to be taken (either by the state or other associations) in order to strengthen the equality among associations.

The two approaches within associative democracy are so diverse that it is

difficult to come to a clear conclusion about the role of associational participation and the appropriate means to achieve democratic goals through
participation. In addition, the pictures drawn by the approaches are either not
really new – for instance, by only taking neo-corporatist and/or consocia-
tional arrangements as examples – or remain somewhat airy – for instance,
the relation between secondary associations and representative institutions
and the issue of the voluntary/compulsory character of associations.
Furthermore, associative democracy seeks to do, perhaps, too much in: a)
overcoming the pluralist problems of faction, thus re-interpreting the role
and the political context for the participation of associations; b) improving
the quality of governance and overcoming state failures; and c) offering the
organisational base for the participation of individuals. These aims are not
free of tensions, which partially explains the meandering of the approaches
between an instrumental and a normative understanding of participation.[40]

Some concluding remarks seem possible, nevertheless. (1) secondary
associations potentially provide the organisational base for bottom-up
processes by stimulating the engagement of citizens in associations. In this
respect, associations could be conceived of as a school of democracy in the
terms introduced above, in the context of normative conceptions of political
participation. (2) In addition to this, the close relationship of associations to
formal political institutions makes them potential agents for information
from the top down to the people, arguably improving the quality of the
implementation and the compliance with decisions. (3) The principles of
autonomy and self-government are potentially strengthened by the increasing
scope of self-regulation. (4) Some form of active state support for the
emergence of a democratic associational landscape is important.

### The participation of organised civil society

*Basic principles*
In recent years, a third type of collective actor has entered the debate about
enhancing the democratic quality of policy-making in and beyond the nation
state in both normative and empirical Political Science, namely, organised
civil society. Unlike the theories discussed above, the democratic potential of
civil society is more deeply embedded into a debate of grand democratic
theories, above all civic republicanism,[41] and, increasingly, deliberative[42]
democracy. Instead of trying to establish a somewhat practical, supplementary model of democratic governance, such as associative democracy, the
deeper theoretical questions of democratic principles and agents are
discussed. Thus, both approaches are not directly concerned with civil society
organisations, but with civil society as such. Nevertheless, the participation of
CSOs is increasingly discussed also within a framework of these theories.[43]

Deliberative democracy situates itself between liberalism and pluralism
(Habermas 1996b) and attempts to offer a path to deal with the challenges of

size and diversity. In addition, it strives to overcome the strong focus on a common good by emphasising the inter-subjective quality of the outcomes of deliberation (see Habermas 1999, Chapter 9). This model is based upon the principle of 'political justification' (Cohen 1996: 99; Forst 2001), the basic idea being that any public policy decision has to rely on good reasons made publicly by political equals in a process of open deliberation.

Since many political scientists are probably intuitively more familiar with the standard model of politics, which is captured by the aggregative model of democracy[44] and the formula of 'one person, one vote', the democratic character of deliberation needs further elaboration. Deliberation *per se* is not democratic if it only focuses on the epistemic quality of deliberation in order to improve the quality of a public decision (whoever decides on the quality of that decision) (Lafont 2006). The deliberation of experts in a small group will probably enhance the epistemic quality of a decision, but can hardly be called democratic.[45] In contrast to the aggregative model, which starts from the assumption of given preferences, the rationale of deliberative democracy is the idea that citizen preferences are not pre-politically given and thus cannot merely be fed into channels of interest aggregation. Instead, individual preferences emerge and change in the discursive practice of deliberation within the public sphere, and, ideally, a common idea about the public interest develops.

Thus, according to the deliberative model, collective choices need to be discussed and justified (rather than aggregated) in a process of public reasoning (and are thus political in nature). The democratic moment of deliberation is that political decisions are 'the outcome of a procedure of free and reasoned deliberation among individuals considered as moral and political equals' (Benhabib 1996a: 68) and that everybody can assent both freely and reasonably to these decisions (Lafont 2006: 8). Consequently, political decisions are not necessarily the *best* decisions in an epistemic understanding, but are, instead, the decisions to which the majority of participants are voluntarily able to consent to out of the totality of the available options in the light of public deliberations; in so doing, the decisions are oriented at the public good.[46]

The public good is neither pre-politically given, nor the aggregate sum of individual interests, but the outcome of a dynamic process of public deliberation among political equals. Deliberative democracy thus avoids calling for the necessity of a strong *demos*, which is allegedly necessary to establish a pre-politically given sense of commonality and solidarity. Instead, by introducing the notion of inter-subjectivity, it offers a way of coming to terms with the unavoidable fact of diversity and plurality in modern political bodies. The preferences of each individual emerge in a public, inter-subjective sphere within a deliberative process. Each preference is therefore integrated into a web of communication, which shapes the interests of others and reacts to the environment (see Habermas 1999, Chapter 9). With this concept, it is possible to overcome the problem that one needs either a metaphysical common good or a homogeneous group for democratic politics. Thus, the door for the possibility of mutual understanding and public action beyond the state is opened.

In particular, the scholars of deliberative theory that stand in the tradition of Jürgen Habermas have paid much attention to the role of civil society. Civil society, according to Habermas, is to be understood as being

> composed of those more or less spontaneously emergent associations, organizations, and movements that, attuned to how societal problems resonate in the private life spheres, distil and transmit such reactions in amplified form to the public sphere. The core of civil society comprises a network of associations that institutionalizes problem-solving discourses on questions of general interest inside the framework of organized public spheres. (Habermas 1996a: 367)

The deliberative paradigm replaces the competition between interests with public discourse, while realist approaches to democracy characteristically adhere to the market paradigm. In his approach to deliberative democracy, Habermas 'shifts some of the burdens for securing democratic outcomes away from the individual virtues of an active citizenry onto the 'anonymous network of communication' in civil society' (Baynes 2002: 134). The idea is that an organised civil society picks up the concerns of individual citizens, gives voice to them in the wider public sphere (weak public), where the issues are discussed, and carries them further to the institutionalised political system (strong public) (see, critically, Fraser 1992). This two-track model seeks to offer a solution to the contemporary problem of socio-cultural complexity: political decision-making in institutions must be open towards the general public without being overly ineffective. Conversely, civil society organisations should also be open to all interested citizens, and, furthermore, should pick up the concerns of disadvantaged people, such as migrants, and of the voiceless, but nonetheless important, issues in the public realm, such as the environment.

*A critical appraisal of the role of participation in deliberative democracy*

Deliberative democracy seeks to integrate both the normative and the empirical dimensions of democracy. Deliberation enhances the epistemic quality of decisions, thus stressing the instrumental aspect. In order to become democratic, deliberation additionally needs equality in the inclusion of all concerns that have a stake in the particular issue and of all those who are generally interested in the particular issue. Thus, deliberative democracy shifts the focus away from the direct participation of physical persons towards the participation of a plurality of concerns, of voices, which are present in the public sphere and articulated by the actors of civil society. In doing so, and in emphasising the principle of justification and the process character of preference emergence, deliberative democracy reacts to the challenges of democracy in modern capitalist states. Size, territoriality and diversity are less threatening if democracy and the democratic legitimacy of political processes are somewhat de-personalised without abandoning central democratic norms, above all, political equality.

Unlike the affinity of the aggregative models of democracy for parliamentary representation, the theoretical assumptions of deliberative democracy do not prejudice specific democratic mechanisms (with, of course, the exception that any mechanism must be deliberative in nature). There are both shortcomings and strengths to this conceptual openness. The strength is its relative ignorance to specific institutional and procedural arrangements. It suggests that there is more than one way of democratising policy-making processes. The juxtaposition of the deliberative and the aggregative model, for instance, implies the mutual exclusion of potentially democratic policy-making procedures.

A deliberative model of democracy seems to be institutionally more inclusive than the aggregative model, because it does not, for instance, rule out institutional practices such as majority voting as the final step in a deliberative decision-making process.[47] As Benhabib points out, 'the deliberative theory of democracy is not a theory in search of practice; rather it is a theory that claims to elucidate some aspects of the logic of existing democratic practices better than others' (Benhabib 1996a: 84).[48] Furthermore, its conceptual inclusiveness and focus on political, i.e. public, justification and reasoning seem to be particularly appropriate for capturing the diversity of policy-making processes in complex modern societies and of offering a deliberative setting for public preference formation.

On the downside, this institutional indecision is potentially problematical in so far as it subjects any attempt to base a democratic evaluation on this approach to the easy criticism of being an *ex-post* rationalisation or justification (and thus a labelling) of non-democratic procedures as democratic. I contend that no model of democracy can avoid questions about its practicability, and, therefore, must, to some extent, also entail a dimension in which it becomes a 'theory in search of practice' (Benhabib 1996a: 84).

While the theoretical effort of an author such as Habermas (1992) to justify the principles of deliberative democracy are considerable, the practical realisation of these principles in a postnational context, which eludes the traditional 'container model of state politics' (Greven 2005: 261), remains unclear. It is questionable as to whether the Habermasian two-track model with its distinction between a strong and a weak public sphere can be easily identified within the EU, given the well-researched deficits of a common European public sphere (Gerhards 2002; Sifft *et al.* 2007) and the multi-centred, heterogeneous polity. On a global scale, these problems abound even more. The proliferation of governance, i.e. of multiple forms and *fora* of decision-making bodies within modern polities, poses considerable problems for this differentiation between an informal weak public sphere, on the one hand, and the formal institutions of a strong public sphere that ultimately make the decisions, on the other.

Against this background, it is possible to argue that deliberative democracy seems to focus too much on the epistemic, argumentative rationality of democratic processes, and tends to forget about the participatory moment of democratic practice.[49] This lack of emphasis on the participatory moment comes at some cost, because deliberative democracy is in danger of losing the critical stance of democratic theories both by accommodating the existing political institutions and by striving primarily to improve the openness and accessibility of the existing decision-making procedures, instead of upholding the aim of a transformation towards a more democratic society.

Moreover, there is little systematic reflection on the possible common conceptual ground between participatory and deliberative democracy (Hauptmann 2001; Hilmer 2010; Vitale 2006), despite some important overlaps. These become visible in the work of Carole Pateman, one of the highly influential proponents of participatory democracy. She claims that 'the theory of participatory democracy is built around the central assertion that individuals and their institutions cannot be considered in isolation from each other' (Pateman 1970: 42). This statement clearly elucidates that participatory democracy depends on an open and interactive relationship among individuals, as well as between them and the political institutions; it furthermore implies that the preferences of the actors are shaped within this interaction. From this, it follows that participatory and deliberative democracy both adhere to the concept of inter-subjectivity. In the face of this conceptual overlap between participatory and deliberative democracy, one can say that any realisation of the latter requires thicker forms of participation than mere voting activities and anonymous debates in the public sphere.

Whereas deliberative democracy in the Habermasian perspective predominantly focuses on the public sphere effects of civil society, the inclusion of civil society organisations in governance arrangements is also of interest, at least in a pragmatic application of this concept in more policy-oriented research. There is, to my knowledge, only one effort to apply the reasoning of deliberative democracy on the participation of civil society organisations systematically (see Nanz and Steffek 2004; Steffek and Kissling 2007). This approach sees organised civil society as providing the appropriate transmission belts between the citizenry and the institutional level of policy-making, and also as the appropriate mirror of the diversity and plurality of the life-forms and concerns in society. With this idea, the approach somewhat resembles pluralism (particularly that of Dahl), although a fundamental difference prevails concerning the mechanism by which democratic policy-making should be functioning, namely, aggregation *versus* justification. Its proximity to pluralism is also accompanied by similar problems, as identified above, especially the problems of asymmetry and equality.

So far, deliberative theorists do not offer practical solutions to these problems and seem to expect (or hope) that the necessary respect for other deliberating actors and the epistemic quality of deliberation strengthen political equality, even in cases of the physical absence of mute or disadvantaged concerns. Consequently, if one adds practical implications to the conceptual considerations of deliberative democracy, the democratic moment of deliberation necessitates the presence of participatory activities. Two things seem particularly urgent: first of all, efforts to increase the inclusion of disadvantaged voices, and, secondly, provisions that ensure the justification of all actors. Certainly, deliberative democracy has gone some way to loosening the tight connection between democracy and the direct presence of the people by introducing the anonymous network of the public sphere and by highlighting the epistemic quality of deliberative practices. Notwithstanding this, there is still a need for some specification regarding the form that the necessary participative practices should take alongside deliberative principles, which, in the public sphere, thus requires an actor-basis, which could be provided by CSOs.

Collective actors are suitable agents for participatory and democratic governance because of their ability to take part both in the weak public, with its overlapping networks and associations of public discourse, and in the strong public of political institutions. In addition, they offer multiple avenues to overcome deliberative elitism, which, for instance, have become visible in the early notions of deliberative supranationalism (Joerges and Neyer 1997).

## Conclusion: the democratic contributions of collective actors

### A synopsis of the theoretical approaches
This chapter has so far illustrated that, upon closer inspection, the concepts of participation and participatory democracy are situated in a discursive field that is more complex than their regular application in everyday political (science) language suggests. Table 2.2 summarises the key issues that have been discussed and which will remain relevant throughout the following empirical sections.

Considering the argumentative level, it is apparent that pluralist and deliberative reasonings are fairly dichotomous, while the different conceptions of associative democracy occupy the middle terrain between both approaches. The range from pluralist, associative, to deliberative accounts of democratic participation shows differing degrees of theoretical abstraction and empirical foundation. Pluralist theory is so strongly interested in the real world that it is hard to distinguish between empirical and normative statements. The different accounts of associative democrats share a critical perspective on pluralism and the state of the art of modern democracy, and seek to make propositions that are institutionally innovative, and, furthermore, advance the theoretical debate. Deliberative democracy is a very abstract normative theory, and from the attempt to use it as an analytical

Table 2.2 Synopsis of the theoretical approaches

|  | *Pluralism* | *Associationalism* | *Deliberative approaches* |
|---|---|---|---|
| Argumentative level | Empirical | Empirical and normative | Normative |
| Democratic will-formation | Aggregative | Integrative | Deliberative |
| Style of Politics | Competitive | Co-operative | Co-operative |
| Conception of participation | Instrumental | Integrative | Normative |
| Role of collective actors | Aggregating and enforcing interests | Aggregation and negotiation | Deliberation and information |
| Character of institutional provisions | Limited, voluntaristic | Determined and regulated | Regulated and flexible |

framework for assessing the participation of collective actors, it becomes clear how difficult it is to bring it back to politics.

The features of will-formation and political style, which characterise the approaches, are related to each other. Pluralist accounts of democratic will-formation are based upon the aggregation of interests that compete with each other for the greatest influence. The comprehensive associations envisaged by Cohen and Rogers also aggregate diverse concerns, but, here, politics is conceptualised as co-operative, rather than competitive. This is also the case within the deliberative framework, whose idea of will-formation is, of course, a deliberative, i.e. process-based, one.

Consequently, the deliberative democratic conception of participation would be a normative one. The main role of collective actors would be to function as a transmission belt between the people and the decision-making *loci* and to improve the deliberative characteristic of policy-making by introducing the requirement of justification. Pluralists, instead, would highlight the instrumental value of participation and ascribe to interest groups the function of aggregating and transporting interests into the policy processes; associationalists can again be placed in the middle between both positions, because they highlight the function of secondary associations as partners in negotiations both with each other and with the elected public institutions.

Although the three approaches are fairly silent with regard to visions concerning institutional design – in particular, the abstract theory of deliberative democracy avoids such discussions – some propositions are possible in order to specify the character of suitable institutions. In a pluralist under-standing, participation should generally be guided by the principle of *laissez-faire*. Only minimal provisions of access rights seem necessary in order to enable interest groups to compete for influence. In the associationalist perspective of Cohen and Rogers, the secondary associations need a much more structured and regulated environment if they are to be able to play an active part at the same level with public institutions. Deliberation can take place in different institutional settings, but the theory's normative emphasis on equality and inclusion strongly suggests that *laissez-faire* would not be the appropriate solution. Instead, rules that oblige all the participants of a policy process to engage in deliberations would seem to be necessary. However, some flexibility within the rules is required in order to offer space for learning processes. This emphasis on the importance of legal rules for democratic participation most profoundly distinguishes associative and deliberative democracy accounts from the pluralist approach.

### The democratic role of collective actors

The participation of non-governmental groups unfolds its democratising potential, on the one hand, in the broad sense of adding to the democratic fabric of a polity and, on the other, in the day-to-day practices of policy-making.

With regard to the polity level, it was shown that associational life is inex-tricably linked to the development of any democratic society. In associations, people gather in order to understand and to shape the context in which they live collectively. Thus, the right to associations are one important (yet not the only) expression of every person's individual freedom to express his or her opinions and to become engaged in activities in order to realise his or her visions. With Philippe Schmitter (1983), one can agree that Alexis de Tocqueville's 'famous hypothesis has stood the test of the time astonishingly well: "For men, to become or remain civilized, the art of association must develop and perfect itself among them in the same measure as the equality of conditions among them grows"' (Schmitter 1983: 908).

At a very fundamental level, these theoretical insights suggest an inter-pretation in which the emergence of globally active civil society organisations is an expression of a democratisation process in the postnational age that has already started. These groups can be understood as the building blocks of a potentially developing global democratic society in a multi-level context. In the polity dimension, they acquire normative significance through their potentially vertical-linking function between the people and the decision-making *loci*, within the complex multi-level structure of democratic policy-making.

In such a broad understanding, the inclusion of these associations in policy-making processes at any level of governance, while respecting political equality, is positive from a democratic point of view because they are expressions of a plurality of shared issues, functions, interests and moral convictions that originate from the wills of the people. To some extent, this normative reasoning remains counter-factual because – as I discussed in some detail above in the section on the idealists' conceptions of participatory democracy – the degree to which participatory activities make individuals better citizens is hard to prove, and the approaches that refer to collective actors do not add new empirical insights to this question. Similar to Jane Mansbridge's argument (see above), I can nevertheless claim that it is highly plausible to assume that both the general existence and the specific activities of a plurality of non-governmental actors directly add to the democratic fabric of a polity.[50]

One central democratic purpose of including non-state collective actors in policy-making arrangements is to relieve the individual citizen of the burden of concerning himself or herself with all of the thousands of political decisions taken in modern political orders – and, in doing so, to counter one of the central reservations against any form of participatory democracy. Since democracy only makes sense if it is also feasible without foregoing its normative essentials, the participation of collective actors is a pragmatic means to increase the democratic character of policy-making. In everyday politics, one could reasonably argue, collective actors have the necessary epistemic ability and capacity to deal with many important decisions.

Furthermore, the theoretical perspectives both acknowledge and welcome the activities of non-state actors in postnational political arenas because they have the potential to break up the diplomatic tradition of secrecy, and, instead, open up the political processes, make them more accessible and subject them to public scrutiny – all of which are democratic requirements.[51] Of particular importance is the deliberative democratic emphasis on a more de-personalised conception of communicative participation, i.e. the inclusion of arguments, rather than necessarily concrete actors. CSOs are thus conceived as institutional condensations within the public sphere, capable of enforcing communicative participation within the strong public sphere. Consequently, their participation – if equal, diverse and inclusive – increases the democratic quality of participatory policy-making.[52]

Overall, the participation of collective actors in day-to-day politics should be understood as complementary, rather than supplementary, to the electoral mechanisms of a representative democracy. It is time to overcome the 'either-or' of participatory *versus* competitive democracy. For pluralists, the participation of groups is complemented by a competition for political leadership; thus, the burden of democratic legitimacy is shared. In associative democracy, the secondary associations co-operate both among themselves *and* with the state, so that their agreements complement the electoral competition. And, for deliberative democrats, at least in the Habermasian sense, the discussions within civil society both inform and shape the decisions of the elected government.

Thus, one should avoid placing the burden of democratic legitimacy exclusively on the shoulders of non-state collective actors, even in the absence of convincing political institutions of representative democracy, as is the case in the supranational context of the EU. These actors can play a democratising part in interactions between democratic institutions within a given institutional frame, a frame which, however, cannot be taken for granted outside nation states. However, as will be demonstrated in Part II, the EU has made some efforts to provide such an institutional frame.

## Notes

1   The fact that this book concentrates on the political dimension of participation and thus excludes cultural and communal activities and the like, such as taking part in a bowling club (Putnam), is not to dispute that the latter are enormously important for any society to be more than an accidental gathering of individuals. I merely want to express that the focus of this study is a different one. In the following, political participation and participation are synonymously used.

2   The policy cycle model stems from public policy analysis and differentiates different stages in policy processes. There are various descriptions of policy cycles, but all contain at least elements such as agenda setting, policy formulation, decision-making and policy implementation (among others, see Howlett and Ramesh 1995).

3   I want to stress that I use the term 'classic' in a temporal form, referring to authors such as Rousseau or J.S. Mill. I do not agree with authors such as Joseph Schumpeter (1947) who construct an allegedly coherent classic doctrine of democratic theory against which one can put one's own argument.

4   Another, but related, distinction would be that between thin and strong democracy as proposed by Barber (2003 [1984]). Of course, empirical approaches are also highly normative in their assumptions, but their emphasis is on an analytical access to the reality of democratic practices rather than to construct ideal theories, as normative approaches do.

5   According to Schumpeter, this doctrine shares the following idea: 'The democratic idea [of the classical doctrine] is that institutional arrangement for arriving at political decisions which realizes the common good by making the people itself decide issues through the election of individuals who are to assemble in order to carry out its will' (1947: 250).

6   This focus on the selection processes of a society's elite triggered a controversy on elitist theories of democracy (see, among others, the following authors for further discussion and more literature: Dahl 1966; Medding 1969). There was a division among authors who called themselves 'progressive' or 'developmental' democrats (such as Peter Bachrach) and empirical theorists of democracy, where the former called the latter 'elitist democrats' with a clear pejorative undertone. It is ironic to see that, in the 1960s and 1970s, the proponents of alleged elitist approaches were criticised by participationists, while, today, the literature on participatory democracy and the role of collective actors in participatory governance is itself accused of elitism by empirical democrats.

7   One of the most prominent and important developments of this parsimonious model of democracy is provided by Downs (1968). In his model of electoral competition, Downs offers a strong, rational-choice based explanation as to why parties tend towards the median voter, namely, because people rationally vote for the party closest

to their preferences. Downs' model thus follows Schumpeter in its credo in a market model of electoral competition.

8   This straightforward researchability, in fact, is one of the reasons why Schumpeter found his model of democracy attractive.

9   Such a mixing of levels of arguments can often be found in Political Science writings, for instance, in Scharpf's critique on participatory democracy (1970). Held also criticises Schumpeter for supposing that 'empirical evidence about the nature of contemporary democracies could straightforwardly be taken as the basis for refuting the normative ideals enshrined in classic models' (Held 2006: 153).

10  See, here, Schumpeter's ambiguous propositions on the self-defining power of a people as a demos, in which he does not rule out the exclusion of minority groups.

11  Speaking about the protesting students, Kaufman (1969b: 202) says, 'They bite the hand that feeds them. And with good reason. For, all the devotion, energy, creative imagination that have been bestowed on material things have tended to turn people into human things.'

12  An important exception to this is, above all, the notable work of Benjamin Barber (2003 [1984]).

13  A brief overview of different degrees of politicisation among writers in the idealist tradition is offered by Schmidt (2000, Chapter 2.6).

14  In the mid-1980s, a theorist of democracy more close to the realist tradition, Robert Dahl (1985), presented a book also on economic democracy, a development that was understood as a sign of convergence in democratic theory (Adamson 1989).

15  Fritz Scharpf tried to include both the realist and the idealist position in his proposal for a complex theory of democracy (Scharpf 1970).

16  Robert Dahl, in particular, strongly argued for responsiveness (1971: 2f): 'I assume that a key characteristic of a democracy is the continuing responsiveness of the government to the preferences of its citizens, considered as political equals ... In this study I should like to reserve the term democracy for a political system one of the characteristics of which is the quality of being completely or almost completely responsive to all its citizens ... I assume further ... that all full citizens must have unimpaired opportunities: (1) to formulate their preferences; (2) to signify their preferences to their fellow citizens and the government by individual and collective action; (3) to have their preferences weighed equally in the conduct of the government, that is, weighted with no discrimination because of the content or source of the preference. These, then, appear to me to be three necessary conditions for a democracy, though they are probably not sufficient.' See, also, a similar overview provided by Teorell (2006) and the centrality of responsiveness in representative systems of government (Fung 2006).

17  Social legitimacy is an empirical concept that is measured via the degree of the peoples' acceptance of the political systems. Democratic legitimacy, instead, is a normative concept that can only be judged according to criteria derived from democratic theory. For the concept of social *versus* normative legitimacy, see, for instance, B. Peters (2003).

18  For the distinction between co-determination and self-determination, see also Birch 1993, Chapter 6.

19  Political equality and freedom are central ingredients in almost all democratic theories, whereas the control function is stressed particularly in liberal theories of democracy (see Kneip 2006).

20  Scaff (1975: 455) chooses a different distinction, namely, between 'participation as interaction' (with a value in itself) and 'participation as instrumental action' (with an objective external to participation).

21  Evidently, these questions refer to the influential concept of input–output legitimacy

as proposed by Fritz Scharpf (1999). For his initial conception of input–output legitimacy, see Scharpf (1970).

22  The original chapter was first published in 1960 in Carl J. Friedrich (ed.), *Responsibility*, New York, The Liberal Arts Press: 266–289.

23  In particular, James Madison, in the Federalist Paper No. 10, highlighted the need to deal with potential 'mischiefs of factions' (Hamilton, Madison and Jay, 2003: 40).

24  A concise overview of pluralism and other group theories in democratic theory is offered in Held (2006, Chapter 6).

25  A good overview of many important issues for Dahl in his long period of writing is offered by Bailey and Braybrooke (2003).

26  For the proximity of American pluralism with the aggregative model of democratic will-formation, see also Young 2000: 18ff.

27  Similarly, Connolly (1969a); changes in the accounts of empirical and normative dimensions of pluralism are addressed in Reutter (1991) and in Scharpf (1970).

28  An assumption which is stronger in older versions of pluralism.

29  This is, in a less explicated form, similar to the transmission belt model of participation of NGOs proposed by Nanz and Steffek (2005).

30  The classic doctrine of pluralism is still very prominent in public political discussions and the media and, arguably, also in many Political Science discourses, although its premises have been under severe attack and were even criticised from within its tradition (see, for instance, the more recent works by Dahl (1982, 1985), where he reflects more thoroughly on economic democracy and the dominance of business in capitalist societies).

31  Though only upon the basis of a personal estimation, it seems that Dahl's classic book on American pluralism (1956) is still more widespread than his re-conception of pluralism in a market society (1985).

32  An excellent overview of different positions in the relation between capitalism and democracy is given by Almond (1991).

33  For overviews of the diverse literature of neo-corporatism, see Wilson (1983), Reutter (1991) and, recently, in a tribute to Philippe Schmitter, Streeck (2006).

34  See, however, Schmitter (1983), and Crouch (2006) for the relation of neo-corporatism and democracy.

35  For a more detailed discussion of different aspects of associative democracy, see, above all, Saward (2000), Hirst and Bader (2001) and Rossteutscher (2005).

36  A rich critique on this approach is offered by Bader (2001b).

37  Hirst himself would perhaps object to being placed too strongly within a liberal tradition by stressing his ideational ancestors, which are, above all, the syndicalist and anarchist thoughts of the nineteenth century and their emphasis on self-governance and mutuality. My point is, nevertheless, that, from a phenomenological point of view, these perspectives meet with liberal considerations about a limited role of the state, voluntarism and the welcoming of self-organised groups. In his emphasis on self-regulation, Hirst certainly goes well beyond the pluralist approach of interest representation.

38  With this position, associative democracy criticises the strong separation in liberal thought between the public and the private.

39  The authors write, that the 'trick of associative democracy is simply [*sic*] ... using conventional policy tools to steer the group system toward one that, for particular problems, has the right sorts of qualitative features. Of course, there is nothing "simple" about this. Doing it right involves judgement. But in this it is no different from any other politics' (Cohen and Rogers 1992: 430).

40  For instance, a clear emphasis of Cohen and Rogers is to portray the democratic quality of associational life, thus wanting to make a normative argument. However,

they do not operate consistently within the realm of normative democratic theory. Already at the outset, they make it very clear that secondary associations 'play a central role in resolving problems of successful governance' (Cohen and Rogers 1992: 394). This is a clear instrumental justification of associational participation that proceeds without further discussion of the relation between efficiency and legitimacy, instrumentality and normativity.

41   Civic republicanism underlines the importance of a common good for a democratic society and thus perceives democracy as endangered by too much pluralism. It 'belongs to the species of anti-pluralist conceptions of politics … that accept the affirmative state and with it a conception of the state as legitimately advancing a common good that extends beyond the ideal of an efficient allocation of resources' and believes that 'the substance of state policy is not fixed by bargaining among interest groups, each seeking its own advantage' (Cohen and Rogers 1992: 406) as suggested by pluralism. In this view, politics is not based upon the aggregation of preferences given in advance, but the aims and objectives are discussed in deliberative forums of the civil society with a view to the common good.

42   A discussion is deliberative if the propositions made are justified by reasoned arguments. There are many different accounts of deliberative democracy, a discussion of which would go beyond the study's argument. An admiringly condensed overview of different deliberative theories and their application to empirical research is given by Chambers (2003).

43   Because civic republicanism's scepticism against plurality and diversity cannot be upheld in a postnational age, and since it does not answer how a common good can exist prior to deliberation, I will focus in the following on deliberative democratic approaches to civil society participation.

44   For an introduction to the common distinction between an aggregative and a deliberative understanding of democracy, see, for instance, Farrelly (2004).

45   However, the opposite seems to be the message of some of the comitology literature in the EU.

46   Jon Elster clearly depicts the issue when he says that 'the notion [of deliberative democracy] includes collective decision making with the participation of all who will be affected by the decision or their representatives: this is the democratic part. Also, all agree that it includes decision making by means of arguments offered by and to participants who are committed to the values of rationality and impartiality: this is the deliberative part. These characterizations are somewhat rough, but I believe they capture the intersection of the extensions reasonably well' (Elster 1998: 8).

47   See also Dahl: 'But if Cohen means to say that mere aggregation is not enough, and that the final vote should be preceded by a process in which citizens can discover their individual, joint, and common interests, then I could not agree more' (Dahl 1991: 230). Therefore, it is subject to dispute whether the high interest in deliberative democracy necessarily signifies a shift 'from "voting-centric" to "talk-centric" democracy' (Fung 2003: 525).

48   As a side remark, it is interesting to note that, despite the new theoretical input of recent democracy theorists and political philosophers, deliberation 'is in fact of ancient lineage' (Lord 2004: 24). According to Lord, as J.S. Mill had already argued, with a view to representative bodies, 'those who are overruled should "feel satisfied that (their opinion has been) heard, and set aside not by a mere act of will, but for what are thought to be superior reasons"' (*ibid.*, quoting Mill, 1861). See, also, Manin (1987) for an excellent account of the essential deliberative character of parliamentarian democracy.

49   Deliberative democracy's emphasis on rationality can be criticised as unrealistic and wrong, because it does not provide space for other, emotional forms of expression,

and implicitly assumes the possibility of a common good. However, I follow Iris Marion Young's (2000: 47ff) more agonistic account by stressing the requirement of reasonableness instead of rationality: 'Being reasonable in a discussion means being open to listening to others and having them influence one's views, and expressing one's own claims upon them in ways that aim to reach their assent or understanding' (*ibid.*: 38). This neither precludes conflicts nor assumes the necessity of consensus.

50   This vertical linkage and the extent to which the ultimate link to the individual person is realised in the political practice lie outside the focus of this study. For this aspect, see the ongoing research project of my Bremen colleagues on 'Participation and Legitimation in International Organisations' within the Collaborative Research Centre 'Transformation of the State' (www.sfb597.uni-bremen.de).

51   This development at a global level might also have repercussions on nation states because many states partaking in global arenas are not used to dealing with plural interests internally. This seems less valid in the European context, although the Central and Eastern European Member States, in particular, have only achieved internal openness fairly recently. The potentiality and factuality of such norm diffusion from the global to the national is, however, not within the scope of this study.

52   I deliberately limit the scope of participation thus conceived to daily policy-making processes. In constitutional issues and in areas of high moral concern, where scientific expertise and methodology cannot provide sufficiently clear solutions/alternatives, other and more direct forms of people's inclusion would be necessary.

# 3

# Researching democratic participation

The particular methodological challenge of this book is the complex interplay of normative insights with empirical observations. The insights of the previous chapter's elaboration of the democratic potential of the participation of CSOs in different democratic theories do not offer straightforward guidance for the empirical reality, because they are ideal theories. Even the most applied of these accounts, pluralism, cannot be taken as a concrete image of the real world. Hence, these theories neither offer immediate criteria to evaluate the participatory structures and practices of the EU, nor criteria for their institutional design. The real world necessarily falls short of ideal theory.

Consequently, the conduct of the empirical analysis requires a mechanism by which the transition from normative democratic theory to empirical democratic practices can be accomplished, always bearing in mind the institutional dimension of participatory practices. By generating images of ideal democratic practices, normative democratic theory offers orientation for scholarly and political activities. As Nicole Deitelhoff (2006, Chapter 1) showed, such normative orientations can be made operational as critical heuristic tools for empirical social science research in the confrontation of facts and norms. The normative characteristics of the empirical reality of participatory governance in the EU will be re-constructed and interpreted in the light of normative conditions of democratic participation, and these interpretations are then used for institutional reflections upon how to improve the institutions by making use of the democratic potential of CSO participation. In re-constructing concrete cases, the critical potential of normative theory is fruitfully employed to open up an institutional perspective.

Given the inevitable normative inadequacy of real world structures and practices, a research strategy that generates hypotheses in order to test the theoretical assumptions is inappropriate. Either the normative theories would have to be refuted because of empirical deviations, or the real world is bound to be judged as being normatively insufficient. Instead, a two-step operationalisation, inspired by the Habermasian concept of rational re-construction (Pedersen 2009), seems appropriate to achieve the transition from normative theory to empirical analysis. The first step focuses on the

issue of political equality as the essential challenge to the democratic participation of CSOs. The second step proposes a set of four conditions of political
equality which, at the same time, possess critical evaluative and institutionally
prescriptive potential. They are used as evaluative guidance by offering
critical yardsticks against which to analyse and to judge the observed participatory regime of the EU. Institutionally, they offer productive guidance by
opening up perspectives for thoughts about institutional design in order to
realise the normative demands.

In the following, political equality as a fundamental principle of
democracy will be introduced, based upon the previous chapter, and a set of
four conditions will be elaborated, before the chapter concludes with some
remarks on the data and methods employed.

## Evaluative and productive guidance of the theories on democratic participation

### Political equality and the democratic participation of collective actors

Although the different democratic theories and their concern with the participation of non-state collective actors, as discussed in the previous chapter,
do not share a common definition of democracy, they do share the conviction
that the plurality of interests and concerns are to be equally included in the
policy-making processes in order for them to possess democratic significance.
The capacity for the self-determination of the people who raise their voice
through non-state collective actors is only enhanced if these actors are equally
included in policy processes.

Certainly, this agreement on the importance of political equality as a
'foundational idea' of democracy (also Christiano 2003; Saward 1998: 15)
does not amount to a fully fledged definition, let alone a justification, of
democracy. But it shares the pragmatic contention that 'no compelling justification for democracy could oppose the view that people ought to be treated
as political equals' (Saward 1998: 15). Thus, it is possible to condense the
previous chapter into the proposition that the participation of civil society
organisations increases the democratic quality of participatory policy-making
only if the universe of concerns is equally included in the actual practices of
policy-making.

Treating political equality as a foundational principle of democracy
implies that it does not forestall specific institutional models of political
implementation. Yet it does point to the importance of taking the institutional context into account, if one aims at critically assessing the concrete
practices of political participation. This means that the theoretical emphasis
on political equality has to be linked to the concrete challenges that equal
participation faces in the existing institutional context of the EU.

It is specifically the Europeanisation and the capability to act on the part of the potential participants, which endangers political equality for civil society organisations in EU policy processes, and which potentially limits the democratic promise of participatory governance. The character of the emerging plural landscape at the level beyond the nation state entails both opportunities and dangers to democratic participation. On the one hand, the absence of a traditional distribution of power, as within a democratic nation state, offers the chance to overcome the established asymmetries. Weaker or nationally disadvantaged interests may obtain the chance to bridge national borders and to form transnational alliances. On the other hand, it seems plausible to assume that the bias towards stronger groups, which the critique on national pluralism has put forward, cannot be better balanced on a global scale. The capability of disadvantaged groups to act could be even more diminished than at national level. Not only the different degree of the organisability of different interests, but also the unequal resources both in financial and in knowledge terms potentially deteriorate in the postnational context.

In addition to this, the absence of a central government, and, in its place, the existence of a multiplicity of political arenas, makes it difficult for the collective actors always to know about the relevant arena to address with their participatory efforts. There is, at best, a partially stable institutional infrastructure that offers the opportunity structure to realise equal participation, and which is capable of accommodating the asymmetrical effects of the different (material and immaterial) resources of the groups. From this, it follows that political equality in the participation of collective actors requires institutional provisions that strengthen equality, and that the question of whether the European level in Brussels is appropriately equipped to guarantee them is an empirical one. The equal inclusion of collective actors in policy processes needs to be institutionalised beyond pluralistic *laissez-faire*, thereby coercing public institutions to render their practices more transparent, accountable and responsive.

### The conditions guiding the empirical analysis

In the national age of electoral democracy, the normative aspect of political equality in competitive conceptions of democracy has – for many people – been convincingly translated into the 'one person, one vote' (OPOV) formula (see, critically, Christiano 1996, Chapter 3). Unfortunately, this operationalisation cannot be upheld with regard to the participation of collective actors beyond the nation state. As already argued in the introduction, even in the highly integrated EU, the growing power of the European Parliament has not succeeded in ending the debates on the EU's democratic deficit. To the contrary, it is particularly the perceived insufficiency of this traditional form of representative democracy beyond the nation state which requires further reflection upon the conditions necessary for political equality in the participation of non-state collective actors.

Nevertheless, the normative functions of the OPOV formula are instructive for the present purpose, because they point to some basic conditions that need to be fulfilled by participatory practices in order to meet the fundamental democratic principle of political equality. OPOV serves as the key feature of the competitive electoral system which is the dominant translation of democratic participation in Western liberal democracies (Nohlen 2000, Chapter 1). The normative assumptions of the OPOV formula, beyond universal suffrage, which are said to be necessary in order to accomplish the key function of democracy, namely, to select a legitimate leadership, are derived from the market logic of competitive democracy. In particular, these are assumptions on complete information about the persons to be elected, on undistorted access to elections, and on the responsiveness of the candidates to the demands of the electorate, if they want to be (re-)elected. Thus, political equality in an electoral democracy rests on the conditions of universal suffrage, undistorted information, access and responsiveness.

If one perceives these conditions as necessary, then any participatory regime for CSOs also has to respect them, even if they are implemented by different participatory means than elections. I propose four conditions – namely, access, inclusion, responsiveness and transparency – which are necessary for a democratically meaningful participation of CSOs, all of which rest – to different degrees – on the three theories discussed earlier.[1]

Equal participation necessitates equal access opportunities and an equal inclusion of concerns in a manner which is both as broad and as diverse as possible. A democratic participatory regime has to avoid the institutionalisation of discriminatory access provisions that would further privilege the already privileged organisations. Consequently, institutional provisions must be designed to guarantee equal access to participation for all actors. Above all, taking up the above-stated communicative conceptualisation of participation, the right to equal communicative access is necessary.

In a pluralist understanding, the guarantee of equal access would suffice for democratic participation, since the different interests freely compete with each other for access. But as the critics of pluralism have convincingly argued, free competition of interests is bound to reproduce the existing societal asymmetries in the realm of political participation. This means that, beyond formal access rights, there is a need for institutional provisions that attempt to mitigate the asymmetries in order to break the 'circle between social and economic inequality and political inequality that enables the powerful to use formally democratic processes to perpetuate injustice or preserve privilege' (Young 2000: 17). Consequently, provisions for enhancing equal inclusion are decisive from a democratic point of view, and add a substantive dimension to the formal conception of political equality as expressed by equal access. Otherwise, strong and outspoken preferences will always triumph over the more hidden and implicit needs of people, as well as over those that are complex and difficult to express (see Teorell 2006: 793).

In particular, deliberative democracy emphasises that inclusion is a necessary condition for democratic participation: the criterion of inclusion seeks to achieve an incremental realisation of democratic equality. In a post-national context in which the interactions with *others* become more regular and important (Brunkhorst 2006: 13), inclusiveness towards the diversity of concerns is important. In this understanding, the inclusion of as many different arguments as possible is a reply to the challenge of political equality under conditions of strong plurality. The inclusion of all those concerned with a political decision is also a necessary condition for the fundamental democratic goal of self-determination. Freedom from domination by others and/or by public institutions is aspired to by policy-making processes that are as inclusive as possible. Otherwise, people would be 'treated as means if they are expected to abide by rules or adjust their actions according to decisions from where determination their voice and interests have been excluded' (Young 2000: 23).[2] Since one cannot assume a naturally given equilibrium among civil society organisations, an empirical proxy for the condition of inclusiveness is therefore needed. In this study, this proxy consists of the institutional, mainly financial, efforts to empower the participation of as many different CSOs as possible.

From the perspective of all three theoretical approaches, an important signifier for political equality is the equal responsiveness of the political processes to the expressed concerns of participating CSOs.[3] Responsiveness is a *content condition* for democratic participation that encompasses more than the establishment of consultative practices for civil society organisations, as these are in danger of being of simulative, instead of substantial, value.[4] From an instrumental perspective, responsiveness must necessarily include success for participants, meaning that the final decision must reflect their concerns. In a more procedural (but not merely simulative) interpretation of respon-siveness, it is essential that concerns are not only heard (as in consultations), but also actively reflected upon by all actors during the policy-making process.

If a procedural framework succeeds in establishing rules for reciprocal justification, one would have a procedure that provokes an obligation to 'die eigenen Gründe und die der anderen auf rationale und offen, faire Weise verstehen und bedenken' ('understand and reflect upon one's own reasons and those of the others in a rational, open and fair manner') (Forst 2007: 254). In this justificatory interpretation, responsiveness is given if all the participants in a policy process recognise the positions of the others and justify their own preferences in the light of those of the others.[5]

In the event that the preferences and the positions of all the participants were responsive to each other and were clearly justified, the accountability of the decision-makers would be enhanced because observers would be enabled to re-construct the emergence of the decision. The civil society organisations could make the different options and interests accessible for wider public scrutiny. However, the ability to re-construct the decision depends on the transparency of the overall process. All the participants need to have the complete information about the issue in question and also need to know the positions of all the other participants – particularly those of the public institutions.

In order to accomplish this, all those who want to participate have to have the possibility of acquiring the complete information about the issue. This transparency, in terms of access to documents for all the participants, becomes a necessary pre-condition that has to be fulfilled by any democratic participatory regime (Curtin 1996). Without this very basic transparency requirement, no access to substantive democratic participation would be possible. Instead, participation would be merely instrumental, meaning that the public institutions would profit most from it by gaining the input of consulted parties.

The four conditions of transparency, access, inclusion and responsiveness are not independent, but mutually dependent upon each other. Each of the conditions relies on the contribution of the others in order to gain a common normative effect. If all these criteria were fulfilled in the participatory regime of the EU, would the EU policy-making then be fully democratic? No, such an understanding would mis-interpret the argument of this book. A democratically structured participatory regime would certainly contribute significantly to the democratic quality of the EU's policy-making; however, it cannot solve all the problems of democratic legitimacy beyond the nation state. Instead of being regarded as a supplement, it should be understood as a complement to other democratising mechanisms, such as the increased role of the European and national parliaments or of EU-wide referenda.

### Models of democratic participation

Having thus established the conditions for both empirically assessing the reality of participatory governance in European policy-making processes and for outlining an institutional vision, it is now possible to bring these conditions together with the different approaches to participation. As illustrated in Table 3.1, the four conditions belong to two different dimensions, namely, a procedural dimension and a content dimension. Access, inclusion and transparency are procedural conditions because they determine the extent to which a political process is subject to regulations that enhance participatory governance. Responsiveness is a content condition because it describes the extent to which the policy-making process is characterised by a struggle about substantial positions.

Pluralistic participation is the normatively most modest of these models. In this understanding, a polity only needs to guarantee basic freedoms, such as freedom of association and of speech, which can be taken for granted within the EU. In order to be democratic, pluralistic participation requires some minimal regulation that prevents the blatant favouritism of a few by offering minimal provisions of access and transparency. The central condition for democratic pluralistic participation is the presence of a diversity of civil society organisations on the political scene, all of which compete for influence. In its aggregative logic of will-formation and its instrumental understanding of participation, the pluralistic conception of responsiveness is output-oriented. What counts is the final result, and not the discursive process of achieving it.

Deliberative participation can be imagined as sitting on the other end of a continuum between non-regulation and over-regulation; its realisation is much more demanding. In order to exert its democratising potential, clear rules are required, which simultaneously force the public institutions to strive for equal inclusion, and, in particular, to enable participants to enter the policy process. It is not only about the presence of civil society organisations, but also about their equal inclusion in the process. Here, responsiveness is process-oriented, because the model assumes a result based upon the justificatory exchanges of good arguments as put forward throughout the process. Confronted with them, some participants might adapt their initial positions.

With regard to associative participation, it is evident how much this is situated between the poles of pluralistic *versus* deliberative participation. It requires not only a sufficient amount of regulation, but also freedom for the associations to self-organise their own affairs. Furthermore, associations are conceptualised as encompassing organisations, and much of the procedural dimension of responsiveness is thus understood to take place within the organisation. A participatory regime based too strongly upon voluntarism could even become democratically deficient, above all, when the public institutions can voluntarily pick and choose those organisations which share their own pre-established positions.

The following empirical analysis of participation in EU policy-making mirrors this distinction between the procedural and the content dimensions, and, consequently, consists of two parts: in Chapter 4, the formal participatory regime of the EU will be examined. Apart from assessing the conditions of transparency, access and inclusion, a historical overview of the relevant legal provisions and the recent participatory developments in governance

Table 3.1 Dimensions and models of democratic participation

|  | Pluralistic participation | Associative participation | Deliberative participation |
|---|---|---|---|
| Procedural dimension (Transparency, Access, Inclusion) | Minimal regulation needed (*laissez-faire*) | A mix between regulation and voluntarism needed | Clear rules needed |
| Content dimension (Responsiveness) | Output-oriented | Linking output with process | Process oriented |

arrangements will be given. The content dimension evidently requires an investigation of concrete policies, which will be the object of Chapter 5.

The empirical part has two main objectives: first of all, it characterises the currently existing participatory regime of the EU and shows the extent to which the institutional provisions of the EU can accommodate inequalities in the participation of interest groups. Upon this basis, it is possible to discuss whether this participatory regime offers a solution for the establishment of democratic participation, and whether it even exerts democratising effects.

The null-hypothesis of the empirical analysis is that, up to now, an instrumental understanding of participation dominates in the EU, and that, at best, the EU has established a pluralistic, *laissez-faire* approach to partici-pation. Thus, in the light of this, the second objective is to identify whether we can currently observe a transition from one (less democratic) participa-tory regime to another (more democratic one), as the discussion on this issue in political and scientific debates seems to suggest.

## Methodological issues

### On data and methods
The differentiation between the content and the procedural dimension has consequences for the research approach, since it requires different methods and different data. Overall, in the empirical analysis, I make use of the key elements of the methodological arsenal of qualitative political science research: (1) extensive analyses of the available documentation of the European institutions and the civil society organisations were undertaken; (2) semi-structured expert interviews (Bogner, Littig and Menz 2002; Rustemeyer 1992; Tansey 2007) with sixteen carefully selected representatives of CSOs, members of the European Commission, the European Parliament and the Council were conducted in June and July 2005; the interviews were systematically evaluated with a computer-based content analysis;[6] (3) another, extensive systematic computer-based content analysis was conducted to identify the responsiveness of the exemplary policy-processes; and, finally, (4) secondary analyses were further important sources of infor-mation.[7]

The empirical analysis of the content dimension, which aims to identify the evolution and to specify the contours of the EU's formal participatory regime is, methodologically, a straightforward undertaking. It is based upon secondary analyses, extensive document analysis and expert interviews. These data are appropriate to assess both the legal rules for CSO access, and the EU's information policy and arrangements to include a multiplicity of CSOs.

The analysis of the procedural dimension is more difficult, because the theoretical approach outlined above and the conceptualisation of the respon-siveness-condition implies that it cannot be observed in a straightforward manner. Responsiveness not only encompasses, but also extends beyond the success of participating CSOs, in order to place some of their issues into the final policy document: in its procedural, communicative conception, responsiveness is given if the argumentative input of CSOs is actively reflected upon by the other actors during the policy-making process. This means that the research tools must be sensitive to capture the changes that occurred during the process, irrespective of the question of whether a final success can be observed or not.

The chosen method is that of a qualitative content analysis (Rustemeyer 1992). At first sight, the choice of content analysis, instead of discourse analysis (Carmel 1999; Keller 2004), might come as a surprise, but the focus of the analysis is not the actual quality of a public discourse, but the different twists and turns of a legislative proposal, instead. Notwithstanding this, a qualitative content analysis epistemologically shares many attributes with discourse analysis, above all the conviction that '[m]eaning is fluid and constructs reality in ways that can be posited through the use of interpretive methods' (Hardy, Harley and Phillips 2004: 21).

The assessment of the quality of a public discourse, of the propositions and justifications made by participants, have resulted in detailed methodological efforts, as the Discourse Quality Index (Steenbergen *et al.* 2003) demonstrates; it shows sophisticated efforts to assess the quality of the actual arguments that are exchanged in a deliberative setting. Clearly, such a discourse analysis approach requires demanding data, namely in the form of either tape recordings of the deliberative meetings themselves, or word-protocols. None of these were available for my research. But responsiveness in terms of (temporal) adjustments to the input of CSOs should – arguably – also become visible in the public documentation of a policy-making process, so that it can be made visible by means of content analysis.

Evidently, these data and the applied method have some limitations, as they are not appropriate to identify the concrete authorship of specific identified positions. It is not possible to distinguish whether the input of certain CSOs *caused* the wording of particular paragraphs, or whether a given Member State has simply held the same position from the very beginning. A more explanatory approach to the influence of CSOs on the concrete positions of national governments would require a fundamentally different research approach, but this is not crucial for my research interest.

Some further remarks about the difference between this research approach and an impact analysis of the contributions of CSOs seems necessary. Whereas an impact analysis would focus on comparing the final result with specified positions of CSOs, by trying to find elements of the specified positions in the final document, the analysis of responsiveness as a measure for the justificatory quality of a process requires a more demanding procedure. In particular, it is crucial to take the temporal dimension into account in order to trace changes over time. This is particularly important because the outcome of a policy-making process could – when analysed in isolation – be found not to have been responsive to CSO input at all. A content analysis in the temporal dimension, however, is capable of tracing possible temporary changes that were excluded in the final document. Such a finding would suggest that CSO input *was* discussed and reflected upon, even if it was not included in the final document. Finding no reflection at all is of different normative significance than finding evidence of unsuccessful input. This means that, by means of content analysis, I will be able to trace the argumentative input of CSOs in the evolution of the key documents of the selected policy processes. What this method cannot account for, however, is whether classical lobbying, instead of deliberation, took place. For this, the expert interviews are an additional source of information.

The actual research process of the content analysis is accomplished in three stages. It begins with the description of the background of the respective policy areas and the concrete policy processes upon which basis the involved actors, key issues and key moments of the process can be identified. In the second stage, I developed a code-book based upon maps of the key arguments of the participants. For this purpose, I analysed the diverse documents of the CSOs:

- official statements (such as position papers) of the CSOs;
- background documents (such as letters) of the CSOs;
- press releases and other forms of media communication (including websites) issued by the CSOs if they were directly related to the policy process; and
- expert interviews.

The input of the CSOs was very diverse, but all forms of data were treated equally. The idea is, that, if common concerns that are shared by several CSOs throughout the whole decision-making period exist, then, one can expect that these organisations put particular emphasis into communicating these concerns, thereby potentially stimulating a discussion – if not the inclusion – of these issues in the public documents. The codes were created upon the basis of induction and were subsequently deductively double-checked by taking the insights of the scientific literature into account. The inductive approach had two sources: firstly, the information which I gathered in the expert interviews, and secondly, the technique of open coding.

Open coding means that I started off by reading the documents, both from official and CSO sources and freely coded the paragraphs that seemed to me to be particularly relevant. After a while, the codes started to repeat themselves. With this achieved saturation, I revised the code list and created, upon this basis, a number of 'code families'[8] in order to identify the key issues that were in question and which were particularly contested in this legislation. Upon this revised code-basis, a consecutive coding of all documents was pursued, and it was possible to summarise a number of codes into code families which established the general themes upon which I focused the respective analysis.

In the third stage, these key positions were analysed in the evolving legislative draft, including the final decision. For this purpose, the respective process is one of splitting them up into temporal sections, ranging from $t_1$ to $t_n$. The aim was to identify all the developments and changes, in order to see whether the arguments and positions put forward by the CSOs were included in the officially drafted documents. In the respective sections in Chapter 5, I will elaborate upon both the key issues and the coding scheme of the procedural dimension.

### The selection of cases

The procedural dimension, which characterises the formal participatory regime of the EU as such, does not require any case selection because it seeks to outline the contours of the EU's participatory regime beyond any policy-area specificities. The identification of responsiveness in the content dimension, however, is only possible by analysing concrete policy-making processes, which entails a two-staged selection process (Gerring 2004), which established (1) the policy areas, and decided (2) on concrete decisions within these areas. The content dimension is analysed in this study in two policy areas, in each of which one key decision was taken as the unit of analysis for responsiveness. This data basis was sufficiently broad to assess exploratively, within the content dimension, the plausibility of the assumed relationship between the participation of civil society organisations and democracy in EU policy processes.

Overall, the case selection approach could best be described as a qualitative case selection, rather than as a quantitative one. The latter would be interested, above all, in questions of representativeness, which is not an appropriate (or feasible) aim of a research strategy that re-constructs empirical evidence in the light of normative conditions in order to make normative assumptions plausible. The qualitative approach implies that both the empirical research and the case selection have to be context sensitive. The choice of policy areas followed the logic of a 'most likely' case selection. In order to find appropriate empirical evidence at all, a sufficiently strong tradition of CSOs working in the respective area appeared to be necessary. But, within this general *likeliness*, the policy areas should entail some variation, thereby attempting to address the issue of representativeness by the choice of typical cases.

The chosen policy areas are environmental and migration policy. Environmental and human rights CSOs are, at global level, among the most well-known CSOs, so that one can expect their presence also at EU level. Yet within this general likeliness, the migration policy area is a harder case than the environmental policy area. There are different reasons for this. Above all, environmental policies have long been considered as low politics. Arguably, the public actors responsible for this policy area, be they the national representatives or the units within the European Commission, have been keen to find allies among civil society organisations in order to strengthen the importance of this issue. Now that environmental policy has been transformed into high politics, in the wake of the climate change discussion, one can, nevertheless, expect long-existing traditions of collaboration. Migration policy, on the other hand, was always conceived as high politics because it directly concerned the key sovereignty of the nation states, namely, whether to decide upon the inclusion or exclusion of people living within their territory. Consequently, one can expect a tradition of secrecy, rather than openness to civil society input, and the analysis will reveal to what extent the CSOs were able to break into this policy area and demand responsiveness.

Beyond the important distinction between high and low politics, a number of other factors potentially influence the intensity of responsiveness. Above all, the integration history of the respective policy field and its belonging to different Pillars of the EU will be of some significance. The area of migration is a very dynamic, rather young, policy area at EU level, in which substantial legislation has been put forward in recent years, while environmental policies belong to the most established policy fields in European integration.

Environment has, for a long time, belonged to the EU's supranational First Pillar, while migration belongs to the more recent intergovernmental Third Pillar. In due course of the analysis, I will come back to some of these structural differences and endeavour to supply some possible reasons for the differences in CSO participation, although these remarks do not lead to a coherent model that explains the variation.

Within these two policy areas, one crucial policy process was chosen as a concrete example in order to carry out the content analysis. The policy process not only had to have been already finalised, but also had to be fairly recent in order to have been potentially influenced by the EU's discourse on participatory governance. I decided to pursue this 'crucial case' research strategy because I anticipated only a limited degree of identifiable responsiveness. If, so the hypothesis goes, a low degree of responsiveness were identified in crucial cases, it would be possible to infer low responsibility in the policy area. However, if a high responsiveness were identified, a similar confident inference could not be made so easily, but would imply that further research was necessary. In addition, this selection strategy seems to be in line with my overall qualitative, context-sensitive research approach. However, given the limited resources of CSOs, one cannot expect them to participate simultaneously in all the legislative activities of their policy field, but one should expect a focus on the crucial cases within their field.

For migration, the case of the *flagship* directive in legal migration (Boeles 2001: 61), namely, the Directive on Family Re-unification, was selected

(Council 2003). This directive is the first case in the post-Treaty of Amsterdam era of migration policies, which has gone through all the political and juridical stages available. In total, it took almost seven years for the Directive on Family Re-unification to be implemented. This long period of contestation provides evidence of the importance of the selected case. Furthermore, its contested nature signifies that it was an important target for civil society organisations and an ideal opportunity for the EU institutions to organise a participatory policy process in order to give a say to all the voices of contestation. Notwithstanding this, the remaining severe disagreements among the participating actors until the very end remain a first sign of the low responsiveness, particularly on the part of the Council, to the concerns of CSOs.

In the area of environment, the Regulation on the Registration, Evaluation, Authorisation and Restriction of Chemicals (REACH) (Council and European Parliament 2006a) is analysed. REACH is of crucial importance, as the activities of the Member States, the lobbying efforts of the chemical industry, and the excitement of the NGOs all show. Given the fact that the NGOs were very much involved in this directive, it seems unrealistic to expect substantial input to other less important legislation.

### A terminological clarification

Before the empirical analysis commences, a terminological question needs clarification, namely, do I speak about interest groups, secondary associations or civil society organisations? If one disregards the different underlying normative assumptions of the democratic approaches discussed above, it is striking that the phenomenology of the actors in question is very similar in all of them. All speak about non-governmental collective actors, the main conceptual distinction being the different conceptions of democratic will-formation.

Pluralists have an aggregative understanding of will-formation, and their conception of democratic participation lies within the instrumental dimension. Deliberative democracy, in contrast, understands democratic will-formation as a dynamic process of deliberation among political equals whose interests and preferences are shaped and changed during this process. Associative democracy is less clear about this, but tends towards the normative dimension of participation. With some over-simplification, one could say that the different approaches address the same phenomena, but use different terms, which are not coherently defined. In particular, civil society is a much debated and amorphous term whose definition depends very much on the theoretical standpoint of an author and/or the empirical context in which it is applied.[9]

Given the phenomenological proximity of the different types of actors, I leave the conceptual debates aside and will adhere to the term civil society organisations. This decision is not made arbitrarily, but is based upon some conceptual reflections. The conception of the political nature of preference-building during deliberative processes – which, as shown above, includes the necessity of participation – is more appropriate to account for the political reality without, however, ignoring the relevance of interests. This – arguably – is particularly relevant in the postnational context, in which the diversity of experience, moral convictions and interests is much higher than within (alleged) homogenous nation states. Thus, CSOs are more encompassing in meaning than interest groups.

Furthermore, the term CSO is the one which captures the communicative conception of participation best. One can imagine CSOs as condensed entities within the public sphere, offering an institutional infrastructure both for the expression of multiple arguments, and for their transportation from the *weak* into the *strong* public sphere.

All in all, the term CSO captures the bottom-up character of the organised groups better than the more static term of secondary associations, and highlights the independence of CSOs from state institutions. Organised civil society includes collective actors, but excludes state-related actors as well as those organisations whose purpose is purely economic (firms and enterprises). I focus on the civil society actors that participate in public matters. In so doing, I exclude mere private activities (such as bowling clubs), and integrate not only social movements or non-governmental organisations (NGOs), but also interest groups that engage in the fostering of economic concerns, because the economy is undoubtedly an important part of society.

To be very explicit, this approach to civil society organisations does not intend to distinguish between good and bad civil society (Chambers and Kopstein 2001). It excludes professional lobbies such as international law firms and consultancies because they follow the interests of individual firms and seek to make a profit from their work; it does, though, include business associations which do not engage in business themselves. However, it is important to note that the term CSO is by no means used synonymously with that of civil society, as such. Instead, CSOs are understood as the institutional core of civil society (see, similarly, Anheier, Priller and Zimmer 2000: 76).

## Notes

1 These conditions mirror the criteria developed in the research project 'Participation and Legitimation in International Organisations' that is part of the Collaborative Research Centre 597 'Transformations of the State' (www.sfb597.uni -bremen.de/pages/forProjektBeschreibung.php?SPRACHE=en&ID=11, accessed 19 February 2010). In this project, these conditions are drawn from deliberative democratic theory, whereas in the present study they are seen as necessary participatory conditions of political equality. In doing so, the theoretical perspective is broadened to other approaches in democratic theory. This seems to be more appropriate because the conditions are not applied in concrete deliberative settings, but rather as tools to identify the participatory character of particular policy-making arrangements.

2  The principle of inclusion transcends the boundaries of a polity, because one cannot be sure that the existing boundaries, with their necessarily exclusionary tendencies, are compatible to the scope of decisions taken within this polity. Put differently: the principle of inclusion challenges the notion of national citizenship towards denizen-ship, and even points further to a need for transnational arenas in which transnational problems can be dealt with on a global scale.

3  '"Democratic responsiveness" is what occurs when the democratic process induces the government to form and implement policies that the citizens want ... Indeed, responsiveness in this sense is one of the justifications for democracy itself' (Powell 2004: 91).

4  Blühdorn proposes the term 'simulative democracy', which, in his view, captures a tendency in modern democracy merely to simulate democratic practices without abolishing their formal frame (Blühdorn 2006).

5  This conception of responsiveness is formulated from a deliberative perspective, but it does not aim at assessing the deliberative quality of political discussions (see, for this, Steenbergen *et al.* 2003).

6  I used the programme Atlas.ti which is constructed on the methodological approach of grounded theory (Glaser and Strauss 1980). This programme is particularly suitable for an interpretative research approach with non-hierarchical, open coding.

7  Lists of the interviews and of the analysed documents are available on request from the author.

8  Please note, in Atlas.ti, a code family usually consists of several issue codes, which themselves are divided into specific instances. In my research, however, I required some hierarchy between different topics and within Atlas.ti – which is a programme based upon the non-hierarchical structure of grounded theory – the only possibility of making the hierarchies among codes visible is via the creation of code families. Therefore, there are some family codes with only one issue code (but several instances).

9  A useful overview of how differently different deliberative theories conceptualise civil society is provided by Hendriks (2006).

# PART II

Participatory governance in the European Union
– the empirical perspective

# Introduction

Having elaborated the theoretical and conceptual reflections on participation, and having specified the democratic contribution of the participation of collective actors, it is now time to turn to the concrete context of this study, namely, the European Union and its lively debate about participatory governance and democracy. The critical potential of normative theory only comes to the fore in a rational re-construction of the concrete political reality. By illustrating the extent to which the intense participatory discourse within the European institutions has, or has not, in recent years, already found entrance into the practice of some European policy-making processes, by discussing the democratic significance of these practices and by speculating about which of the above-specified participatory models the EU seems to be heading towards, it will be possible to clarify the actual contribution that the participation of civil society organisations has on the democratic character of European policy-making processes.[1]

Chapter 4 deals with the procedural dimension of this study, in which the outlines of the formal participatory regime[2] of the EU will be presented. It starts by presenting an overview of the development of the formal rules that regulated the participation of non-state actors until the Treaty of Maastricht. It will be demonstrated that the scope of participatory rights has been gradually expanded throughout EU integration history, starting with firms, then including social partners, and finally opening up to the plurality of civil society. This expansion of actors took place in three phases, which are not mutually exclusive and still co-exist to this very day, and has to be considered in the context of an increasing focus on new forms of governance arrangements in European policy-making.

Overall, a shift away from interest representation to participatory governance can be detected. Whether the evolution of the formal provisions and the widening scope of actors have an impact on the grounds of political action will be the subject of Chapter 5, which focuses on the content dimension by investigating concrete policy processes in two different policy fields, namely, migration and environmental policy.

## Notes

1   To make it very clear, I am neither interested in the strategies of civil society organi-
    sations in pursuing their participatory activities, nor do I attempt to find a model that
    explains their (non-)participation. The results presented below serve as illustrations
    to plausibilise the theoretical assumptions empirically and to outline the contours of
    a possibly evolving democratic European participatory model.
2   Throughout this study, a participatory regime will be understood as a set of rules that
    coherently regulate participatory governance across all policy areas.

# 4

# The participatory regime for organised civil society in the European Union

## The history of participatory rights for non-state actors in European policy-making

Today, Brussels and its European quarter is known as an 'insiders' town' (Greenwood 2003: 2), in which people regularly meet on a 'cocktail circuit' (Lahusen 2004: 57), and establish a flow of continuing discussion among public and private actors. But how did this come about? What rules – if any – does this circuit follow? What legal provisions have been developed over time? These aspects will be elaborated on by presenting three phases in the development of participatory rights in the EU.

### Phase 1: access to the files for individual economic actors

After the failure of the establishment of a European Political Community in the 1950s, European integration became mainly an economic project. Hopes for further political integration were hidden behind the (neo-)functionalist Monnet-method, which entailed – for some – the promise of political spillover from seemingly technical policies (Rosamond 2000). Following this logic, it is not surprising that the first bricks of political participation were placed within this specific field where the European Economic Community possessed genuine competences, namely, in competition policy.

Initially, it was not the planned action of the European Commission that pushed the development of political participation rights forward. Instead, the actors that had been the direct addressees of European policies, namely, firms and other economic agents, had an intrinsic interest in obtaining the right to make their cases directly heard at the level where their fates were determined.

Today, firms have the power to make themselves heard because they are, despite having no formal status, the 'principal player[s] outside the arena of governments and public institutions' (Middlemas 1995: 435). It was due to the existence of the rule of law that those concerned were enabled to make themselves heard. When firms felt an unjust burden had been placed upon them, they asked the European Court of Justice (ECJ) for support – and often received it. It was, above all, the ECJ that was responsible for the establishment of participatory rights for non-state actors in EU policy-making, providing early evidence for those who speak about integration through law (for the latter, see for example Hix 2005, Chapter 4).[1]

First of all, the ECJ introduced the principle of the inclusion of all those concerned with a decision by the European Commission. In a decision from 1974,[2] the Court introduced a general rule that 'a person whose interests are perceptibly affected by a decision taken by a public authority must be given the opportunity to make his point of view known' (Bignami 2003: 5). This general rule had not been pre-established in the treaties, but was introduced by the Court, apparently based upon the considerations of the British Advocate General on the principle of natural justice in the English law tradition (*ibid.*: 5). However, it only applied to those actors who were directly (negatively) affected by a decision of the Commission.

Parallel to this, the ECJ commissioned a 'general right of access to the file' (*ibid.*: 6f) to these actors. Several procedural elements were included to enable firms to exercise this right: the Commission has to issue a statement of objections to which the concerned parties can hand in a written reply. Moreover, an oral hearing between the parties must be held, and the Commission has, in order to finalise the process, to publish a detailed decision in which it accounts for its position in the light of both the hearing and the written contestation by the parties. In the meantime, these rights were further developed and included in the Charter of Fundamental Rights (CoFR), which established a right to good administration (Article 41 CoFR), including the 'right of every person to have access to his or her file' (Article 41 (2) CoFR) and the right to be heard if a decision has direct affect (see below).

It is remarkable that these rights, established in competition law, were quite far-reaching. In fact, Bignami calls the procedures in competition law the 'Community Rolls Royce of administrative adjudication' (Bignami 2003: 7). This relatively early development in the integration history of the EU seems explicable because, in this policy field, the scope of a Commission decision is circumscribed and includes only clearly assigned parties who are adversely affected (for instance, sanctions in cases of abuse of market power) by a decision. From both an administrative and a democratic theory perspective, it is thus fairly straightforward to determine who should be included and given access, to whom the political institution needs to be responsive, and to whom they should guarantee transparency in order to foster the democratic fundamental principle of political equality. As will be argued below, it is far more difficult to uphold such high standards in cases in which a lot more actors, or even the general public at large, are concerned.

Nevertheless, one can see, at this point, that participation rights have to be complemented by institutional legal measures that empower the potential participants to make use of these rights, and which force the public institution, the Commission, to make itself accessible. In this first phase, it was the right to be heard that needed complementation by the general right to access to the relevant documents in the course of a legislative procedure as well as the duty, for the Commission, to justify its position.

However, one should bear in mind that it was not the intention, neither of the ECJ, nor of the Commission, to democratise its proceedings or even to create measures of participatory democracy that would have made the policy-making processes, as opposed to the administrative processes, more open and accessible. Instead, it was more about introducing elements of basic procedural fairness into European administration. Despite their limitations, these developments can be re-interpreted, in the light of democratic theory, as instances in which developments in the politico-legal sphere cautiously approach normative ideals, which might – even if unintended – lead to what one could call a normative spillover.

### Phase 2: The self-determination of collective economic actors in the social dialogue

In the 1980s, as economic integration accelerated with the formulation of the internal market in the Single European Act (SEA) in 1986 and the prospects of a common market programme with a single currency (put forward by the Treaty of Maastricht in 1993), it was recognised by some actors, above all by the influential incoming new President of the European Commission (1985), Jacques Delors, that European economic integration had to be flanked by a social and employment dimension. For the participation of non-state actors, this expansion of the scope of European integration had significant consequences, for the mere inclusion of individual economic actors in administrative and legal proceedings within the limited policy area of competition was deemed to be insufficient. A new focus on the self-regulative abilities of collective economic actors, the European social partners,[3] occurred. Two developments towards the widening of the scope of participation are to be highlighted and subsequently outlined, namely, the Social Dialogue that aimed at collective actors, and the European Works Council Directive, which sought to empower individual workers to participate in their businesses across national borders.

In 1985, stimulated and supported by the European Commission, a European Social Dialogue was initiated with the so-called Val Duchesse process, named after the first place of meeting in January 1985. This was an attempt to revive the failed processes of concertation between the social partners and the Commission of the 1970s (for a historical explanation, see Falkner 1998, Chapter 2, and Falkner 2006; also Johnson 2005, Chapter 3; for a legal analysis, see Smismans 2004, Chapter 6). Today, there are several Social Dialogues (Smismans 2004, Chapter 6), which include both bipartite and tripartite[4] arrangements, as well as sectoral dialogues. Its formal recognition took place through its insertion into the EC Treaty of the SEA (see, now, Articles 138 and 139 EC) and the subsequent strengthening in the Treaty of Maastricht.

From the perspective of the participation of non-state collective actors, this invention of the Social Dialogue is notable because the EU had already been, since the Treaty of Rome in 1957, in possession of an institution that was designed to bring labour and capital together, namely the European Economic and Social Committee (EESC).[5] The EESC consists of nationally nominated representatives of labour, capital and various other interests. In its early days, it was an open question as to whether the EESC would even become stronger than the Parliamentary Assembly, a decision which was, however, decided long ago. Arguably, the EESC never succeeded in establishing itself 'as more than a discussion forum where capital and labour could find each other, launch their prepared papers and mature a certain sense of interdependence' (Middlemas 1995: 385). Above all, unlike the Social Dialogue, it never acquired the power for making binding decisions.

This leads to the essence of the Social Dialogue, in its bipartite and most prominent form. Under the Treaty of Maastricht's Social Protocol,[6] a co-decision right of the European social partners was established, meaning the initiation of institutionally guaranteed rights for them to formulate their own regulatory frameworks. The mandatory consultation of the social partners on Commission proposals in the area of social affairs was introduced, and an option was given to the social partners to negotiate framework agreements. Such agreements among the social partners are generalised by adoption in the Council. One can thus speak of the introduction of a 'principle of horizontal subsidiarity' (Platzer 1998: 110) to European social policy-making. From a democratic viewpoint (above all associative democracy), this was a significant move which strengthened the ability for the key actors to obtain self-determination via the introduction (and possible failure – see Streeck and Schmitter 1994: 185ff) of corporatist structures (Falkner 1998).[7]

Parallel to these evolving corporatist forms at European level, issues of worker participation and European industrial relations had been on the agenda since the early 1970s as supplements to the economic integration and the evolving common market (EIRR 1991: No. 207; 1994: No. 245; Hall 1992; ILR 1995; Streeck 1997). But it was only in 1994 that the Council adopted the Directive on European Works Councils (EWC) (Council 1994), after the Commission had broken the impasse, having been enabled by the Treaty of Maastricht's social protocol to play the 'treaty-base game' (Héritier 1999), i.e. to change the legal base of the proposal and to make use of the new Social Dialogue procedures.

This directive is potentially far-reaching towards the establishment of economic citizenship in Europe, since it does not address specific situations, such as mass redundancies or workers' efforts to co-determine their fate within their companies. Instead, it lays down general rules to ensure that workers in multinational companies and consortia are informed and consulted. However, in the end, the social partners did not come to a common agreement, due to the late withdrawal of the British employer association, the CBI, but the Council did decide upon a directive that was heavily influenced by the positions achieved by the Social Dialogue.

The directive's final content shows that self-regulatory mechanisms such as the Social Dialogue do not necessarily lead to more encompassing individual participation at the workplace, as is demanded by participatory democracy (Pateman 1970). The directive was severely watered down in the Social Dialogue negotiations, and, after its failure, not re-strengthened by the Council. Community-scale undertakings or groups of undertakings with a minimum of 1,000 employees, and at least 150 employees in two or more Member States, are obliged to establish an EWC or an information and consultation procedure. Moreover, neither the extant structures in enterprises, nor the national rules of worker participation are affected by this directive. Hence, the directive's scope and influence is considerably restricted so that the outcome has to be taken as a voluntaristic approach to social regulation (see, more positively, Falkner 1996; critically, Streeck 1997). It does not provide strong participatory rights for workers, nor is it an example of successful self-regulation at EU level.

This second phase saw an expansion of actors, from individual firms to the collective actors, the social partners, and the first steps to strengthen individual participation. The policy-scope for which participation became important was also significantly expanded to comprise social and economic policies. The story of these institutional inventions can be told in a neo-functional manner, interpreting them as a political spillover from the economic realm to the realm of social and employment policy, which was seen by some actors, such as the European Commission, as a necessary complement to the project of economic integration. Thus, the co-evolutionary process between European integration and participatory forms had once again become visible.

The main focus of the new measures was on self-regulation as a democratically meaningful mechanism, although the scope of the Social Dialogue fell well short of establishing encompassing associations as were envisaged by associative democrats. Yet, in line with the latter, the limited outcome of the Social Dialogue and the problems that became visible, for instance, following the European Works Councils Directive, all underline the importance of rules set by the public institutions to regulate the process and the EU's capacity to step in as legislator if self-regulation fails.

### Phase 3: Broadening the scope of actors – the civil dialogue

The third and most recent phase in the history of the expansion of European participation rights provides the framework for this study. Consequently, I will only sketch the beginnings of the phase, which will be analysed in greater detail below.

Like the invention of the Social Dialogue, the initiation of this phase was part of the European Commission's efforts to strengthen the social dimension of Europe in the context of the EU's Economic and Monetary Union (on

European social policy, see, amongst others, Cram 1997; Hantrais 2000; Kowalsky 1999; Leibfried and Pierson 1998). In the mid-1990s, the European Commission initiated a Civil Dialogue, based upon the example of the Social Dialogue. The efforts of the European Economic and Social Committee (EESC) to re-invent itself as a more relevant actor by stressing its linkage function between the EU and the so-called European civil society, a term not least brought into the debate by the EESC, played an important role (Smismans 2003).

During this phase, one can observe a gradual convergence of the political and academic debates on interest representation and participatory democracy through the introduction of normative questions of democratic legitimacy into a discussion that was initially concerned with lobbying and consultation.[8] This convergence can be exemplified by two approaches on the part of the EU towards non-state collective actors in the early 1990s. The 1992 communication on 'An open and structured dialogue between the Commission and special interest groups' (European Commission 1992a) expresses the viewpoints of the European Commission towards lobbying activities. It distinguishes between non-profit and profit-interested lobby groups without making a normatively justified distinction between them, as is done in the current discourse on CSOs. On the contrary, the Commission is – to date – convinced of the normative superiority of an approach towards lobbying 'which is as open as possible [towards] all interested parties' (European Commission 1992a: 1) and does not seek to privilege any particular type of organisation.

Parallel to this communication, non-state collective actors other than the social partners or special interest groups were addressed in Declaration 23 of the Treaty of Maastricht,[9] not least due to the insistence given by the German government to the eminent role of welfare associations within the German welfare system and their fears of European intrusion (Kendall and Anheier 1999; Kuper 1997). The declaration stresses the importance of co-operation between the European Community and charitable associations and foundations as the institutions responsible for social welfare establishments and services, but it largely remained an example of 'symbolic policy-making' in the EU's social policy realm (Kendall and Anheier 1999: 288). These two different ways of conceptualising both the nature and the role of non-state collective actors show that the Commission's attitude was principally dominated by functional interests, such as gaining expertise or improving the quality of genuine EU-level legislation. Other voices stressed the fact that these actors possess a normative quality that is important for the construction of a European people.

One important step towards the fusion of the instrumental and normative characteristics of the participation of non-state collective actors – a fusion that today tends to blur the differences of both dimensions – was the invention of the term Civil Dialogue[10] by Padraig Flynn, Commissioner of the then Directorate-General V for Employment and Social Affairs in the mid-1990s. It must be admitted that, at the beginning, the Civil Dialogue was also perceived more from a functional perspective, because the Directorate General V felt the need to find allies that would speak up for European social policy in order increase its own influence, given the hostility of many Member States to social policy initiatives in the early 1990s. However, as will be shown in greater detail later, it is interesting to note that the inclusion of non-state actors has lost some of its last resort or second-best tone, as the European Commission is now more favourable to the role of such actors as important agents in the soft modes of governance and has taken increasing notice of the '"legitimacy capital" of such a civil dialogue' (Smismans 2002: 11).

In any case, in 1996, the first European Social Policy Forum took place and brought together over 1,000 participants, mainly from social policy NGOs. It aimed at starting a consultation process with regard to the general principles of a European social policy, and resulted, among other things, in the establishment of the Platform of European Social NGOs, which is, to date, one of the key actors in the civil dialogue. Following the second Social Policy Forum in 1998, the Commission and the Social Platform agreed to establish a biannual consultative meeting between them (Cullen 2005: 5). Other than this, and unlike the Social Dialogue, the civil counterpart still lacks any more concrete institutionalisation, and it took until the Commission's discussion paper entitled 'The Commission and Non-Governmental Organisations: Building a Stronger Partnership' (European Commission 2000a) for it to overcome the confines of social policy.

In the meantime, a normative undertone had entered the discourse, first, in the Commission's 1997 communication 'Promoting the role of voluntary organizations and foundations in Europe' (European Commission 1997), which linked the Commission–NGO relations to Declaration 23 of the Treaty of Maastricht under the concept of voluntary organisation, in the NGO discussion paper which already speaks about participatory democracy, and, of course, in the influential White Paper on European Governance (European Commission 2001b). Now, words such as 'lobbying' or 'special interest groups' were pushed to the back of the discourse.

As Stijn Smismans (2002) elaborated, the credit goes to the EESC for finding a wording which turned out to possess sufficient conceptual imprecision, because it captures many different forms of organisations and participatory activities by simultaneously upholding a positive normative connotation. With its opinion, 'The role and contribution of civil society organisations in the building of Europe' (European Economic and Social Committee 1999), the EESC – stuck between the EP and the Social Dialogue, and in search of a new identity and relevance – tried to re-invent itself as an interlocutor between the European institutions, the European citizens and the organised European citizen.

In an act that was theoretically remarkable, the EESC made some efforts to show that the participation of CSOs adds to the flourishing of democracy, and argued that it, the EESC, would be the appropriate institutional forum for organising the civil dialogue as the appropriate form of participatory democracy in Europe (Armstrong 2002: 116ff; Cullen 2005: 21ff).[11] The committee defines CSOs as 'the sum of all organisational structures whose members have objectives and responsibilities that are of general interest and who also act as mediators between the public authorities and citizens' (Paragraph 7.1) and distinguishes different types of CSOs, namely, the social partners, other social and economic players, NGOs, community-based organisations and religious communities (Paragraph 8.1).

This conceptualisation of CSOs, the ascription and elaboration of their normative function for achieving European democracy, and the catalogue of CSO types, proved to be very influential, and is frequently picked up, *inter alia*, in the Commission's White Paper on Governance (European Commission 2001a: 14). In this study, too, the actors analysed mainly follow the typology proposed by the EESC.

In the end, this third phase is not characterised as a phase that has seen an expansion of participatory rights for CSOs, but as an attempt to introduce new soft mechanisms of participatory governance. In addition, this phase has largely been dominated by conceptual struggles. Finally, the term 'civil society' succeeded other terms, such as voluntary associations or NGOs, and now dominates much of the political and academic discourse on participatory governance and democracy in Europe.

It is only very recently in the currently ongoing debate surrounding the European Commission's European Transparency Initiative (ETI) (see below) that this discourse regained a more practical edge. However, there is the possibility that the focus on institutional inventions might only be on the responsibilities of the participants, rather than on those of the receiving institutions as well.

Be this as it may, today we are faced with a situation in which the full picture of normative and functional approaches towards participatory governance, as well as the diversity of actors, are on the table. This broad scope, which the discourse captures, has proved to be stimulating for many practitioners and observers, but has also led to a new complexity. It is far from easy to distinguish whether normative concerns about European democracy, or whether concerns for better governance and efficiency, have triggered the debate. Similarly, it is unclear which role is played by the self-interest of the European institutions to increase their own legitimacy and relevance on the European stage. Finally, the complexity of the discourse obscures observations of the possible steps towards the establishment of elements of a participatory democracy in a postnational setting.

## The procedural dimension: the EU's formal participatory regime

In this section, the procedural dimension will be examined, in order to try to illustrate the outline of the currently existing formal participatory regime of the EU. Here, it will be examined to what extent the intense participatory discourse within the European institutions has already trickled down into the terms and conditions of CSO participation.

Before doing so, an overview will be given of the legal provisions and their recent developments, focusing on the three conditions of the procedural dimension – transparency, access and inclusion – and distinguishing between the three major EU institutions – the Commission, the European Parliament, and the Council. It will be crucial to identify the extent to which the participatory regime of the EU offers appropriate opportunity structures for participatory activities, and whether these structures are regulated or whether they rely on a *laissez-faire* approach.

In an instrumental understanding of participation, the provisions of transparency and access would be sufficient because all the divergent groups would seek to be included and thus demand influence on the political institutions. However, the more demanding normative understanding of participation would require some provisions by the EU institutions designed to guarantee equal inclusion and responsiveness, in order to strive for fair and equal justification processes among all concerns. This means that the more the participatory regime were characterised by *laissez-faire*, the more it would be conducive to an instrumentalised aggregation of interests and, vice versa, the more the participatory regime were regulated, the more it would possess democratising potential.

### Transparency – access to information

Transparency[12] of the agenda and the policy process, as well as of the positions of the actors involved in such processes, is an essential condition for any meaningful participation, both in instrumental and in normative terms. The most basic, but also most fundamental, transparency requirement to achieve this is certainly access to documents for all those interested in the particular issue in question. It is the *sine qua non* for democratic interest representation (Curtin 2003). I believe that one can justifiably argue that, without a regulated transparency regime, it would be all too easy for public institutions to set the terms of the conditions for access to information every time. However, it is important to understand that, despite being a necessary condition for democratic participatory governance, a regulated transparency regime alone would not prejudice a concrete model of democratic participation because it 'allows for scrutiny of public decision-making but leaves influence to existing political and legal mechanisms' (Bignami 2003: 15).[13]

Since the early 1990s, the EU institutions have started to develop mainly independent transparency approaches, which include both formal rules and soft approaches. It took almost ten years to overcome this independence, when, 'after a long, bitter set of negotiations' (Bignami 2003: 11), Regulation 1049/2001 EC on the Access to Documents of all three major EU institutions,[14] which entered into force in December 2001, was decided. Below, I will briefly trace the path that the European Commission, the European Parliament and the Council took in drawing up this regulation, and the more recent events (for more detailed analyses of the earlier stages, see, amongst others, Curtin 1996; Davis 1999; Harden 2002; Lodge 2001; Öberg 1998).

*The European Council and the Council*
In 1992, a 'Declaration on the Right of Access to Information' was annexed to the Treaty of Maastricht.[15] This was the first explicit link between transparency and democracy on the part of the European Council,[16] albeit in a lofty and soft language.[17] Nevertheless, in an attempt 'to respond to the concerns raised in the recent public debate',[18] the European Council reiterated, in the Birmingham Declaration in 1992, its dedication to 'ensure a better informed public debate' on EC activities. The issue was again picked up by subsequent summits in Edinburgh (December 1992) and Copenhagen (1993), finally resulting in a common 'Code of Conduct concerning Public Access to Council and Commission Documents' (December 1993).[19] However, the implementation of this code had to be undertaken by specific administrative regulations within each institution itself.

This development shows that the initial usage of a language that brought forward the normative dimension of transparency by highlighting the relationship between transparency and democracy, had subsided to a more narrow conception of transparency that only focused on better administration, rather than on better communication with the people (see also Curtin 1996: 98). The Council implemented the Code in the Council Decision on Public Access to Council Documents.[20] While the concrete measures and exceptions to access are of less importance here, it is crucial to note that the decision does not capture the disclosure of preparatory information or render documents fit for disclosure by the blanking out of names, numbers, etc. (*ibid.*: 108). This excludes, for instance, documents such as Council minutes, which would have been crucial in order to know the positions of the different Member States. Furthermore, in cases where documents were authored and classified by Member State institutions, no appellation to counter this classification was possible. With a view to the increasing importance of a common security and defence policy, the secrecy regime was even enforced by a Council Decision in 2000 (Council 2000).

In the meantime, however, the right of access to information has gained power from its inclusion into the Treaty of Amsterdam (Article 255). But it took until the above-mentioned Regulation 1049/2001 EC (Council and European Parliament 2001) for the issue of transparency to be again placed more explicitly into the context of democracy and citizen participation

(Paragraph 2). The regulation makes some improvement compared to the Council decision of 1993; most notably, it applies to all the documents of the institutions (Paragraph 11 and Article 2 (3)), i.e. even to information surrounding the activities in question.

Furthermore, it also includes documents that do not originate from an EU institution, so that the relevant documents from the Member States are no longer directly exempted from access, although the Member States have to request (albeit without justification) the EU institutions not to disclose a document without their explicit consent (Article 4 (6)). Moreover, if only parts of a document are judged as classified, this no longer hinders the accessibility, but, instead, obliges the institution to censor the sensitive parts and hand over the rest of the document. While the earlier legislation only required biannual reports on its implementation, the new regulation demands all institutions to draw up annual reports, which are, of course, also available publicly.[21]

With regard to other provisions of transparent and open government, the Council has traditionally been 'cloaked in secrecy' (Curtin 1996: 104), a situation that has slightly improved only very recently. In 2005, in a decision of 21 December, the Council acknowledged a transparency deficit and announced that it would open its meetings to a wider audience on all the issues that were decided under the co-decision procedure. However, the European Ombudsman criticised this move as being insufficient, and urged the Council to open its doors to *all* meetings that deal with concrete policy measures (Press Releases No. 2/7/13, 2006).[22] Nevertheless, it seems reasonable to argue that the Council's attempt to put the main burden of transparency on the administrative practices (mainly of the Commission) has resulted in undesired consequences for the practices of the Council (see, similarly, Lodge 2001, Chapter 4).

After the successful ratification process and the coming into force of the Lisbon Reform Treaty in December 2009, the right of public access to documents obtained the status of a fundamental right of the EU, because of the inclusion of the Charter of Fundamental Rights and its Article 42 into the treaty.[23]

### The European Commission

In spite of the widespread agreement that the European Commission 'interprets its role as guardian of the treaty in an open and relatively un-secret way, less secret than most national governments at home' (Middlemas 1995: 463), it is remarkable to note that, initially, it was not in the interest of the Commission to provide free access to information. As Curtin (1996: 100ff) underlines, it was, above all, a ruling by the European Court of Justice (ECJ) in 1990[24] that forced the Commission to reconsider its position towards greater transparency in its administrative proceedings. But, in the context of the internal market programme as well as the Maastricht referenda shock, the

Commission became more active in promoting transparency. However, these different sources of motivation for transparency activities opened different avenues for the Commission to act on transparency and only today is the Commission trying to come up with a coherent strategy. I will mention three of these avenues:

(1) The Maastricht-*problématique* triggered growing awareness of the need to structure the contacts with lobby groups and NGOs. Consequently, the Commission commenced by linking, albeit only loosely, the issues of transparency with the participation of CSOs. This point was made in the Commission's 1992 Communication on Special Interest Groups (1992a: 1). However, the rest of the communication mainly discussed measures about how to administer the interest groups better – via a directory and a code of conduct – instead of adopting a reflexive perspective about the responsibility of the Commission and the possibility that it would link the issues of transparency and participation in order to promote democracy. This was also not solved in the twin communication on increased transparency in the work of the commission (European Commission 1992b), although the Commission did explicitly see both communications as being complementary to each other.

In the transparency communication, the Commission promised to take certain steps to improve its working by, amongst other things, making more use of (the consultative) Green Papers, and by publishing annual work agendas and the like. With regard to the linkage with special interest groups, it only expressed its conviction that 'More public participation in the work of the Commission enhances more open government and can increase public confidence' (European Commission 1992b: 8), but left it 'for the competent service to decide the appropriate moment when and from whom it should seek advice' (*ibid.*). How this leverage was to guarantee that an inclusive and balanced participation was not further elaborated.

In the 1997 Communication on Voluntary Associations (see above), which, amongst other things, introduced the civil dialogue, the tenor was also on how to make use of these actors in order to increase the legitimacy of EU policies. It proposed some measures, including budgetary provisions, in order to support their role as transmission and dissemination agents (see, for example, p. 7), but it did not reflect upon organisational changes within the Commission and the EU institutions that might also have had supportive effects, such as the improvement of transparency and access to information.

(2) Under the influence of the Treaty of Maastricht and also requested by the various previously mentioned presidency conclusions that referred to transparency, the Commission engaged with the Council in the formulation of the common Code of Conduct about Transparency. In preparation of this code, the Commission published – as requested by the Birmingham European

Council – two communications in 1993, one directly on public access to the institution's Documents (European Commission 1993a), and the second on openness in the Community (European Commission 1993b).

The former was a stock-taking exercise, which assessed the existing transparency regulations at EU and Member State level. It outlined general principles of how access to information should be granted and pointed to the limits to transparency – points that can be found in its later decision on access to information (European Commission 1994). The Commission once again stressed its conviction that the transparency principle 'should be shared by the other institutions and Member States' (European Commission 1993a: 3) and invited them to co-operate in the development of a common approach.

The second communication on openness had several purposes. First of all, it took stock of how the promises made in the 1992 Transparency Communication had already been put into practice (clearly, it had been satisfied). Secondly, it expanded on the earlier 1993 Access Communication, preparing its decision on access to information. In this decision, the Commission focused, as did the Council, predominantly on better administration without improving its direct communication with the people. The decision simply adopted the Code of Conduct and pointed to the internal Rules of Procedure. However, it did not open the perspective to the wider issue of the legitimacy crisis of the EU.

(3) The Commission's administrative and instrumental approach to better information had been stimulated fairly functionally by the upcoming Single Market Project. The so-called Sutherland Report (Sutherland 1992) was requested by the Commission in March 1992 in order to learn about how to improve its administrative proceedings in the internal market. A High Level Group on the Operation of Internal Market undertook an empirical investigation among 23 business and consumer associations and some firms. Among the Report's 38 recommendations, several concerned issues of transparency and access. For instance, the Commission was asked to develop a communication strategy that was to include all community institutions, national administrations and affected NGOs 'in a systematic and co-ordinated way' (Recommendation 5) and urged better consultation, which included the making available of background information at the earliest stages possible (Recommendation 8).

Although the intentions of these recommendations as well as of the other avenues towards transparency were mainly not intentionally normative, in that they did not aim at democratic improvements but were instrumental in nature, focusing on administrative improvements, these developments are important in the present context. They demonstrate that instrumental and normative mechanisms and approaches are often two sides of the same coin, which means that instrumental changes have normative repercussions and vice versa.

As was noted above, since the year 2000, the linkages between democracy, participation and transparency have become stronger. But, notwithstanding this, the sheer number of different steps taken and initiatives launched by the Commission suggests that a master plan about how to improve transparency as a means of strengthening democratic participation did not exist. Diversity is still an indicator of the internal segmentation of the Commission and of a lack of a consistent vision as a side-effect of the regularly changing personnel, both at administrative staff level, as well as at the highest level of the Commissioners. I will subsequently sketch four of these more recent developments.[25]

(1) In the 2000 discussion paper on strengthening the partnership between the Commission and NGOs (see also above), the importance of transparency and a better information policy was underlined in order to build a 'true partnership' with the NGOs (European Commission 2000a: 7). In particular, it was highlighted that the European Community is a signatory to the convention on access to information, public participation in decision-making and access to justice in environmental matters, the so-called Århus Convention (June 1998).[26] Although the Convention, which was agreed by the United Nations Economic Commission for Europe (UNECE), was supposed to come into force in 2001, the EU only agreed in 2003 on two decisions for a partial implementation of its substance. Furthermore, only on 17 February 2005 did it ratify the convention, albeit in a watered-down version that excluded access to certain types of documents, and, above all, denied NGOs access to the European Court of Justice.[27]

(2) The Commission's White Paper on Governance (European Commission 2001a, see above) was a hallmark for the political and academic debates about participation, governance and democracy. Other authors have already presented their critical remarks on this White Paper (Armstrong 2002; Magnette 2003), and thus I will focus here only on the aspects that refer to transparency of information. The White Paper did not add much that was new, but mainly limited itself to referring to the 2001 regulation. The Commission argued that much had already been achieved with this regulation. Nevertheless, it is interesting to note that transparency and information do not appear as one of the guiding principles of good governance – those named specifically are 'openness, participation, accountability, effectiveness and coherence' (European Commission 2001a: 10) – and only in the sections on openness was a little said about the need for the EU and the Member States to '**communicate more actively with the general public on European issues**' (*ibid*:, emphasis in original), pointing at the new technologies and the the Eur-Lex portal where one is able to gain access to existing and proposed EU legislation.[28] This notion fell short of the demands raised by CSOs in the major consultation conducted in the run-up to the White Paper. These actors, asked, among other things,

firstly for a clarification of the conditions under which consultations prior to a decision are conducted. Who is consulted on what? More transparency, rigour, foreseeability and equity are wanted. This is particularly important since the use of 'soft' legislative tools, recognised as effective in certain cases, may also generate major inequalities through lack of transparency. (Governance Team of the European Commission 2001: 7)

The major issues of transparency were being raised here, and, it is clear that the CSOs felt that the 2001 Regulation on Access to Documents did not deliver sufficiently on these issues.

(3) Moving forward in the discussion line on contacts with NGOs, the Commission published, in 2002, the communication entitled 'towards a reinforced culture of consultation and dialogue – general principles and minimum standards for consultation of interested parties by the Commission' (European Commission 2002a). This communication aimed to implement some of the issues raised in the White Paper on Governance, and, above all, it sought to make the consultation processes with CSOs 'more consistent' (European Commission 2002a: 3). It set out to formulate 'general principles and minimum standards for consultation by the Commission' (ibid.: 15), without, however, over-ruling any of the already existing practices by individual Directorates-General or Departments.

To what extent this communication has the potential to render consultation processes more consistent is not debated in the document and is subject to empirical research (see below, Chapter 5). This communication appears to be a collection of more or less useful steps to administer consultation processes better, asking its own civil servants to act with more transparency and to be publicly accountable, but it fails to be a decisive step towards strengthening democratic participatory governance. As explicitly expressed at the beginning of the document, the rationale of the communication is to enhance the social legitimacy of the Commission itself, as well as to improve the quality of its policy measures.

Thus, the Commission seeks to make instrumental use of participatory activities by CSOs. This becomes visible when it is said that a more transparent consultation process makes the Commission more accountable (ibid.: 3), or that internal coherence and learning processes should be enhanced (ibid.: 4). Although administrative improvements are certainly important stones in building democracy, in this context, however, the Commission's intentions regarding these improvements are introspective, i.e. interested in enhancing its own role and perception, rather than outward looking, striving for the empowerment of the self-determination of civil society.[29]

Consequently, with regard to transparency, not much that is new is said. The communication merely re-iterated the fact that the EU is a signatory to the Århus Convention and referred to the additional measures that were under consideration at that time (and, indeed, decided upon the following

year). Yet the genesis of the document itself is a fine example of how participation processes could be further developed. Following the White Paper on
Governance, the Commission published a consultation paper and
commented on the major issues raised by interested parties in the communication, in an attempt to justify its own position. Hence, one could argue that
this communication is possibly less important due to its content, but more
important regarding better consultation practices.

(4) In November 2005, the current Commission launched a European
Transparency Initiative (ETI)[30] (see next section). To some extent, the ETI
was an attempt to combine the two sources of participation of non-state
collective actors in the EU, namely, the one in lobbying and interest representation, and the one in the discourse about bringing the Union closer to its
citizens, with the administrative discourse on good governance. Whether it
will be possible to relate these issues in a way that has an impact is still
undecided. From a democratic point of view, however, it is worth attempting
to democratise lobbying, to strengthen the participation of citizens, and to try
to render administrative practices more transparent.

In the earlier documents of the ETI, it again becomes clear that the
Commission sees itself as having already done a great deal to guarantee transparency in terms of access to information, most notably with the 2001
regulation.[31] Consequently, it is remarkable that the Commission, in the
meantime, changed its mind and launched a Green Paper on public access to
documents held by institutions of the European Community (European
Commission 2007a), followed by an online consultation (until 31 July
2007).[32] This Green Paper was a reaction to the eventual ratification of (parts
of) the Århus Convention by the EU as well as a response to several
complaints launched by the European Ombudsman and by the Case Law of
the Court of First Instance (CFI) and the ECJ.

Moreover, it was a reaction to the EP's proposal to amend Regulation
1049/2001. It poses eight questions to all those interested in this issue, and
covers issues such as a better definition of what constitutes a document, how
to strike a balance between data protection rights and the right to information, and how to improve the online databases for easier access. Meanwhile,
the Commission summarised the main points of this consultation.[33]

If all these measures were taken together, the self-image of the European
Commission as an open administration would probably stand comparison
with many national executive administrations. However, higher demands on
the Commission are justified, given its double nature as the EU administration, on the one hand, and as the executive with the monopoly of legislative
initiator, on the other. It is, in particular, the latter function that requires the
upholding of democratic standards.

*The European Parliament*
If one considers Lodge's statement that the European Parliament has 'consistently advocated a right of access to administrative documents' (2001: 358), and if one also takes into account that the EP is, 'by its very nature' (Curtin 1996: 112), interested in being accessible and transparent in its proceedings, it is remarkable that the EP decided about the rules for public access to its documents only in 1997 (European Parliament 1997). This document does not add significantly to the previously discussed rules by the Commission and the Council, and, consequently, I will not explore it further.

Despite this delay, the EP was not inactive in promoting transparency. Notably, on 12 July 1995, the EP appointed the European Ombudsman, and this proved to be of some significance for the transparency regime of the European Parliament. The Ombudsman's main task is to investigate instances of alleged maladministration, and it is notable that it is particularly the case of transparency and access to information that has been at the centre of his work. Consequently, in 1996, the Ombudsman undertook an inquiry on his own initiative into the provision of public access to documents by all European institutions and bodies and dedicated his first ever special report to the EP on precisely this topic in 1997.[34]

In this report, he urged the EU institutions to come up with a common transparency regime, and, if this were not realistic, he asked every single institution to draw up its own rules. In particular, he made a case for a transparency regime based upon rules, instead of upon soft measures, which he called, in his inquiry, the information strategies of individual institutions, because only rules can secure that the 'legitimate interest [of citizens] in the organisation and functioning of institutions and bodies that are paid for from public funds [is respected]. This may lead to requests for administrative documents, which are not usually covered by an information strategy' (see the report's section on Information Policies). To some extent, the EP's move to decide upon access rules was a reaction to the Ombudsman's special report.

*Conclusion*
The overview of the transparency provisions of the key EU institutions shows that some progress has been made towards access to information. Above all, it shows that the right of public access to information does not distinguish between different groups of persons and no justification or special interest is required. Thus, the provisions are principally inclusive and respect political equality.

However, the overview also illustrates the limits of the chosen strategy. The practical implications drawn in the context of the discussions surrounding the Maastricht referenda shock mainly took place at an administrative level; the reforms of the inter-institutional balance (among others, the Council *versus* the EP) or the secrecy of the Council's working style have only emerged in recent years (see, similarly, Lodge 2001, Chapter 3). Democratic governance requires transparency, as much as it also necessitates institutional reforms – a point that I will come back to in Chapter 7 of this study.

Even more so, the given overview does not dig deeper into the politics of the emerging transparency regime. It thus obscures the fact that the visible expansion towards a more coherent approach did not go as smoothly as the preambles to the legislation suggest. On the contrary, a brief glimpse into the politics of the transparency regime shows two factors that are important for its development – as well as for the democratic character of EU governance,[35] namely, the role of law and the importance of CSOs.

Since the early days of the transparency provisions, progressive Member States, such as the Netherlands, or active CSOs, such as Statewatch, have launched a number of complaints in the CFI and the ECJ.[36] Furthermore, Statewatch and other CSOs, such as the European Citizens Action Service (ECAS), have also launched complaints of maladministration with the European Ombudsman. These organisations found many reasons for their complaints. In a preliminary analysis made two years after the Regulation had been in existence, for instance, ECAS complained that 'at the very most, the Institutions fulfilled the minimal requirements' (Ferguson 2003: 1) and noted that refusal rates for access to documents were actually rising.[37]

In 2006, Statewatch won its complaint against the Commission before the European Ombudsman, because the former had failed to produce its annual Report on the Implementation of the Regulation 1049/2001.[38] To date, the Ombudsman has already cited almost sixty cases of complaints since the coming into force of the regulation (European Ombudsman 2007: 1). Hence, these illustrative examples show the importance of judiciable rights for the enhancement of democratic governance, since they can be used as a trigger to enhance the quality of the provisions in force. They also show the significance of participatory activities for the strengthening of democracy in the EU.

Despite the shortcomings, the CSO representatives who were interviewed revealed that, in principle, they were satisfied with the accessibility of documents. In particular, the improvements that accompanied the new information technologies were mentioned, although the consultation on the Green Paper on Access (see above) showed the desire for single access points that merge the many different search tools available on the Europa website. In addition, there was a call for the extension of the types of documents. Many interviewees would particularly welcome the publication of the positions of the individual Member States. This means that they call for the accessibility of the footnote papers of the Council working groups.

Other statements indicate that it would be important for effective participation if the procedures were made more transparent. For CSOs, to obtain 'access to the agendas' of the European institutions at an early stage would be as important as 'access to documents', as this would grant them sufficient time to prepare themselves and to develop positions in co-operation with their national sections.

This latter remark points to a difference between the right to access documents and the right to know. Here, the latter is necessary in order to exercise the former. However, the current provisions only focus on the former. Thus, as long as the European institutions do not broaden their conception of transparency and openness, and more actively offer information about agendas, planned activities, etc., which includes the accessibility of background documents and 'grey literature', the transparency regime remains a tool which is suitable only for those already informed, and would exclude all those potentially affected and interested in the activities of the EU.

### Access to the policy-making process

Equal access to policy processes can be described, as was elaborated above, as something akin to the lowest common denominator for all theories of participatory democracy. If one leaves aside the early pluralist assumption about an equilibrium of interest group influence, some form of institutional provisions that strive for equality in access appears essential for participatory activities that do not wish to fail a democratic test. Thus, access, and the way access to policy-making processes is granted to civil society organisations, is decisive for determining the EU's participatory model and for judging the extent to which this model is suitable for producing democratising effects on EU governance.

The particular challenge for the condition of access is the danger that public institutions, which have, after all, to establish the condition of access, will be tempted to install rules that favour their own – mainly instrumental – needs, rather than more abstract democratic requirements. In the EU context, access provisions are predominantly discussed under the framework of consultation. I will subsequently discuss each of the three major EU institutions again, in turn. This differentiation is essential because, unlike other international organisations[39] such as the United Nations,[40] the EU does not possess a common formal accreditation scheme that establishes participation rights. Consequently, each institution applies its own rules, and it is only in the ongoing debates in the context of the transparency initiative that a more integrated access regime is thoroughly discussed. I will briefly touch upon those issues that were already introduced in the section on the civil dialogue above.

### The European Council and the Council

Interestingly, in recent research about the regulation of CSO participation by EU institutions, such as those by Bignami (2003), Chabanet (2007), Knodt (2005) or Smismans (2005a), the Council and the European Council are hardly ever addressed in great detail.[41] This stems most probably from the fact that not much can be said about the Council's rules and provisions concerning access, since it does not deviate from its reputation as the least open and least accessible of the European institutions when it comes to access for CSOs.[42] In fact, in its rules of procedure, the Council does not mention its relations with lobbyists or CSOs at all.[43] Consequently, CSOs have no formal consultative status and there is, to my knowledge, no framework in place for regulating the relations between them and the Council.

One exception to this rule is the contact between the Council and the Social Platform which forms part of the Civil Dialogue. In 2000, the Portuguese Presidency invited the Platform to an informal Social Affairs Council Meeting and provided them with speaking rights (Alhadeff, Wilson and Forwood 2002). These meetings were repeated until the Presidencies of Italy and Greece stopped this invitation. The British Presidency in 2005, however, re-established these meetings.

It is apparent that the Council is lagging behind in its effort to become more open and more accessible to civil society. Informally, however, and below the level of the Council and the European Council, there are many access points for lobbyists – less so for CSOs. These access points are to be found in the complex committee system, both the Council working groups and the comitology committees. This committee structure opens access points at European level, but also via the national route, and poses severe challenges for democratic participation (Huster 2008).

*The European Commission*
In stark contrast to the Council's approach, the European Commission adopts a different strategy. It has long since stipulated that it wants to 'maintain a dialogue which is as open as possible'.[44] This had already been expressed in the 1992 Communication on special interests, which stated that:

> Explicit Commission rules (such as accreditation, registration, code of conduct) towards special interest groups do not exist. However, the Commission has a general policy not to grant privileges to special interest groups, such as the issuing of entry passes and favoured access to information. Nor does it give associations an official endorsement by granting them consultative status. This is because the Commission has always wanted to maintain a dialogue which is as open as possible with all interested parties without having to enforce an accreditation system. (European Commision 1992a: 1)

This position was confirmed and reinforced in the Commission's 1993 Communication on 'Openness in the Community'. It only adds the plan to establish, together with the EP, a common database that should contain information about all organisations with whom the two institutions are in contact. But it stresses that 'inclusion in the directory will not imply any form of official recognition, nor will it confer any privileges' (European Commission 1993b: 10). This refusal of an accreditation scheme was valid until very recently.

This preference for a somewhat unstructured openness apparently met with some challenges from within the Commission. In its 1997 Communication on Voluntary Organisations, the Commission acknowledges that a 'high level of political commitment exists at European level to ensure that more systematic consultation with the voluntary sector is instigated, as regards both the development and implementation of policy' (European Commission 1997: 9.7). However, the only concrete example is the civil dialogue in the social policy area and the Commission's support in establishing the Platform of European Social NGOs (the Social Platform[45]).

Concrete proposals for improving access and participation are lacking, beyond the rather lofty prose that the 'Commission will maintain and further develop a continuous exchange of information and points of view by establishing systematic and regular dialogue and consultation with the sector' (*ibid.*: 13). Lack of progress is implicitly acknowledged by the 2000 NGO Discussion Paper, which states that, for many NGOs, the fragmented nature of consultation practice is strenuous, and that a more coherent approach would be welcome. Such an approach would, of course, require a minimum set of rules, which were not proposed in the paper.

Some progress towards a better regulated access regime was made in the White Paper on Governance, in which the Commission admitted that there 'is currently a lack of clarity about how consultations are run and to whom the Institutions listen ... [and that] ... it needs to rationalise this unwieldy system not to stifle discussion, but to make it more effective and accountable both for those consulted and those receiving the advice' (European Commission 2001a: 17). The Commission calls for a '**re-inforced culture of consultation and dialogue**' (*ibid.*: 16, emphasis in original) that encompasses all major EU institutions, in particular the EP, and promises a '**code of conduct that sets minimum standards**' (*ibid.*: 17, emphasis in original). Furthermore, the Commission points to the promises of the new information technologies by pointing at its initiative for online consultation, called Interactive Policy-Making (IPM) (see below).[46] In addition to these measures, the White Paper testifies to an interesting new edge in the discussion on the participation of CSOs. Even before it presents its own plan, it states that:

> **With better involvement comes greater responsibility.** Civil society must itself follow the principles of good governance, which include accountability and openness. The Commission intends to establish, before the end of this year, a comprehensive on-line database with details of civil society organisations active at European level, which should act as a catalyst to improve their internal organisation. (*ibid.*: 15; emphasis in original)

With this statement, a turn towards the responsibilities of CSOs is introduced, which has subsequently become stronger, as will be shown below in the context of the Transparency Initiative, and which moves away from the responsibilities of the public institutions to introduce an access regime that fulfils democratic expectations.

The promised minimum standards were published by the Commission in its 2002 Communication on minimum standards for consultation, in which it underlines its position which 'does not intend to create new bureaucratic hurdles in order to restrict the number of those that can participate in consultation processes' (European Commission 2002a: 11). On the other hand, it introduces the figure of targeted consultation where only those that have relevant interests should be consulted (*ibid.*). Given the absence of clear rules, it remains at the Commission's discretion to define whose interests are relevant and whose are not. In terms of access rules, the communication states the following:

> Thus consultation processes run by the Commission must also be transparent, both to those who are directly involved and to the general public. It must be clear:
> - what issues are being developed;
> - what mechanisms are being used to consult;
> - who is being consulted and why;
> - what has influenced decisions in the formulation of policy.
> It follows that interested parties must themselves operate in an environment that is transparent, so that the public is aware of the parties involved in the consultation processes and how they conduct themselves.
> Openness and accountability are thus important principles for the conduct of organisations when they are seeking to contribute to EU policy development. It must be apparent:
> - which interests they represent;
> - how inclusive that representation is.
> Interested parties that wish to submit comments on a policy proposal by the Commission must therefore be ready to provide the Commission and the public at large with the information described above. This information should be made available either through the CONECCS database (...) or through other measures, e.g., special information sheets. If this information is not provided, submissions will be considered as individual contributions. (*ibid.:* 17)

Again, the dual melody of requirements for both the Commission and for the CSOs appears. While in this quotation, the Commission speaks about an obligation for transparent and clear access rules (it uses 'must'), in its more concrete guidelines for the Commission's civil servants, this language of obligation is watered down to an envisaged aim (using merely the word 'should'). It therefore remains unclear what the target group of this communication is: either the civil servants, or the outside world? However, the obligation for the CSOs to register on the closed online database CONECCS[47] (Consultation, the European Commission and Civil Society), was not changed to an invitation. Disregarding the soft language of the minimum standards, their content could make a difference from a democratic perspective, if they were implemented properly. The Commission distinguishes five minimum standards:

- Clear organisation of the consultation process;
- Clear justification and consultation to define target groups;

- Publicity of the consultation procedures;
- Sufficient time for the participation; and
- Public summaries of the positions raised throughout the consultations. (*ibid.*: 19–22)

However, the implementation of these standards within the Commission is unclear. It is still subject to detailed policy analysis of whether the practice of consultation has improved since the launch of this communication. Scepticism remains because the Commission's earlier acknowledgement about the need for a more coherent access regime is contradicted in this communication. It states that the Commission favours a de-centralised approach to access, saying that its 'different services are responsible for their own mechanisms of dialogue and consultation', thereby rejecting 'an over-legalistic approach [which] would be incompatible with the need for timely delivery of policy' (*ibid.*: 10).

Based upon a widely agreed opinion of the interviewees, and with a view to the later case studies (Chapter 5), I agree with the rather disillusioned findings of Pauline Cullen, who states that '[t]he only tangible results from these initiatives were a Commission website with a registration system, and the use of Internet portals as cyber or virtual consultations' (Cullen 2005: 6). Here, Cullen refers to the online database CONECCS, and the Internet consultation scheme Interactive Policy-Making (IPM). CONECCS was a database where CSOs could (or should) voluntarily present themselves to become better known to the Commission and their potential co-operation partners. However, many CSOs did not make use of CONECCS. Although the Commission hoped that virtual consultation would have been used by Commission staff in order to identify an appropriate mixture of partners for consultation, its *de facto* usage fell far short of this goal.

Both CONECCS and the IPM are relatively unknown among both CSO representatives and civil servants; in fact, ignorance is dominant, and there is no structured intra-institutional strategy for disseminating relevant information.[48] Only detailed future research would be able to show whether this website will remain what it currently is, i.e. a voluntary, non-conditional database for information, which has failed to improve the *de facto* consultation procedures (as Cullen would suggest), or whether it will develop into an incremental foundation for a system of 'access leagues', as Greenwood and Halpin argue (2005: 5).[49]

This overview of the key documents shows that the discourse on access and consultation has moved towards the acknowledgement that a more regulated approach would be recommendable by the European Commission. Practical progress, however, remains scant. All these papers and communications on the relationship with CSOs do not add very much that is new to the initial quotation from the 1992 Communication, and a formalised access regime to the Commission is yet to be established. On the contrary, the

Commission's emphasis on openness and accessibility favours informal access rules. Rather than a formal conditionality approach which spells out the rules and conditions for access, the Commission explicitly favours a self-regulatory model. The rationale behind this approach seems to be the wish to avoid the instalment of access barriers – and thus favours equality. However, it does have serious drawbacks. The lack of explicit conditions for access comes together with a lack of explicit rights to access. CSOs that wish to participate in a policy process have no opportunities to demand their access. On the contrary, it was shown that a gradual focus on their responsibilities was observable.

This move has been even more strengthened in the Commission's recent transparency initiative.[50] As stated previously, the ETI is the latest step taken by the Commission in the context of the overall discussion on participatory governance and democracy. In its earlier documents, the focus was clearly on improving the administrative practices of all EU institutions in order to increase the confidence of the European people in their work. The Commission stressed that:

> the main challenges are to enlarge the debate beyond the European Commission and engage the other EU institutions. In the eyes of the public, there is one, single 'European ethical space' and while rules may vary, different ethical standards across the institutions are neither desirable, nor explainable. By launching the debate, the Commission openly signals that it considers itself part of the challenge and part of the solution.[51]

However, in the ETI Green Paper, which was launched in spring 2006 to accelerate the transparency initiative (European Commission 2006a), the ambitious goal for a common transparency and access regime of all institutions seems not to have survived the internal discussions. In the follow-up to the Green Paper (European Commission 2007b), a lofty invitation 'to examine the possibility of closer co-operation' (European Commission 2007b: 6) is the only remainder, an invitation that does not even include the Council. Thus, instead of progress in this area, the focus is more limited to the Commission's consultative practices, here, above all, the 2002 Communication on minimum standards for consultation, and the regulation of interested parties.[52] Yet, in the follow-up, there was a clear tendency to favour the second aspect.

With regard to the consultative practices, the Commission has failed to consider the introduction of new measures that would render its consultative practices more transparent, more credible and less arbitrary. It says that 'it is not intended to review the content of the consultation standards at this stage' (European Commission 2007b: 6) and its shortlist of measures, whose application is to be re-inforced,[53] does not create much confidence that the 2002 minimum standards will be further developed into a clear access regime in the foreseeable future.

As for the second aspect on regulating interest representation, the debates are livelier and the envisaged measures by the Commission are much more concrete. Three issues are highlighted in particular. First, the Commission cancelled CONECCS in spring 2008 and replaced it by a single register where any lobbyist wishing to participate can include himself or herself.[54] This register is to be voluntary in order not to spoil the favoured self-regulatory (instead of rights-based) approach, but it might well be another step towards access leagues (see above). The Commission is considering granting those that register additional rights, such as the more extensive transparency rights of the Århus Convention (*ibid.:* 5). Moreover, it might end up that only registered actors can participate in online consultations. Secondly, a code of conduct[55] for interest representatives is being considered.

An online consultation about this code was conducted (from 10 December 2007 until 15 February 2008) and 165 contributions issued by different kinds of actors.[56] At the time of writing (early January 2008), only three contributions have been made so far. The code is a one-page document that seeks to promote the principles of openness, transparency, honesty and integrity, so that lobbying can take its legitimate role in a democratic system. The vision of strengthening democracy by fostering democratic participatory governance no longer exists. Interest representation is merely said to be a legitimate part of a democratic system. The interest representatives are asked to disclose some basic information about their funding and their allegiance. However, it is too newly established to say more about its relevance.

But severe limits remain. The code only applies to instances in the context of a public consultation, i.e. there is apparently no intention to illuminate the shadowy corners of everyday lobbying. Furthermore, transparency is questioned since the representatives may ask for their contributions to be treated confidentially if 'such publication would harm his or her legitimate interests' – but it remains unclear what establishes a legitimate interest and upon what basis this will be determined.

It is still undecided whether the Commission is willing to establish an access regime based upon clear rights for the participants, or whether it will remain in its soft language that leaves the door open for instrumental participation alone. In the strong words of an engaged observer, the Commission is now:

> faced with the stark choice of 'double or quits'. It can press on with its mini-mandate to encourage a self-regulatory system under the shadow of mandatory imposition. This will satisfy no one, but will continue to damage the reputation of public affairs. Alternatively it can recognise that its aims can only be achieved on a basis of all institutions, all countries and all public affairs practitioners. If it takes this high road it will need to start by establishing a consensus with Council and Parliament on how to reshape the system.[57]

For this purpose of this book, the recent change in vocabulary is telling.

As I described in the historical overview, there was a development that merged different actor types, in particular special interest groups and voluntary organisations, under the umbrella of CSOs. One important reason for this was the normative promise that resonates with the concept of civil society. Now, the more profane term 'lobby group' is again predominantly used. Whether this signifies a farewell to the democratic aspirations of participatory governance remains to be seen. However, if one considers the turn that the transparency initiative has taken, it becomes apparent that the Commission has managed to shift the debate away from improving its own procedures about participation and consultation towards the lobbies. It is up to them to prove that they are representative, accountable, open and transparent in order to be worthy of inclusion.

Although there is a certain appeal to placing some normative standards of accountability on the participating agents,[58] this turn entails the danger of colonising CSOs 'both in terms of their organisational forms and their rationalities' (Obradovic 2005: 32). It is very unclear how the requirements could ever be fulfilled given the opaqueness of the terms applied. To name but a few of unclarities: to whom should CSOs be accountable – to its members (often, they do not have individual members) or to the Commission, or to somebody else? Should they be territorially representative, or rather functionally representative? One could well imagine an approach that would not focus on organisational structures, but on substantive issues, instead. One could, for instance, demand a credible assertion from the organisations that they respect the rule of law and support democratic standards in a non-violent manner. Otherwise, the Commission remains in the comfortable position of being able to pick and choose only the organisations which it wants to hear.

*The European Parliament*

The European Parliament is an interesting case with regard to an access regime. On the one hand, it has well-developed informal contacts with CSOs, and, as Smismans states, 'is seen as very receptive to the demands of the NGO sector' (2002: 18); on the other hand, however, the EP is considerably more sceptical concerning too much emphasis on participatory democracy, a somewhat unsurprising fact for an institution of representation.[59] Instead of having been a driving force in the discussion on CSOs and participatory governance, the EP already had a record of attempts to establish an access regime – attempts about which the Commission's key ETI documents – interestingly enough – do not provide information.

According to Chabanet's detailed analysis (2007: 2ff), the EP was the first EU institution that considered the regulation of interest representation. Back in 1991, while it was increasingly becoming the target of lobby activities because of its gaining decision-making powers, the EP's 'committee on rules of procedure, the verification of credentials and immunities' was asked by the plenary committee to submit proposals for a code of conduct and a public register of lobbyists in the EP. The committee's chairman, Marc Galle, became *rapporteur* and, after conducting a public hearing, the so-called Galle Report was published in 1992 (European Parliament 1992).

The general gist of the report is worth noting, because it comprehensively aims at both the lobbyist and the Members of the European Parliament (MEP). It proposes both the formulation of a code of conduct and a register of lobbyists that would offer those registered access rights to the EP's premises (in the form of a one year access badge) and would ensure them the right to obtain documents (thus, well before the other initiatives had had results, see above). In addition, MEPs and their staff were to be obliged to disclose their financial interests regularly. However, no provisions were foreseen regarding a list of contacts between MEPs and lobbyists, and thus the actual lobby activities would have remained hidden.

The report's proposals for a basic regulation of lobbying runs counter to the self-regulatory approach promoted by the European Commission ever since its 1992 Communication on a dialogue with special interest groups. Here, it was stated that the 'Commission therefore encourages the sectors concerned to draw up their own code of conduct', thus expressing once again the initial objections of the Commission to the regulation of lobbying. Moreover, as Chabanet highlighted (*ibid.*: 10), this communication was created in close co-operation with business lobbies. In fact, even the proposals of the ETI were not much more far-reaching than those of the Galle Report. However, as Chabanet elaborates (2007: 4f), the report met with resistance not only from the Commission, but also within the EP, so that it was never discussed, let alone any decisions made, in the plenary committee.[60]

In the following years, the parliament's College of Quaestors[61] managed the lobby activities, mainly following the Commission's 1992 proposals. Thus, effectively, no regulation took place until 1997, when a Code of Conduct for the representatives of interest groups[62] was adopted by the EP, formalising the existing practice of the Quaestors. Neither the long time-span during which the code remained undecided, nor the code's content are particularly glorious chapters in the EP's history. The reason for this is that, in the years in between, both central issues of the Galle Report, namely regulating lobbying and the disclosure of the MEPs' financial interests, were debated and connected to each other.

Apparently, however, the interests of many MEPs and their assistants to maintain secrecy, rather than adopt transparency *vis-à-vis* their independence from lobbyists were too strong and prevented both significant measures and a linkage between the two issues. Consequently, in the final reading of the code of conduct, two amendments were rejected by the plenary committee, the first obliging the lobbyists to submit an annual report about their activities in order to receive a renewable pass for accessing the EP premises, the second allowing access only to the assistants who worked exclusively for the MEPs, and who were not on the payroll of some business or lobby. In this meeting, the Greens regretted that, from that point on, it would be impossible to link the lobbyists' activities with the financial interests of MEPs.[63]

Rule 9 on Members' financial interests, standards of conduct and access to Parliament of the current EP rules of procedures[64] brings both issues together without linking them substantially. As for the disclosure of financial interests, it refers to Annex I of the Rules of Procedure, whose provisions, such as the Declaration of all Financial Interests and Support Received by Third-Parties in their Political Work, are apparently not followed too strictly by a significant number of MEPs (see Chabanet 2007, Chapter 2). Annex IX comprises the provisions of Rule 9 (4) on lobbying, and includes the code of conduct for lobby representatives, but without real sanctions. Lobbyists have to register at the Quaestors' in order to obtain a long-term pass (valid for one year) to access the EP.

The recent increase in the number of lobbyists has led to a tightening up of the issuing of these passes. Only six persons of any given organisation, which needs to be based in Brussels, are given permanent passes to the EP. It was particularly the latter aspect which met with resistance even among the interviewed civil society organisation representatives, since it hinders the work for organisations that are not based in Brussels. Furthermore, the impression among the interviewees was that the tightening up of the rules of access were security-driven in the wake of anti-terrorism activities after the attacks of 11 September 2001. In Annex IX, the assistants to the MEPs are also covered, and they are obliged to disclose their eventual linkages with lobby interests to the Quaestors. This information, which is different from the information about the MEPs, does not have to be made available to the public.

*Conclusion*

This overview of the access provisions by the central European institutions reveals a more ambiguous situation than in the case of transparency. While the Council remained mainly silent on this issue, both the EP and the Commission have acted on access. The EP, however, started rather ambitiously, but only came up with soft measures on regulating lobbying. No transparency obligations concerning the number or the content of contacts are in place, nor is there a (physical) access right to all CSOs. Although this was seemingly rather unproblematical in the daily work of the organisations, recent developments are restricting their access to the EP.

An explicit link to democracy has not been forged – beyond some rhetoric in the preambles. The EP's approach makes its scepticism with regard to participatory governance visible. In the case of the Commission, the opposite tendency is observable. Having started with significant emphasis on the self-regulatory capacities of special interest groups, the overall discussions on good governance and democratic participation have had a clear impact on its approach to a better-regulated access regime. However, whether the ETI will bring results is still an open question – and there is some scepticism with regard to this issue.

Hence, all in all, despite a lively discussion on the participation of CSOs at European level, repeated calls from CSOs (see for example Platform of European Social NGOs 2001), and some Commission initiatives to strengthen consultation, the EU has still a long way to go for CSOs to acquire a 'right to be heard' (Bignami 2003: 3). The ratification of the constitutional treaty could have substantially accelerated this process. The envisaged Title VI of the constitutional treaty included Article I 47 on participatory democracy, which establishes a clear connection between civil society participation and democratic governance in the EU. Furthermore, this article obliged *all* European institutions, i.e. even the Council, to be both transparent and open to consultation. The entering into force of this article would probably have stimulated reflections about the inclusions of CSOs in EU policy-making processes. The Reform Treaty of Lisbon (2009), however, falls short of this proposal. In its new Article 11, the principle of participatory democracy does not appear; instead, only a reference to a regular dialogue to representative associations and the civil society is made. In doing so, the EU has not grasped the opportunity to make itself – even on paper – more accessible to the participatory activities of the people of Europe. However, in the wording of Article 8, the provisions of the Constitutional Treaty have survived almost unscathed, so that there is some legal leverage for further developing a regulated model of participation in the EU.

For the time being, the access of CSOs has to be characterised as participation by grace and favour, meaning that there are no rules that could better regulate the extent of participation and consultation, which, until now, mainly hinges upon the discretion of officials – if one leaves aside the open online consultations. Practices differ widely both across and within the institutions. Thus, when it comes to a preliminary judgement about the usage made of the democratic potential of equal access, the results are modest and one must concede that recent debates on greater participation have been largely implemented on a soft and voluntary basis.

### The inclusiveness of policy processes
For the public institutions, the condition of inclusiveness, i.e. the inclusion of all those who have a legitimate interest in a discussed policy initiative, is, from an instrumental perspective, of minor importance compared to the expertise provided by a limited number of CSOs to whom they can give selective access. However, for democratic purposes, be it from a pluralist or a deliberative perspective, the equal consideration of all who are affected by a decision, and all those who, for good reasons, are interested in it, is a central value. Inclusiveness is crucial for the fair and equal participation of all who wish to partake.

The condition of inclusiveness is a demanding condition that could not be rectified by the provision of far-reaching consultative rights for an exclusive group of selected (encompassing) organisations, as corporatists (and perhaps associationalists) would argue. Such a focus on a few (even important) groups would violate political equality and foster exclusionary tendencies that would be hard to counter. Efforts for inclusion into the participatory processes are particularly important for the CSOs of vulnerable groups (such as migrants) or voiceless issues (such as the environment), which are difficult to organise, and/or cannot afford (or are unable) to set up an office in Brussels, or lack the modern telecommunication resources necessary to make use of e-governance.

To some extent, as was argued in the previous chapter, inclusiveness and access are complementary conditions. Inclusiveness makes access more equal by aiming at acting against the existing inequalities among CSOs. However, inclusiveness is of a contra-factual nature, because it is empirically impossible to observe whether all those possibly affected and/or whether all interested persons really are included and have their say in a concrete policy process. The fulfilment of the conditions of transparency and access can thus be framed as necessary for achieving inclusiveness, because, without the potential knowledge of a specific policy measure, and without access to its process, no inclusiveness would be possible. But they, alone, are insufficient, because – as was argued in Chapter 3 – institutional measures for enabling CSOs, which aim to enhance political equality, are also necessary.

The increased use of e-governance mechanisms, such as online consultations, could constitute elements of such institutional efforts, because, in doing so, they not only lower the costs of participation, but also somewhat de-territorialise consultation and participation. However, e-governance is not able to balance the disadvantages in the capability of raising one's own voice. It does not substitute efforts to support the inclusion of these concerns actively. Next to extending the basic access provisions (see the section above), it is, above all, the allocation of financial provisions, in support of the organisations of vulnerable, disadvantaged and voiceless concern-groups, which would seem to constitute a suitable institutional effort to foster equal inclusion. The extent to which the EU engages in (financially) supporting the CSOs of vulnerable groups and the overall CSO landscape is thus the pragmatic levelling board for the condition of inclusiveness.

Whether such attempts are successful can only be tentatively determined on a case-by-case basis (see Chapter 5). On a general level, a brief overview of the budget lines offered by EU institutions to support the work and existence of CSOs follows here.[65]

The European Commission tries to support civil society organisations financially. The legal basis for such provisions is laid down in the Commission regulation (European Commission 2002b) which implements the rules stipulated by a Council regulation on the financial regulation of the general budget of the European Communities (Council 2002).Article 108 of the Council's Regulation on Grants opens the door to finance:

(a) either an action intended to help achieve an objective forming part of a European Union policy; or
(b) the functioning of a body which pursues an aim of general European interest or has an objective forming part of a European Union policy.

Furthermore, Article 110 clearly states that grants have to be awarded by respecting 'the principles of transparency and equal treatment'. These provisions are specified in the Commission regulation, which defines bodies pursuing an aim of general European interest as the following:

(a) a European body involved in education, training, information or research and study in European policies or a European standards body; or
(b) a European network representing non-profit bodies active in the Member States or in the candidate countries and promoting principles and policies consistent with the objectives of the Treaties (Article 162, Commission's regulation).

These provisions open the possibility for the Commission to support not only the projects or research activities of CSOs, but also to contribute to the functioning of such organisations by offering core funds. However, they also make it evident that CSOs that wish to obtain financial support need to align themselves to the overall aims of EU integration. To what extent this excludes certain actors is hard to tell, but at least it opens the door to discretionary funding, as the following quotation from an e-mail communication with the Directorate-General for Budget (January 2008) reveals:

In general, there are no NGO-specific budget lines. There is no EU-wide definition of NGOs for the purposes of the implementation of the EU budget. NGOs take different forms in different EU countries according to the sector concerned. NGOs can and do of course receive EU funding but are not a specific category of organisations and there are no specific rules for NGOs. (Personal e-mail communication with the Commission)

The exact way in which these provisions are put into practice, with regard to CSOs, even the Commission cannot exactly say.[66] In its NGO discussion paper in 2000, the Commission only estimated that approximately €1,000 million is allocated per year to CSOs, the bulk of which goes to NGOs in the policy field of external relations and consists of project funding (European Commission 2000a: 2) at EU and national level.[67] It says there that several hundred NGOs receive EU funding and NGOs appear to be a major recipient of the direct funding of the Commission (*ibid.:* 22). Despite the Commission's acknowledgement in this discussion paper that the whole financing system is somewhat complicated and opaque, improvements, it maintains, are somewhat difficult to make.

There is no single access point for NGOs (or scholars, for that matter) to find out about funding opportunities. Instead, the activity-based budget approach by the Commission means that all the budgetary lines of each policy area must be examined in order to find the appropriate information. Funding can be received for different reasons, such as the core funding of an organisation, as payment for the implementation of a project, or for research activities. CSOs have to apply for grants or enter competitive calls for tenders, tasks which already require a certain amount of administrative expertise that is rather detrimental to the accessibility of funds for weak groups, and violations to the requirement of equal treatment are easy to imagine (see also European Citizen Action Service 2004: 4). Interestingly, the official position of the Commission contradicts this judgement and understands the calls for tenders and grants as the means of achieving transparency and equal treatment:

> EU funding is awarded either 1. Through calls for tenders (contracts) or 2. Through calls for proposals (grants). Both processes are open (transparent) and competitive (equal treatment). (Personal e-mail communication with the Commisison)

However, one has to acknowledge that the Commission is, given its history of fraud, under significant pressure for budgetary accountability, which hinders low-threshold accessibility to funds for CSOs. Existing research points to the danger that these efforts may create hindrances for CSOs to obtain funding. In order to organise the funding system somewhat better, the Commission aspires to be more restrictive on smaller grants, which evidently challenges many small organisations (see Smismans 2002), and to substantiate budget lines. This means that the Commission forces CSOs to squeeze themselves under the headings of policy objectives, to the detriment of the organisations which do not necessarily conform to these objectives.[68]

To name just two instances from policy: firstly, there is the current focus on anti-discrimination, but not all social CSOs are engaged in this field (see, similarly, Cullen 2005). Secondly, and interestingly for this study, there is an emphasis on promoting European citizenship. The Council decision on 'establishing on the period 2007 to 2013 the programme *Europe for citizens* to promote active European citizenship'[69] opens the gates for CSO funding, highlighting their role as 'intermediaries between Europe and its citizens' (Paragraph 13) and their contribution to active citizenship and thus to the development of democracy in Europe (Paragraphs 5 and 9).

The decision strives for some inclusiveness by opening up the programmes' funds to the European Free Trade Association (EFTA), and to candidate and Balkan countries. However, with regard to the structural funding of CSOs, it severely limits its scope by naming three organisations which are to receive structural support for the years 2007–2009, namely, the already mentioned Social Platform, the European Movement,[70] and the European Council on Refugees and Exiles (ECRE),[71] all of which play an important role in the policy field of migration (see Chapter 5). It is interesting to see that the language of participatory democracy has trickled down even to the budgetary publications. For instance, budget line 04 04 09 in the EU budget's Section concerning Employment and Social Affairs, which regulates the 'support for the running costs of the Platform of European Social Non-governmental Organisations' (in 2007, €620,000), states that:

> This appropriation is intended to cover the running costs of the Platform of European Social Non-governmental Organisations (NGOs). The Social Platform will facilitate participatory democracy in the European Union by promoting the consistent involvement of social NGOs within a structured civil dialogue with the EU institutions. It will also provide added value to the EU social policy-making process and strengthen civil society within new Member States.[72]

The bulk of CSOs are forced to make significant efforts in order to receive more specific funding through grants, projects and other calls for tenders. This has potential exclusionary effects because it favours stronger and well-established organisations.

### Conclusion

This chapter has illustrated that the EU has gone a considerable way to establishing a formal participatory regime. The recent developments of participatory governance provisions are grounded both in a gradual expansion of participatory rights and in the scope of the actors who are grouped under the heading of participation and consultation. The current practice developed in an evolutionary process, which has accompanied the ongoing integration process. Throughout integration history, the increasing institutionalisation and the regulation of the channels of (formal) participation which accompany informal and unregulated lobbying activities have been identified.

This formalisation included, as was presented above, *inter alia*, the access of firms to the ECJ in the 1970s, the increasing role of the social partners since the mid-1980s, and the adoption of transparency rules by the European institutions from the early 1990s. In the last few years, this process has gained momentum in the governance debate that surrounded the European Commission's White Paper on Governance (European Commission 2001a), and eventually resulted in the already-mentioned clause on participatory democracy in the failed draft constitutional treaty.

The evolving participatory regime for non-state actors has not only been influenced both by the actors themselves, who seek to attain access and influence at the progressively more important European level, but also from the top, which had strong interests in a developing lively participatory culture. From the very beginning of European integration, the European Commission, in particular, was the institution most eager to consult external interests and experts (see also Streeck and Schmitter 1994: 182f), thus pursuing several goals: first, it tried to compensate for its chronic under-staffing, trying to attract external expertise and to profit from new ideas; second, it sought to gain diverse stakeholders as allies for its legislative proposals, and thus strengthened its own position *vis-à-vis* the Council; and third, the Commission hoped for better compliance and public support.

This interaction between the efforts from below and from the top was convincingly conceptualised as a co-evolution of the emerging European political system and the landscape of interest representation (Eichener and Voelzkow 1994; on this, see also Kohler-Koch 1997). Thus, at a general level, the current participatory regime has, first and foremost, been shaped by the interaction between the European Commission and non-state collective actors.

However, these efforts have not yet succeeded in establishing a coherent, transparent participatory regime which significantly overcomes the well-known characteristics of lobbying. It was the unanimous opinion of the interviewees – and this will be supported in the following analysis of the participatory pattern of concrete policy processes – that the Commission favours well-established CSOs with a high reputation and expertise, so that the functionary can expect not only 'opinions' and 'unrealistic wishes', but also 'competent' aid and 'technical expertise' (expressions from several inter-views of both CSO and public institution representatives). Moreover, the budget lines available to CSOs have been put in place to pursue the EU's policy goals and, potentially, to exclude CSOs with different agendas. As a result, one can say that the existing EU rules of participation do *not* guarantee broad and equal inclusion, although, at the same time, they are not funda-mentally detrimental to the participation of stakeholders, either.

### Notes

1  The legal information of the following largely relies on the excellent paper written by Bignami (2003). However, the interpretation of the information is my own.
2  Case 17/74, Transocean Marine Paint Association v Commission, 1974 ECR 1063.
3  European Trade Union Confederation (ETUC); BusinessEurope (former UNICE); European Association of Craft, Small- and Medium-sized Enterprises (known by its acronym UEAPME after the French name – *Union européenne de l'artisanat et des petites et moyennes enterprises*); European Centre of Enterprises with Public Participation and of Enterprises of General Economic Interest (known by its acronym CEEP after the French name – *Centre européen des entreprises à participation publique et des entreprises d'intérêt économique général*).
4  In form of the macro-economic dialogue, called the 'Cologne Process' from 1994, see Johnson (2005, Chapter 3).
5  In today's post-socialist language, one usually speaks about *management* rather than

*capital.*

6   Initially, the United Kingdom opted out of the social protocol but the New Labour government under Tony Blair opted in, eventually, agreeing to the incorporation of the protocol into the Treaty of Amsterdam (1999).

7   The Social Dialogue has succeeded in developing five European Framework Agreements to date. (1) on parental leave concluded by UNICE, CEEP and ETUC on 14 December 1995 (transformed into Council (1996)); (2) on part-time work, concluded by UNICE, CEEP and ETUC on 6 June 1997 (transformed into Council (1997)); (3) on fixed-term work concluded by ETUC, UNICE and CEEP on 18 March 1999 (transformed into Council (1999)); (4) on telework, concluded between ETUC, UNICE/UEAPME and CEEP on 16 July 2002, which has not been transformed into a Directive, but is to be implemented by the partners autonomously through their national members; (5) on work-related stress, concluded between ETUC, UNICE, UEAPME and CEEP on 8 October 2004 (source: www.eurofound.europa .eu/areas/industrialrelations/dictionary/definitions/frameworkagreements.htm; accessed 19 February 2010).

8   For instance, on the European Commission's website 'The European Commission and Civil Society' lists both documents relating NGOs as well as classical interest groups. See http://ec.europa.eu/civil_society/index_en.htm (accessed 19 February 2010).

9   *Official Journal of the EU* (hereafter OJ) C 191, 29 July 1992.

10  For the Commission, the Civil Dialogue has two main objectives: 'to ensure that the views and grass roots experience of the voluntary sector can be systematically taken into account by policy-makers at European level so that policies can be tailored more to real needs, and to disseminate information from the European level down to the local level so that citizens are aware of developments, can feel part of the construction of Europe and can see the relevance of it to their own situation, thus increasing transparency and promoting citizenship' (European Commission 1997: 7).

11  See also the more recent statement made by the President of the ESC, Mr Dimitris Dimitriadis, at the 2nd regional meeting of the Economic and Social Committees and Similar Institutions of South-Eastern Europe and the Black Sea Region, Sofia (Bulgaria), 25 June 2007, available at: www.eesc.europa.eu/organisation/president /speeches/index-en.asp (accessed 19 February 2010).

12  In the EU language, transparency usually refers to the decision-making process, whereas openness means the access to documents. The present usage of the term transparency differs from this convention.

13  Evidently, in this respect, transparency is also an essential requirement for public accountability, for, without it, the CSOs cannot fulfil their function as transmission belts for information into the public sphere.

14  OJ L 145/43, 31 May 2001.

15  This declaration says the following: 'The Conference considers that transparency of the decision-making process strengthens the democratic nature of the institutions and the public's confidence in the administration. The Conference accordingly recommends that the Commission submit to the Council no later than 1993 a report on measures designed to improve public access to the information available to the institutions.'

16  In this section, I do not distinguish between the European Council of the Heads of States and Governments and the Council of Ministers.

17  On this website, the Council offers an overview of all legislation and reports concerning its policies regarding access to its documents. See www.consilium. europa.eu/cms3_applications/showPage.ASP?id=305&lang=en&mode=g (accessed 19 February 2010).

18  Paragraph 2 of the Birmingham Declaration (European Council 1992).

19   OJ L 340/41, 31 December 1993.
20   Council (1993). However, this administrative approach did not remain uncontested.
     The Dutch government, which brought the issue initially to the Council's table (see
     Curtin 1996: 101ff), unsuccessfully sought the annulment of this decision at the ECJ
     (European Court of Justice 1996), triggering a debate about whether transparency in
     terms of access to information is a fundamental right for the citizens in Europe
     (Verhoeven 2000).
21   Just to give a short impression of the numbers, in 2006 the Council reported of a total
     of 17,712 communications from the public (including 11,070 petitions), and 4,811
     requests for information, of which 3,913 were forwarded by e-mail and 898 were sent
     by letter. See www.consilium.europa.eu/uedocs/cmsUpload/ENacces2006int.pdf,
     p.12 (accessed 22 February 2010).
22   See http://ombudsman.europa.eu/release/en/default.htm (accessed 19 February
     2010).
23   With the exceptions of Poland and the UK, see the 'Protocol on the Application of the
     Charter of Fundamental Rights of the European Union to Poland and to the United
     Kingdom', annexed to the Lisbon Treaty, available at: http://eur-lex
     .europa.eu/LexUriServ/site/en/oj/2007/c_306/c_30620071217en01560157.pdf
     (accessed 19 February 2010).
24   Case C-2/88 Zwartveld, OJ C 84 04–04.
25   On Council and European Parliament (2001), see, above, the section on the Council.
26   See www.unece.org/env/pp/welcome.html (accessed 19 February 2010).
27   See the relevant legislation under the Århus Convention. Council and European
     Parliament    (2003a),   Council    and    European    Parliament    (2003b),    at
     http://ec.europa.eu/environment/aarhus/index.htm. A legal analysis of the relation-
     ship between the Århus Convention and the EU is provided by Rodenhoff (2002).
28   See http://eur-lex.europa.eu/en/index.htm (accessed 19 February 2010).
29   A similar argument is made by Peterson (1995) already in the mid-1990s, where he
     elaborates that transparency measures are an attempt to improve its internal
     coherence and proceedings and less aimed at the outside world.
30   See  http://ec.europa.eu/transparency/eti/index_en.htm#1  (accessed  19  February
     2010).    More    directly    concerned    with    access    to    documents    is
     http://ec.europa.eu/transparency/index_en.htm (accessed 19 February 2010).
31   See amongst others COMMUNICATION to the Commission from the PRESIDENT,
     Mr Kallas and Ms Wallström for an orientation debate on a possible European
     Transparency Initiative SEC (2005) 644/4 (17 May 2005) and the COMMUNICA-
     TION to the Commission from the PRESIDENT, Ms Wallström, Mr Kallas, Ms
     Hübner and Ms Fischer Boel proposing the launch of a European Transparency
     Initiative,    available    at    http://ec.europa.eu/commission_barroso/kallas/doc
     /etik-communication_en.pdf (accessed 19 February 2010).
32   See http://ec.europa.eu/transparency/revision/index_en.htm#4 (accessed 19 February
     2010).
33   See  http://ec.europa.eu/transparency/revision/docs/report_on_the_outcome_final.pdf
     (accessed 19 February 2010). By the end of the year 2007, following the consultation, the
     Commission announced a legislative proposal in the first quarter of 2008. However, this
     has not happened and the Commission now merely states that it 'will consider what
     concrete measures it may be appropriate to take in order to enhance transparency in the
     EU': see http://ec.europa.eu/transparency/eti/index_en.htm#4 (accessed 19 February
     2010).
34   See, for both documents, http://ombudsman.europa.eu/special/en/default.htm
     (accessed 19 February 2010).
35   For more details on the politics of the merging transparency regime, see the online

book by Tony Buyan (2002) on 'Secrecy and openness in the European Union – the ongoing struggle for freedom of information', available at the Statewatch website at www.statewatch.org/foi/foi.htm (accessed 19 February 2010).

36 Statewatch's informative website on the EU's freedom on information policies lists 6 decisions and 26 pending cases, see again www.statewatch.org/foi/foi.htm (accessed 19 February 2010).

37 European Commission: from 19% in 1999 to over 33% in 2002; Council: from 16% in 1999 to almost 29% in 2002 (for documents that were released wholly). See Ferguson 2003: 4.

38 The reports are accessible at: http://ec.europa.eu/transparency/access_documents /index_en.htm. For the EP, see www.europarl.europa.eu/RegWeb/application /registre/guideAccessDoc.faces (accessed 19 February 2010).

39 I do not want to enter into the debate about the nature of the EU here – whether it is still an international organisation, something *sui generis* or a polity-in-the-making – because this is not of particular relevance for the present purpose. The conditions for democratic participation in policy-making processes that I sketch out here are applicable to all political systems that engage in policy-making.

40 See www.un.org/dpi/ngosection/index.asp (accessed 19 February 2010).

41 Even in cases where this is examined, there are no hints to any formal or informal rules concerning access to the Council; see, for instance, Bouwen (2002).

42 On the secrecy of the Council, see Butt Philip (1985: 55ff).

43 http://eur-lex.europa.eu/LexUriServ/site/en/oj/2006/l_285/l_28520061016 en00470071.pdf (accessed 19 February 2010).

44 See http://ec.europa.eu/civil_society/ (accessed 22 February 2010).

45 See http://www.socialplatform.org/ (accessed 19 February 2010).

46 See http://ec.europa.eu/yourvoice/ipm/ (accessed 19 February 2010).

47 Until its closure in spring 2008; see below for further details on the newly established register for interest representatives.

48 For instance, within the Commission, knowledge dissemination about IPM depends exclusively on the small IPM unit within Directorate-General (DG) Internal Market (interviews with IPM personnel).

49 To my knowledge, there was only one – albeit prominent – instance of rejection. Statewatch's application to be included on the CONECCS database was rejected by the Commission, which argued that Statewatch was not a representative organisation because it does not have members. As Curtin (2003: 60) puts it: 'Such practices do not inspire any confidence in the manner in which the Commission is attempting to come to terms with the difficult exercise of conceptual delimitation. Moreover, attempts are being made by the Commission to insist that in order to be considered part of civil society for the purposes of being part of a consultative network, the organization in question must have a structure and activities covering "at least three European countries". This seems to draw on the practice that the Commission has developed with regard to the social partners where the criterion of 'being organized at a European level is especially important'.' It remains to be seen whether the new interest representation register will change things significantly.

50 For a good overview of the ETI, see www.euractiv.com/en/pa/transparency -initiative/article-140650 (accessed 19 February 2010).

51 See, again, http://ec.europa.eu/commission_barroso/kallas/doc/etik-communication _en.pdf, p. 5 (accessed 19 February 2010).

52 The third point of the ETI, which will not be covered here, is the issue of disclosure of the recipients of EU funds. For this, see amongst others the website of Commissioner Kallas, at: http://ec.europa.eu/commission_barroso/kallas/work/eu_transparency /recipients_en.htm (last accessed 22 February 2010).

53    'Training and appropriate awareness raising among staff; sharing information and good practices on stakeholder consultation between the Directorates-General; reviewing the practical guidelines for stakeholder consultation; creating a new standard consultation template to improve the consistency of open public consultations' (European Commisison 2007b: 7).

54    See https://webgate.ec.europa.eu/transparency/regrin/welcome.do    (accessed    19 February 2010).

55    See https://webgate.ec.europa.eu/transparency/regrin/infos/codeofconduct.do (accessed 19 February 2010).

56    18 from the public sector, 73 by the private sector, 50 from NGOs, 17 by individual citizens   and   7   other   contributions:   see   http://ec.europa.eu/transparency/eti /contributions.htm (accessed 19 February 2010).

57    See www.euractiv.com/29/images/SpencerTransparencyInitiative_tcm29–157730.pdf (accessed 19 February 2010).

58    See the B5 project at the Special Research Centre 'Transformation of the State' at the University of Bremen.

59    The introduction of participatory forms of governance is controversially debated between EU institutions; see, in particular, Bouwen (2007).

60    In fact, Chabanet implies (p. 5) (without sources, however) that the Commission's move was deliberately done in order to defuse the parliament's initiative.

61    The College of Quaestors is the responsible parliamentarian body for administrative and financial matters directly concerning Members and their working conditions. See www.europarl.europa.eu/parliament/expert/staticDisplay.do;jsessionid=63BC9BE03 A78264267D27096DDC8FEA5.node2?id=53&pageRank=6&language=EN   (accessed 19 February 2010).

62    OJ C 167/14, 2 June 1997.

63    See the procedure file of the EP's legislative observatory, Reference number REG/1996/2055.

64    See   www.europarl.europa.eu/sides/getLastRules.do?language=EN&reference=TOC (accessed 19 February 2010).

65    This section deviates from the two above, because it focuses only on the European Commission as the European institution that has the control of the genuine EU budget. The EP's budgetary powers are, as is well known, constrained. The situation with the Council, however, is more complex, given the shared management of the EU's budget, meaning that the bulk of the EU budget is not spent by the Commission alone but in co-operation with the Member States. As the Commission underlines in its ETI Green Paper (p. 13), 75.7% of the budget falls under this category. Who exactly the beneficiaries of these funds are is apparently not in the knowledge of the Commission, since, as it continues in the ETI Green Paper, Member States' law often does not allow the disclosure of this information. The Commission has established a website where it tries – not yet really successfully – to increase financial transparency: see http://ec.europa.eu/grants/beneficiaries_en.htm (accessed 19 February 2010).

66    'As NGOs are not marked as a separate category of beneficiaries of EU funds, information on funds allocated to them is governed by the same rules as for other beneficiaries.' (Commission e-mail communication, see above).

67    'With regard to projects managed directly by the European Commission (the so-called direct management, some 20% of the total EU budget), by 30 June each year the Commission departments publish on the Europa website lists of grants that they awarded during the previous year, with the exception of those awarded in the form of scholarship to individuals (see http://ec.europa.eu/grants/beneficiaries_en.htm). As regards projects managed by Member States ("shared management", some 80% of the total budget), it will be mandatory for Member States to disclose the names of bene-

ficiaries of EU funds as of 2009 for agriculture, and at the latest by the end of this year for structural funds. Some Member States do it already on a voluntary basis' (Commission e-mail communication, see above).

68  As ECAS (2004: 7) expresses it: 'A pre-determined and over-rigid approach can stifle creativity.'
69  OJ L 378, 27 December 2006.
70  See www.europeanmovement.eu/ (accessed 22 February 2010).
71  See www.ecre.org/ (accessed 19 February 2010).
72  See http://eur-lex.europa.eu/budget/data/D2007_VOL4/EN/nmc-titleN118C7/nmc-chapterN1232B/articles/index.html#N60651660651–0 (accessed 19 February 2010).

# 5

## Participatory governance in the practice of EU policy-making

The previous chapter on the procedural dimension of the EU's participatory regime analysed the development of the formal provisions of the EU's participatory regime. It was demonstrated that the hardening of the participatory provisions and the intensity of the debate about democratic participatory governance negatively correlate with each other. Consequently, there are no provisions at hand (yet) that allow excessive optimism about a coherent strategy for the equal participation of CSOs on the part of the European institutions. However, it might well be that the intense discourse on participatory governance has left some traces in the daily work of policy-making, which might be useful as starting points for its democratisation.

The analysis of the content dimension of the EU's participatory practices will be the subject of the following two sections. This will be done by approaching two policy fields (environmental policy and migration policy) and a key decision in each of these fields (the chemical regulation REACH, and the Directive on Family Re-unification) as empirical examples.

This chapter leaves the level of formal processes behind and takes a closer look at the operational level of participatory practices in EU policy-making. The aim is to illustrate the extent to which the decision-making processes in these selected cases were responsive to the input of CSOs. The content analysis is contextualised by overviews about both the position of the respective policy fields in European integration and the role which CSOs play in the areas. This contextualisation is necessary in order to provide an idea about who actually participates in the concrete policy processes analysed. Each presentation of the content analysis is preceded by an introduction into the decision in question. Upon this basis, I am able to highlight the crucial points in the concrete decision.

## Participation in EU migration policy

### *Migration policy in the European Union*

The policy field of migration constitutes one of the most dynamic areas of EU integration in recent years. In the early days of European integration – to give a very brief overview of the history of this policy field – collaboration on migration issues mainly took place horizontally, between nation states, i.e. on a purely intergovernmental basis outside the realm of the European institutions. As Guiraudon (2000, 2001a, 2003) has convincingly demonstrated, the national ministers of the interior have used the European level, particularly since the early 1980s, to avoid national vetoes in order to pursue their security-led agenda of restricting migration; accordingly, their policy style was secretive, rather than open.

Since the Single European Act (1987), however, other actors than the ministers of the interior have entered the stage of migration policies. Functional spillovers from an accelerating European integration process required closer co-operation. The momentum of the Single Market Programme and the envisaged internal market has a tension inscribed between internal openness and external closure. The four freedoms of person, goods, capital and services – which have almost constitutional importance in EU law – demand the eradication of internal borders, but have met with national scepticism towards open borders because of the influx of immigrants from third countries. The Schengen regime, which, for a long time, was a purely intergovernmental agreement outside the treaties, was an important attempt 'to resolve the free movement versus immigration control dilemma' (Favell 1998: 606). In the due course of this development, a Third Pillar on matters of Police and Judicial Co-operation was established in the Treaty of Maastricht (1992).

However, this step only *de jure* transformed multi-lateral intergovernmentalism into 'formal intergovernmentalism' (Geddes 2003: 136) under the roof of the European Union. The decision-making procedures proved inefficient and incapable of solving the tension between the economic-driven freedom of movement and the security-driven control of migration. Finally, the Treaty of Amsterdam (1999) endorsed significant procedural changes in the decision-making rules of the EU's Asylum and Migration Policies. Most of its provisions were transferred from the intergovernmental Third Pillar, to the supranational First Pillar – but not so the issue of legal migration. Now, after a five-year transition period, a simultaneity of horizontal co-operation and an increasingly strong vertical dimension of supranational competences can be observed.[1]

After the end of a transitional period on 1 May 2004, and after a required additional unanimous decision by the Council to abandon unanimity and the consultation procedure in all fields except legal migration by 1 April 2005, qualified-majority voting (QMV) in the Council and co-decision with the EP have recently become the rule (see Peers 2004, 2005). Hence, the secretive tradition of policy-making has been challenged by these more recent changes in procedures and in the primary law, which is now part of a strong supranational frame within an interesting policy style that has been called 'intensive transgovernmentalism' (Wallace 2000: 33). Legal migration, however, remained in the intergovernmental Third Pillar, until it was integrated into the Treaty of Lisbon (2009) and subjected to the ordinary legislative procedure (Article 79).

In addition to the procedural developments, there has been considerable political support to further European integration in this policy field. In October 1999, the Special European Council on Justice and Home Affairs in Tampere, Finland, gave migration policies considerable political momentum by setting the goal of constructing an Area of Freedom, Security and Justice across the Union. The ambitious Tampere Programme[2] formulated a five-year agenda for substantial legislation; it has recently been replaced by the The Hague Programme (European Council 2005), which does not, however, seem to have the same political support (or dynamism). It adds little to the development of legal migration, which 'would likely move only forward significantly once the Constitutional Treaty enters into force' (Alegre et al. 2005: 52).[3]

Commentators vary in their opinions about the state of European migration policies. One prominently held view is that migration policies are dominated by a security agenda, with the repressive 'fortress Europe' looming in the background (see Huysmans 2000). Other voices, however, interpret migration policies as 'a potentially progressive source of postnational rights' (Geddes 2003: 26) that may adopt a 'citizenship paradigm' (Guiraudon 1998: 11) which would include political and civic rights for migrants at EU level (see, for instance, Geddes 2000; Kastoryano 1998, 2003). In fact, the second position would be supported if it turned out that migrants' voices – or third-country nationals (TCNs), to use EU parlance – are heard in EU policy-making processes. Others, again, hold on to the economic motivation of mobility in the EU, arguing that 'the image and argument of fortress Europe are correct about the aims but wrong about the outcomes' (Favell and Hansen 2002).

However, it suffices to say that, in recent years, one can observe a parallel development of tighter security initiatives and intensified police co-operation, and, simultaneously, initiatives concerning economic migration and the improvement of integration efforts. A more detailed analysis would, however, be necessary to come to a definite conclusion about the nature of the EU's migration policies. For the current purpose, it is sufficient to be aware that migration policies are situated in a complex discursive frame in which often antagonistic objectives are pursued by different actors, so that one can expect a high degree of contestation in concrete policy processes which, however, also potentially offer access points for the participation of civil society organisations.

### Civil society organisations in EU migration policy

Following the ongoing Europeanisation of migration policies since the mid-1980s, both the EU institutions and national migrants' movements started to realise that the EU level might become an important locus for civil society activities on migration issues. In particular, the European institutions which were mainly excluded from the intergovernmental processes at that time – namely, the European Parliament and the European Commission – played a well-known game in European integration, aiming at 'the expansion of their own realm of competence' (Guiraudon 2001b: 167). In contrast, the European Commission was always interested in supporting the organisations of vulnerable groups, such as migrants, in their efforts to organise themselves better at European level.

However, such engagement is not necessarily pure altruism; the Commission often acts as a 'purposeful opportunist' (Cram 1997) in trying to pull new policy areas up to the EU level, and, for this purpose, it seeks to build up its allies. Consequently, both the EP and the Commission were actively involved in supporting the emergence of European migration CSOs.[4] Arguably, both the excluded institutions *and* those affected by the new policy framework had an interest in becoming stronger in order to play a better role in this framework. Consequently, a push and pull dynamic for civil society organisations in European migration policies created a potential win-win situation for both sides.

The European Member States, on the other hand, in the shape of the Council, realised, only belatedly, that the increasing supranationalisation of the migration policies from the Treaties of Maastricht and Amsterdam might force them to change the secrecy of their intergovernmental policy approach. Such insights into the importance, for democratic and fairness reasons, of including those who are the very objects of migration policies – and often already living in EU Member States – in the formulation of European policy initiatives at EU level became visible at the Tampere Special European Council in 1999. The presidency conclusions state the following:

> The area of freedom, security and justice should be based on the principles of transparency and democratic control. We must develop an open dialogue with civil society on the aims and principles of this area in order to strengthen citizens' acceptance and support. (European Council 1999, Tampere Conclusions, Paragraph 7)

To some extent, the delay of the European Council to address issues of transparency, democracy and civil society openly in the context of migration policies is explicable with the changes of the Treaty of Amsterdam. Even the Member States could no longer claim that migration was predominantly an economic issue of freedom of movement which only requires some regulation for worker mobility, and had to face the fact that migration had become a highly political issue with increasing demands for democratic legitimacy (see also Favell 1998: 607). Whether this statement is of any practical relevance will be subsequently assessed by taking the long and disputed process leading to the Family Re-unification Directive as an example. The beginnings of this directive go back to the context of the Tampere Programme, so that one can expect some effects of the expressed intention to develop an open dialogue with CSOs, even more so in the light of the general discourse on civil society participation in European governance.

For migrants' movements, the shift in the decision-making location towards Brussels created a fairly complicated situation. They face impediments that hinder a powerful formation of their movements at EU level. Some impediments, such as the lack of resources, are shared with other disadvantaged groups; others, such as the 'Tower of Babel problem' (Guiraudon 2001b: 167), which signifies the difficulties in associating these socially very multi-faceted groups, aggravate the problems of association for migrants. Furthermore, the needs and goals even for migrants of the same origin, but who are situated in different Member States, may be very different and difficult to co-ordinate, given that the diverse integration provisions in the Member States create different demands.

On the other hand, migrant groups potentially gain a level of action that might help them to circumvent some of the often restrictive national policies. And indeed, as Guiraudon (*ibid.*) underlines, the EP and the Commission tend to support the position of migrants, particularly when their claims are framed as human rights concerns. Moreover, Declaration 17 of the Treaty of Amsterdam, which states that, on matters of asylum policy, consultations with the UNHCR and other international organisations should be established, is interpreted by some CSOs as being a 'window of opportunity' (ECRE, ENAR, MPG 1999: 2) by means of which they can increase their inclusion into asylum and migration affairs, as well.

Would we be able to observe a migrant presence that would allow inclusive participation at EU level, if the policy processes were participative? Given the relative novelty of migration policies at European level, it comes as no surprise that there are very few CSOs in Brussels that focus solely on migration issues. On the Commission's online register of interest groups, of the 29 listed organisations linked with the keyword migration,[5] only half are, more or less, closely related to migration issues (including religious groups). The others are industrial associations, such as the German Constructor's Trade Union, the Association of European Producers of Steel for Packaging, or think-tanks such as the European Policy Centre.

Many CSOs only partially deal with legal migration issues, but are mainly concerned with the subjects of integration or the human rights situation of refugees and asylum-seekers. Some of these organisations operate quite actively on specific migration issues. Among them are church-based agencies, such as the Churches' Commission for Migrants in Europe (CCME), or Caritas Europa, the European Network Against Racism (ENAR) and the

European Council on Refugees and Exiles (ECRE), which are prominent, outspoken agents on migration issues. In addition, a few other organisations deal with migrant interests if the special interests of their organisations are concerned. The European Union sections of the International Lesbian and Gay Association (ILGA), and Save the Children show the diversity of the actors' active in this field. Interestingly, expert organisations, such as the Immigration Law Practitioners' Association (ILPA) or Statewatch's European Monitoring and Documentation Centre (SEMDOC),[6] which offer expertise, circulate policy proposals, and comment critically on the EU's migration policies, were registered at CONECCS, but did not register in the new system.

The case of Statewatch is particularly telling with regard to the limits and the exclusionary tendencies even of voluntary registers such as CONECCS or the renewed lobby register, thus exemplifying the impact of the EU's institutional context on the opportunity structures of the activities of the migrant associations at EU level (for this, see Geddes 1998). Statewatch is an independent organisation that aims to provoke widespread discussion by publishing discussion papers and providing detailed information on the issues affecting both legal and illegal migrants in Europe. Thus, it is not a grass-roots NGO, but an expert organisation. But Statewatch's application to be included into CONECCS was not rejected by the Commission on grounds of doubts concerning their organisational capacity, but instead 'on the basis that they are not a "representative" organisation and did not have "members"' (Curtin 2003: 7).

Thus, the Commission only conceives of these organisations as being part of the civil society if they have members – irrespective of whether they are individual or collective in nature – and if the organisation has offices in at least three EU Member States. The Commission does not consider whether an organisation contributes to publicity and transparency, and thus enables public discourse on certain issues – which, in itself, would be an important function of civil society. Instead, the practice resembles the one developed in the context of the Social Dialogue, in which the Commission always stresses that being organised at European level is especially important. Consequently, it is not possible to gain a complete list of migrant CSOs or of all the organisations working on this issue that are active at EU level.

Furthermore, the moderate presence of migrant CSOs at EU level also becomes clear from the weak horizontal network structures. In policy areas such as environmental, development or social policy,[7] the present CSOs are not only working individually, but are also increasingly striving for collective action by forming such structures. In the migration area, though, it is, interestingly, the Brussels Office of the United Nations High Commissioner for Refugees (UNHCR), i.e. an international organisation and not a CSO, which currently hosts and supports the co-operation and co-ordination of migration CSOs at EU level. It hosts a regular, albeit loosely organised, Migration and Asylum Network, which has established a migration sub-group. This sub-group, in turn, is currently organised by the Migration Policy Group – again, not a genuine CSO, only a group of experts. Thus, overall, the awareness of the growing importance of European level migration policies among national CSOs appears to increase only gradually (Migration Policy Group 2002).

From a standpoint of inclusion, it is interesting to note that migrants themselves are currently not directly represented at EU level. Attempts by both the EP and the Commission to establish respective structures at EU level have had no lasting effects, and the impediments for national migrant groups seem to be too strong to change the situation. In the mid-1980s, the EP had started to support migrant associations financially in order to further their co-ordination among themselves and to integrate them better into Europe (Kastoryano 1998: 8ff).

In 1991, supported by the EP, the European Commission established the European Migrants' Forum 'with a mandate to deal with the position of third-country nationals within the European Union' (Niessen 2002: 81). The European Migrants' Forum was structured alongside the nationality criterion, which caused severe internal tensions between certain nationalities (Geddes 2000: 638ff; Guiraudon 2001b: 170). One major aim of the Forum was to strive for the political and legal rights of migrants so that they would be equal to those of European citizens. However, the best path towards this aim remained contested within the organisation.

Due to such internal problems and, in particular, because of managerial and financial irregularities, this Forum lost the support of the Commission and eventually ceased to exist. It tried to contest the Commission's decision of July 2001 to terminate its financial support, but it lost its appeal to annul this decision at the Court of First Instance (see European Court of Justice 2003b). Since then, there has only been loose talk in Brussels about a renewed initiative (Geddes 2000).[8] The case of the Migrants' Forum exemplifies some of the difficulties that migrant organisations face at EU level, and offers a good example of the efforts of the Commission to create its own civil society (De Schutter 2002).

Overall, the presence of migration issues at EU level is rather limited (Migration Policy Group 2002: 4; Niessen 2002: 81), which is also mirrored by the Commission's attempt to introduce an open method of co-ordination on migration (European Commisison 20001c; Migration Policy Group 2002: 3f), an initiative, however, which did not provoke much echo outside academia.[9] This meagre presence is contrasted with the area of refugees, and some refugee CSOs are nowadays also covering the field of legal migration.

The organisations that are present at EU level are very visible and proactively try to make their voices heard, as is shown by detailed and knowledgeable proposals of how to enact the objectives foreseen in the Treaty of Amsterdam and specified in the Tampere Programme (see ENAR, ILPA, MPG 2000). The MPG also attempted to compensate somewhat for the lack of the direct involvement of migrants by initiating an Engaging Stakeholders Project (Migration Policy Group 2002) which has now further developed into the European Migration Dialogue.[10] In this dialogue, the MPG – supported by the Commission – brings together the representatives of the CSOs from 20 EU Member States on an annual basis in order to follow the EU agenda and in order for the MPG to learn about the particular concerns at national level.

Irrespective of any criticisms of such influence on the part of the Commission, and disregarding the particular grounds of the failure of the Migrants' Forum, it is notable that the EU neither uses EU citizenship to preclude TCNs from the establishment of associations, nor as a criterion to exclude them from the informal, soft forms of participation and consultation. Thus, there are no legal impediments against a abroad inclusive participatory pattern in EU migration policies, and the case is still open as to whether the EU migration regime might be a source for a postnational polity (for example, Kastoryano 1998, 2003), although, to date, it cannot be given fully fledged empirical support.

### *The content dimension: responsiveness in the case of family re-unification*[11]

Above, I argued that the three process conditions of democratic governance – transparency, access and inclusion – necessarily have to be substantiated by a content dimension. I further argued that both instrumental and normative theories of democracy place particular attention on the content condition of responsiveness. Pluralists, in particular, emphasise that the final policy outcomes have to reflect the interests in question in the particular case.

Normative theories, however, in a deliberative guise, place less weight on the final outcome, but, instead, underline the importance of a mutual justificatory process. Concerns raised in participatory activities should be taken into account and discussed throughout a policy-making process, and rejections of intake should be based upon justified arguments. Since participatory practices are complex communicative interactions within a given institutional setting, the first step towards assessing responsiveness has to consider the context of the decision-making process. Secretive procedures and dominant actors reduce the likeliness of responsiveness, but public contestations also offer the first indications of the crucial substantial elements of the issue in question, and can thus serve as a basis for the second step of assessing responsiveness by means of a qualitative content analysis. This section looks, first, at the context of the empirical case and its decision-making process, before presenting, in the second step, the main results of the content analysis.

### *The context and decision-making process of the empirical case*

There are many reasons why people migrate. Publicly visible via the media are predominantly those forms of migration which are caused by natural or socio-economic catastrophes. But the most powerful motivation for non-violent migration is more hidden: it is people's desire to live together with

their own families. The right of families to live together without public interference is one of the central human rights that have been codified since the
1948 Universal Declaration of Human Rights (in particular, Article 12[12]) and,
particularly relevant for the European context, in the 1950 European
Convention on Human Rights (Article 8).[13]

The regulation of this form of migration is of paramount importance.
The number of transnational marriages is increasing; EU-internal mobility is
facilitated by provisions concerning the free movement of persons; many
persons who originate from outside the EU are naturalised or possess long-
term residence permits; and extra-EU immigration continues. All these
groups of people have multiple bonds outside their new home countries, or
create new bonds during visits to their birthplaces, and are thus potential
addressees for the regulation for family re-unification. A few recent Eurostat
numbers can demonstrate the potential scope and need for family re-union in
the EU. In 2007, the EU-27 was inhabited by about 495 million people, of
whom about 28 million were living in a country to which they did not have
citizenship. Variations among the Member States are extremely high, from
very low numbers, for instance, in some new Member States, up to almost
30% in Luxembourg. More than half of the foreigners were EU citizens. Many
people in the possession of citizenship were, however, not born in that respective country. For instance, in 2005, more than 720,000 people were
naturalised throughout the EU Member States, so it is clear that a huge
amount of people have transnational family bonds.[14]

These numbers illustrate the EU's twofold interest in regulating family
re-unification. First, as the Commission repeatedly argues in its legislative
proposals, uniting families is important for the well-being and eventual integration of the migrants already lawfully residing in the EU. Second,
demographic concerns call for making immigration to EU countries more
attractive. A clear and favourable regulation of family re-unification is an
important element in such efforts. The importance of family re-unification
for the realisation of the principle of freedom of movement was already
acknowledged by the European Communities in the Regulation on Freedom
of Movement of Workers in 1968 (Council 1968a).

It took until the late 1990s, however, for the economic concerns to be
complemented by a human rights discourse. Now that both considerations
were able to join forces, the combination of economic considerations and
human rights concerns established the driving force for the European Union
to issue a Directive on Family Re-unification. This history makes it understandable that the Council Directive on the Right to Family Re-unification
has been called the flagship directive in legal migration (Boeles 2001: 61) –
although it does not, as the title suggests, cover all instances of family re-
unification, but only addresses the so-called third-country nationals (TCNs).
Its major purpose is to establish the conditions for the exercise of the right to
family re-union for TCNs legally residing in an EU Member State. The

directive defines family re-unification as 'the entry into and residence in a Member State by family members of a third country national residing lawfully in that Member State in order to preserve the family unit, whether the family relationship arose before or after the resident's entry' (Article 2(d)).[15]

The adoption of the directive in September 2003 took place upon the basis of both the new provisions in the Treaty of Amsterdam and the aims specified by the Tampere programme. The legal basis of this directive is Article 63 (3) of the EC Treaty, from which Denmark, the UK and Ireland have opted out. Decision-making is based upon Article 67 of the EC Treaty, including unanimity voting and mere consultation of the EP, which also remains the legal basis for legal migration after the end of the five-year transition period towards qualified-majority voting (QMV), as was agreed in Tampere.

Despite the manifold conditions facilitating the context, if one regards the outlined grounds for regulating family re-union, the new provisions of the Treaty of Amsterdam and the political support for the migration theme as signified in the Tampere programme, it is remarkable that it took four years for the directive to be finally adopted. The process had already started shortly before the Tampere European Council, when the European Commission's unit for legal migration of the then Directorate-General Justice and Home Affairs[16] prepared informal discussion papers on certain issues of family re-unification and used them, just before Tampere on 8 October 1999, for an early consultation with civil society organisations (Niessen 2001: 422).

Such early consultations in a policy process are both quite common and quite effective for CSOs, as the subsequent textual analysis of responsiveness will show. The original aim of the Commission was to regulate family re-unification for all people living within EU borders, i.e. not only for third-country nationals but also for EU citizens – an intention that eventually failed, although the final title of the directive did not specify it. Only two months after Tampere, in December 1999, the Commission published the first proposal of the family re-unification directive (European Commission 1999). This initial proposal followed a human rights logic and was consequently welcomed by many CSOs. However, rather unsurprisingly, the Commission's approach was far too liberal for many Member States, and, since there had hardly been any progress in the Council, the Commission presented an amended proposal in October 2000 (European Commission 2000b), which took several of the proposed amendments of the EP into account (Boeles 2001).

Notwithstanding this, the Council negotiations remained thorny. One important reason for this was the obstructive attitude of Germany and its then Minister of Interior, Mr Otto Schily. Germany had blocked all progress to date because of its pending new immigration law in which strong political currents still had difficulties in acknowledging that Germany was, indeed, a country of immigration. After the matter had finally been decided upon,

Germany ceased its obstruction in the Council,[17] so that the Laeken European Council could invite the Commission to redraft the proposal again (December 2001). In this redraft, which was issued in May 2002 (European Commission 2002c), the Commission gave in to the Council's main thrust of turning family re-unification from an issue of migration rights into an issue of immigration control (Peers 2002a, 2002b, 2003), but was finally able to break the deadlock in the Council. In February 2003, the Justice and Home Affairs Council reached a political agreement on the directive.

However, problems remained. The final adoption of the directive, in September 2003, took place under politically problematical circumstances and was contested for reasons of its content. At the time of the Council's initial agreement on the directive in February 2003, the governments of the 15 Member States had not waited for the consultative resolution which the European Parliament issued only in April 2003 (European Parliament 2003), i.e. two months after the political agreement on the content of the directive.

Above all, reservations persisted with regard to two articles – Article 4 (1 & 6) and Article 8 – that potentially restricted the admissibility of children above 12 and above 15 years of age by giving the Member States leeway to introduce (restrictive) integration requirements, such as language tests for those aged 12 years and over, and up to two years waiting for those aged 15 years and over. In its consultative report, the EP expressed substantial reservations about these provisions of the directive. In the light of these procedural and substantial disagreements and conflicts, the EP took action against the Council at the European Court of Justice in December 2003 (European Court of Justice 2003a), arguing that these provisions were in contradiction with the European Convention on Human Rights. These two contested articles show an ambivalence inscribed in the directive, which can also be identified in the Court's ruling. There is an apparent tension between the human rights objective to grant the members of a family the right to live with each other, and with the objective to oblige the members of the family waiting for a re-union to prove their capacity to integrate into the new country (Ruffer n.d.: 2).

The parliament's move to the Court stalled the directive's envisaged coming into force in October 2005, as the judgment was issued only on 15 June 2006. Several civil society organisations welcomed the call for the annulment by the EP, since they shared the EP's reservations and doubted the conformity with the existing human rights conventions. The EP's appeal to the ECJ might be considered to be a success for CSOs, many of whom called on the EP to take legal action after the adoption of the directive in 2003.

The ECJ dismissed the appeal, basically arguing that no annulment of parts of a directive was possible if these changes substantially altered the character of the overall directive; otherwise, so the argument goes, the ECJ would directly influence national legislation (for a detailed legal discussion, see Ruffer n.d.).[18]

*The responsiveness to civil society arguments*

The condition of responsiveness captures the content dimension for the assessment of democratic participation. It is based, as was detailed above, upon a qualitative content analysis of 48 civil society documents, which were published during the four years of the decision-making process of 14 different civil society organisations,[19] and 10 official documents published by the EU institutions during the official decision-making process.

In attempting to capture both eventual success in terms of CSO positions which are identifiable in the official documents and instances of justification, the decision-making process that led to the Family Re-unification Directive was split into four periods, taking the three proposals and the final directive as reference documents for structuring the process. This means that four content analyses were conducted, based upon the same coding scheme in order to identify instances of responsiveness in both of these periods, and not only in the last stage of the final document. Hereby, I reconstructed the drafting process with the purpose of identifying the changes in the wordings which may (or may not) be related to the input of CSOs.[20] The aim of the textual analysis was to identify instances of responsiveness in the policy-making process. The codes that I specified for this analytical exercise represent the topics that were of special concerns for several CSOs (see Table 5.1).

At the very basic level, the personal scope naturally encompasses the central provisions of the directive. Who is eligible for re-uniting his/her family (i.e, who is the sponsor)? Does it include everybody, i.e. all people living within the confines of the EU, or only TCNs – leaving the provisions for EU citizens to national legislation? Is there a further specification of TCNs that creates a hierarchy among different groups of people, depending upon their legal status? Which family members are eligible for migration? Only the core family (i.e. spouses and children of low age)?

Upon the basis of the defined personal scope, the conditions for exclusion and admission can be specified and can be controversially debated. How restrictive are the administrative rules imposed on the sponsor and the members of the family? What material supplies have to be provided by the sponsor? Which integration requirements are imposed on the members of the family? Once the members of the family have succeeded in entering the new country, their endowment with rights is crucial for their ability to lead a self-determined life. But what happens if, for instance, a marriage breaks down, or a child comes of age? Do they acquire a status independent from the sponsor? What access do they have to the educational system, the labour market, the social system?

On a more general level, even the legal scope of the directive was contested. Was the directive to set minimum or maximum standards? Was it to be flexible or to aim at harmonisation? All these issues expressed in the questions were important topics for the CSOs, and were intensively discussed throughout the policy-making process – some of them from the very

Table 5.1 Summary of the coding scheme in family re-unification

| General themes (code families) | Issues (issue codes) | Instances (coded quotes in the text) |
|---|---|---|
| Personal scope | Sponsor[a] | i.a., legal status, time of residence in host country |
| | Family | i.a., narrow or broad definition, age of children, same sex partners |
| Conditions for exclusion and admission | Vis-à-vis the sponsor | i.a., material provisions, adherence to administrative rules |
| | Vis-à-vis the members of the family | i.a., Integration provisions |
| | Public reasons | i.a., public health, security |
| Endowment with rights | For the member of the family | i.a., independent status, access to education and the labour market |
| Legal scope | EU v. National law | i.a., the degree of flexibilisation, provision of a standstill clause |

[a] The sponsor is the person who wants to be re-united with one or more members of his or her family.

beginning, such as the personal scope, others only in later stages, such as the legal scope.

The purpose of this section is neither to give a detailed account or an exegesis of the directive's content, nor to inform about every step of the analysis. Instead, it aims to present the core results of the extensive analysis, focusing on a central element of each of the specified general themes.[21] I begin with the personal scope, and will then move on to some conditions for exclusion/admission, before I discuss the the endowment of the newly arrived family member with rights. I end with the theme of the legal scope. Each time, I start by presenting the changes in the Commission's drafts until the final directive; thereafter, I demonstrate the positions of the CSOs. Upon this basis, it will be possible to show whether there is convergence, divergence or a parallel development in the positions of the public documents and the CSO input.

*Personal scope I – the sponsor*

Two groups of persons are potentially addressed by family re-unification regulations, namely, EU citizens and third-country nationals. With regard to the first category, there was an interesting gap between those who made use of the freedom of movement and those who did not. The former could rely on the EU rules on family re-unification in the context of the principle of free movement of workers/persons,[22] while the latter had to adhere to the often more restrictive national rules. In its initial proposal (1999), the Commission stated in the commentary on Article 4 that:

> As Union citizenship is indivisible, the gap must be filled. (European Commission 1999)

It aimed at a scope that included both TCNs and EU citizens, thus pursuing a strategy of legal harmonisation of the family re-unification provisions throughout the EU. Civil society organisations were more concerned with TCNs than with EU citizens – beside the demand for the equal treatment of both groups of persons, as ENAR expresses it:

> The ultimate goal is that third country nationals enjoy these rights in the same way as European citizens do. (ECRE, ENAR, MPG 1999)

With regard to TCNs, ECRE announced the call for a broad personal scope of the directive, saying that it:

> recommends that family reunion should not be limited to people meeting the criteria of the 1951 Convention but also be extended to people granted a complementary protection status. (ECRE 1999)

With regard to TCNs, Article 3 of the 1999 proposed directive shows a broad agreement with this position. The Commission – either due to an intrinsic human rights approach to family re-unification, or as a consequence of the pre-draft consultative meeting with CSOs – envisaged a comprehensive coverage of TCNs, which included persons with a subsidiary status of residence and only excluded asylum-seekers whose final status was undecided:

> (a) a third-country national residing lawfully in a Member State and holding a residence permit issued by that Member State for a period of at least one year;
> (b) a refugee, irrespective of the duration of his residence permit (European Commission 1999)

In its first amended proposal (2000), the Commission had already restricted the personal scope, a move that triggered some debates. Namely, it 'excludes persons enjoying a subsidiary form of protection and calls for the adoption without delay of a proposal on their admission and residence', (Point 2, European Commission 2000b), arguing that there is no harmonised definition of the subsidiary status. But this was only the first restrictive step.

In its third draft proposal (2002), only one clearly defined group of TCNs remained within the draft's scope, namely, those lawfully residing TCNs with a residence permit of at least one year (thus also excluding many students) and with – a new restriction – a reasonable prospect of obtaining permanent residence. All other persons such as refugees, persons with temporary permits, and EU citizens were excluded. This restrictive version succeeded in convincing the Council and found entrance in the final directive. It clearly shows that the original intention of the first draft, which was largely drafted in the spirit of human rights, was transformed into rules of immigration control.

The CSOs had been very content with the first draft directive and therefore did not put much emphasis on the issue of the sponsor. However, unsurprisingly, the restrictions introduced in due course of the process triggered harsh criticisms, and CSOs tried to argue for the incorporation of at least some of the persons originally included. Reacting to the 2002 amendment of the draft proposal, the UNHCR – which I include here because of its close connection to the European migration CSOs – argued the following:

> While the original version of the Proposal accorded the right to family reunion to beneficiaries of subsidiary protection who met certain specified conditions, the Amended Proposal excludes this category of persons from its scope of application. Considering that the humanitarian needs of persons benefiting from subsidiary protection are not different from those of Convention refugees, UNHCR submits that there is no valid reason to treat these two categories of persons differently as regards their entitlement to family reunification. UNHCR's concern about the exclusion of beneficiaries of subsidiary protection from the scope of the Amended proposal is heightened by the absence of any provisions on the right to family reunion in the draft Directive on minimum standards for the qualification as a refugee or beneficiary of subsidiary protection. (UNHCR 2002)

In this quotation, the extent of the directive's turn away from the human rights framework – which was the original intention by the Commission, considering the extensive reference to international human rights conventions in the explanatory memorandum of the initial proposal – towards an immigration restriction objective becomes particularly visible.

### Personal scope II – the family
Similar conflicts are observable with regard to the scope of the members of the family who are entitled to migrate – once the sponsor's scope is settled. From civil society, the equal treatment with EU citizens was highlighted, as is summarised by the Migration Policy Group:

> After three years of employment or self-employment, long term residents would acquire the right to family reunion equivalent to that of EU citizens exercising their free movement rights. This includes the spouse, children under 21 years of age and relatives of all generations who are dependent upon them. (ECRE,

ENAR, MPG 1999)

Other CSOs go further and also include non-married partners irrespective of sex. The International Lesbian and Gay Association (ILGA) states that:

> It seems unfair and contrary to the harmonising objective of the Directive if the right to family life fundamentally varies depending on the Member State concerned. Moreover, this conflicts in principle with the commitment to non-discrimination on the ground of sexual orientation stated in Article 21(1) of the EU Charter of Fundamental Rights. The Directive would actually institutionalise the uneven standards which already exist in this area ... Therefore, we recommend that the Directive provides a right to be joined by an unmarried partner, including of the same sex, of third country nationality in all Member States, irrespective of the recognition of unmarried partners in national law, and equally applicable to both EU nationals and third country nationals. (ILGA 2001)

Here, it becomes evident that CSOs are not always in accordance with each other, since the question of marriage and same-sex partnerships is a hotly contested issue throughout Europe. The ILGA would even object to the equal treatment of EU citizens, because Regulation 1612/68 on the Freedom of Movement of Workers, which was, until 2004, the legal basis for the family re-union of EU citizens, only covers married partners. For the ILGA, this would be in violation of the EU's principle of non-discrimination.

However, as was the case with the sponsor, the change of the directive's character from being human rights based to being immigration restriction based is also mirrored in an increasingly restrictive definition of the family. In the initial proposal, the Commission tried not to enforce harmonisation, but to use the principle of non-discrimination as leverage to emphasise the human rights character of the directive:

> Point (a) concerns the applicant's spouse, or his unmarried partner (who may be of the same sex). The provision on unmarried partners is applicable only in Member States where unmarried couples are treated for legal purposes in the same way as married couples. This provision generates no actual harmonisation of national rules relating to the recognition of unmarried couples; it merely allows the principle of equal treatment to operate. To avert the risk of abuse, unmarried partners must be in a stable relationship, backed up by evidence of cohabitation or by reliable testimony. (European Commission 1999, Article 5 (1a))

Children who are regarded as minors and even parents, if dependent upon the sponsor, were also included in the definition of the family. In the final directive, the scope of the term 'family' – with regard to the partner – has been greatly simplified and comprises 'the sponsor's spouse' (Council 2003, Article 4 (1a)).

The migration of children may now be restricted by Member States if:

> If a child is aged over 12 years and arrives independently from the rest of his/her family, the Member State may, before authorising entry and residence under this Directive, verify whether he or she meets a condition for integration provided for

by its existing legislation on the date of implementation of this Directive. (*ibid.*, Article 4 (1))

There are no further propositions that specify what 'a condition for integration' could mean. As Save the Children laments:

> Subjecting children, in addition, to a vague 'integration test' which they may fear or which they may not comprehend, is not likely to represent a 'humane' approach. (Save the Children 2003)[23]

While Christian organisations, unsurprisingly, do not object to the focus on married partners, their criticisms concerning the provisions for children could not be stronger:

> we had particularly welcomed the clarification that considers as minors the children who have not reached the particular Member State's age of majority. We are now most concerned about the possibility for a Member State to derogate from this principle in the case of children aged over 12 years. (Christian Organisations 2002)

Interestingly, the restrictive turn of the directive is also severely criticised by other EU institutions, which suggests that the input of both CSOs and EU consultative organs was marginalised in the course of the process (for instance, the Committee of the Regions (CoR) 2002, 1.4). In its 2002 amended proposal, the Commission clearly explicates that it 'has incorporated the compromises reached in the Council' (European Commission 2002c, Pt. 1),[24] thereby abandoning its earlier and more favourable positions.

*Conditions for exclusion and admission – the members of the family*
There are many rules and procedures pre-dating family re-unification, even if the persons fall under the scope of the directive. Sponsors have to fulfil certain material conditions, members of the family have to be abroad and prove their ability to integrate, and public reasons such as health, public policy and security could still hinder re-unification. However, I cannot retrace every thread of the analysis here; suffice it to say that the drafts did not change throughout the process with regard to the public reasons for exempting re-unification, even though many CSOs made the case for exempting health reasons as a justification for the denial of the right to migrate.

Administrative hurdles such as waiting periods and visa requirements were also contested. With regard to the sponsor, the CSOs tried to make the case for standards that are not higher than for a resident family of comparable size and social status, and tried to obtain consideration for the often precarious financial situation of TCNs, particularly of refugees. One issue discussed was that of housing, and this is one of the rare examples where one can follow, quite directly, the interaction between the draft proposals and the CSO input. The Commission's initial 1999 draft stated, in the commentary to

Article 9 (a), that:

> The evaluation of the accommodation is left to the discretion of the Member State, but the criteria adopted may not be discriminatory. Criteria as to size, hygiene and safety may not be stricter than for accommodation occupied by a comparable family (in terms of number of members and social status) living in the same region. (European Commission 1999)

This formulation was, for many CSOs, too unspecific, leaving too much room for Member State manoeuvre. Christian organisations proposed, in reaction to the above clause, the following wording:

> Instead of adequate housing we suggest the wording 'sufficient living space in comparison to the lowest level in the respective Member State' in Art. 9, 1 (a). We would welcome, if Art. 9, 1 (b) could be complemented by the obligation to provide access to affordable insurance schemes. (Christian Organisations 2000a: 5)

And, indeed, the 2000 draft saw a changed and specified wording that came closer to this position, which now spoke of social housing standards:

> adequate accommodation, which is at least equivalent in size to that provided as social housing and which meets general health and safety standards in force in the Member State concerned; that is to say accommodation that would be regarded as normal for a comparable family living in the same region of the Member State concerned. (European Commission 2000b, Article 9 (a))

The Christian organisations recognised this adaptation, saying that:

> We welcome the changes in Art. 9, 1 (a), which adapt the criteria of the accommodation to the basis of minimum social welfare, thus making them more just, objective and measurable. (Christian Organisations 2000b)

Yet their satisfaction did not last long, because the 2002 draft proposal saw once more a tightening of the planned provisions. Article 7 (1, a) – which was also taken up in the final directive – refers to

> accommodation regarded as normal for a comparable family in the same region and which meets the general health and safety standards in force in the Member State concerned. (European Commission 2002c)

Particularly interesting in this context is the Commission's explanatory note to this proposed Article 7, which states that:

> [f]ollowing the debates in the Council, the optional conditions as to housing and resources have been fleshed out without jeopardising the spirit of the original proposal. (European Commission 2002c)

Thus, the Commission apparently takes the position that it did not fall back on the initial proposal which was formulated after CSO consultation. However, the fact that reference is made to a normal condition in a Member State without specifying any standards or duty to accommodate the special social circumstances of many migrants casts doubt as to whether the final clause was a mere fleshing out or whether it represents a restrictive move. The latter is, at least, the opinion of the Christian organisations:

> We regret the changes made in Art. 7, 1 (a), which in the criteria of accommodation to be proved reintroduce the concept of 'normal accommodation', thus making them once again difficult to measure. (Christian Organisations 2002)

### Endowment with rights

When all definitional and administrative hurdles had been overcome, and the family, thus defined, had been re-united, the endowment with rights of the newly arrived migrants had to be clarified. The extent to which they acquire rights which are independent of the sponsor is a central indicator for placing the final directive between the poles of a human rights and an immigration control document. Several issues were discussed under the heading of endowment with rights, for instance the access of the members of the family to the educational system and to the labour market.

In addition to this, and a signifier for the human rights quality of the directive, is the question of whether, and if so under which circumstances, the members of the family acquire an independent right for residence in the new state, even if changes in the relationship with the initial sponsor occur, for reasons such as illness, death, or divorce. The Commission's initial proposal foresaw the following provisions:

> If the applicant leaves the Member State of residence or if the family links are broken, the Member States may not withdraw the residence permits issued to members of the nuclear family. This autonomous right of residence is given no later than after four years' residence. (European Commission 1999, explanatory note to Article 13 (1))

> A change of family situation (death, separation, divorce) authorises family members to apply for autonomous status before the four years are up. After one year's residence, if the applicant is in a particularly difficult situation, the Member States are under an obligation to issue an autonomous residence permit. (European Commission 1999, explanatory note to Article 13 (3))

Thus, those persons belonging to the nuclear family, including parents, who fall within the scope of the directive, are entitled to autonomous residence permits after a certain time period in order to prevent abuse. These provisions did not change in the 2000 amendment, but were tightened up in the 2002 version and in the final directive. There, the time period for an independent residence permit – but now only on application – was prolonged from four to five years. But the scope was even more restricted by giving the Member States even more leeway for individual regulation:

> Member States may limit the granting of the residence permit referred to in the first subparagraph to the spouse or unmarried partner in cases of breakdown of the family relationship. (Council 2003, Article 15 (1))

Even more so, a newly added clause shows that the directive no longer aims at any real harmonisation of family re-unification. It grants the Member States the competence to lay down those 'conditions relating to the granting and duration of the autonomous residence permit' (Council 2003, Article 15 (1)), according to their national law. Hence, the treatment of TNCs and their families may differ significantly across the EU. It will thus remain to be seen to what extent the practices of the Member States will flesh out these provisions as a human rights document, or as a tool to avoid immigration, instead. In any case, equal treatment of TCNs and their families is not secured by this legislation.

While CSOs seemed to have been fairly content with the earlier proposals – if one disregards the calls for a shorter waiting period for the autonomous residence permit or for an abstention of any time period in cases of extreme hardship, such as domestic violence – the 2002 proposals and the final directive caused some unease among them:

> ENAR strongly supports the intention to establish provisions ensuring the granting of an independent residence permit in the event of particularly difficult circumstances, such as widowhood, divorce, separation or death. We would request that such provisions under this Directive be clarified in order to avoid any sort of discrimination or different treatment of persons in such situations within the EU. (ENAR 2002)

*Legal scope*
Besides the material provisions for family re-unification, a legal issue was also central to the debates throughout the years of the policy-making process. As has already been indicated several times above, the Commission initially envisaged the harmonisation of family re-unification, because, in doing so, it would substantially strengthen the EU's competence for legal migration, and, furthermore, would guarantee equal treatment of migrants and the members of their families across the EU. However, CSOs seemed to anticipate the difficulties that the directive eventually encountered in the Council.

Hence, although they were generally satisfied with the first two proposals, they anticipated that the proposal might end up by merely setting minimum standards. As a result, many CSOs argued for a flexibilisation and a standstill clause; the former would allow the Member States the discretion to deviate positively from the minimum standards of the proposal, and the latter would avoid a race-to-the-bottom by forbidding the Member States to lower their existing standards. The demands for both clauses were contained in the following quotation:

> The right of Member States to introduce or maintain more favourable provisions and practices in their national legislation should also be clearly set out. (ECRE 2000)

This position was shared – or adopted – by the EP's amendments to the initial proposal. In its first reading, the parliament called on the Commission to add a new article with the content of the position expressed by ECRE, putting particular emphasis on a standstill clause:

> The implementation of this directive may in no circumstances be used to justify lowering the level of protection already guaranteed by the Member States in regard to family re-unification in the areas covered by the directive. (European Parliament 2000, Amendment 9)

In its 2000 draft proposal, the Commission expressed its reaction to the EP's requests.

> Amendment 9: The Commission cannot accept this amendment introducing a standstill clause and allowing more favourable arrangements to be maintained since it is not compatible with the objective of aligning national legislation. A number of the directive's provisions already offer a considerable degree of flexibility. (European Commission 2000b)

It is apparent that the Commission still hoped to achieve broad harmonisation of family re-unification, while CSOs continuously called for the inclusion of flexibility and standstill clauses. Eventually, after the long and difficult negotiations in the Council that followed this second proposal, the Commission came to realise that its aim of real harmonisation was not achievable, and abandoned its resistance to having greater flexibility and a standstill clause included. Although conscious that this 2002 draft proposal added a number of new restrictions which substantially changed the character of the directive, the Commission announced that it had taken a new approach.

> The new method acknowledges that, to achieve harmonisation of national legislation on family re-unification, there are several stages to be gone through. The amended proposal is only the first of these. It is inspired by a certain concern for flexibility on the basis of two main parameters: first, as regards substance, the use of a standstill clause. Second, as regards the time-frame, a deadline for the next stage. (European Commission 2002c, Point 2 of the explanatory memorandum)

Thus, Articles 19 and 20 introduced the deadline for a regular review of the provisions that offer the greatest flexibility in order to initiate further progress in harmonising admission policies.

### Conclusion

The analysis demonstrates that the final responsiveness of the Council directive to concerns from civil society organisations was fairly minimal. Only the defensive position about flexibilisation and standstill clauses found entrance in the final directive, but only after the Commission had realised the impossibility of obtaining real harmonisation.

It is particularly interesting that one can, over time, observe a gradual exclusion of issues that were important for CSOs. In the beginning, the

Commission's encompassing, human rights approach for regulating all instances of family re-union, very much matched the concerns put forward by CSOs. Consequently, the comments of all CSOs on the early two drafts, particularly on the first one of 1999, were very positive. One can assume that the Commission was receptive to their proposals during the early consultation before the first proposal. In contrast, the scope of the second amended proposal (2002) was considerably restricted. Having seen their stakes disappearing over time, all CSOs became united in their disagreement over the new proposal and over the final directive:

> The Co-ordination can no longer ask associations to support the new proposal as it did for the two previous ones. On the contrary, it expresses its complete disapproval of a step backward and calls on associations and organisations of the civil society to persuade the representatives and governments of their countries to oppose its adoption. With regard to family re-unification, it would be better to have no European directive than to have one that endorses violations of the right to family life perpetrated by certain Member States. (See, for example, Coordeurop 2002)

> National negotiations on immigration law have strongly influenced and dominated EU negotiations. A very progressive standpoint was taken during the special meeting of the European Council in October 1999 in Tampere and general guidelines were published, which indicated the intention to design a human rights oriented immigration policy for the EU. Three years after Tampere the NGO community observes a tendency not to follow the standpoints taken in Tampere. (ENAR 2002 (t3))

Low responsiveness, however, not only affects civil society input, but also other institutions that were only to be consulted in the process. For instance, the CoR challenged the general direction which the directive acquired with the 2002 proposal:

> [The CoR] is concerned that the revised proposal indicates a move away from a rights based approach to family re-unification to a procedural approach and deplores the fact that the original objective to 'set the right to family re-unification', as formulated in the initial proposal of the Commission in 1999, has been diluted to set a minimum common base of 'conditions in which the right to family re-unification is exercised'. (2002, 1.2)

The evidence strongly suggests that the political interests of the Member States in the sensitive area of legal migration dominated in the policy-making processes which led to the adoption of the directive. The complex policy-making processes of the EU, the tussle back and forth between the EU institutions and the secretive work of the Council did not prove to be very conducive to participation. The intensive discourse on participatory governance has not, it seems, found significant entrance into this policy process.

## Participation in the EU environmental policy

### Environmental policy in the European Union

Having started with no environmental provisions in the Treaty of Rome (1957), it is remarkable that, today, the EU's environmental policy 'adds up to considerably more than the sum of national environmental policies' (Jordan 2005: 2). It represents a complex system of multilevel governance that offers many opportunities to public and private actors, and entails a substantial legislative corpus that 'contributes significantly to the view of the Union as a "regulatory state"' (Sbragia 1998: 241).

Throughout the history of the integration of environmental policy, impulses from the global sphere and from the role of the leader states – such as Denmark, the Netherlands and Germany – pushed the environment into becoming a major policy area in the EU with high regulative standards (Jordan 2005; Sbragia 2000). In 1973, stimulated by a UN conference the previous year, the co-ordinated European environmental policy began with the European Commission's first Environmental Action Programme. In these early years, the environmental policy's reputation as low politics was conducive to its silent progress and to its role of strengthening political integration (Jordan 2005). Similar to the situation in migration policies, national environmental ministers – often rather marginalised at home – made use of the European level in order to increase their importance (Sbragia 1998).

It was only with the Single European Act (1987) that environmental policy received a clear legal basis (see Hildebrand 2005: 34ff). Moreover, the strategy of issue linkages between environmental and single market issues (see Lenschow 2005), in order to use the qualified-majority voting rule, further advanced legislation. The treaty reforms of Maastricht (1993) and Amsterdam (1999) expanded QMV to environmental policy and upgraded it to a general principle of the EU, which was guided by the principles of precaution and prevention. With the Treaty of Amsterdam, sustainable development became a general objective of the EU.

However, in recent years, environmental concerns have been put increasingly on the defensive from different sides. After the enlargement to 27 Member States, one can expect less progress, since the new Member States already have to grapple to implement the existing environmental *acquis communautaire* (Lenschow 2005: 12).[25] Furthermore, institutional rules have been tightened (ibid.) and new policy initiatives – such as the Lisbon Strategy[26] – are dominated by economic reasoning. Nevertheless, the environmental policy evolved from a sectoral theme into a horizontal issue in which general principles – in particular, the principles of sustainability and of precaution – are supposed to be respected across all EU policies.

On the one hand, this mainstreaming strengthens the weight given to the environment; on the other, these general principles are in danger of conceptual overstretching. As the analysis of the REACH case clearly exemplifies, despite being part of everybody's rhetoric, political support for the precautionary principle remains, at best, opaque and undifferentiated. Moreover, environmental policy has increasingly lost the secrecy of low politics, in which policy processes are the primary realm of expertocratic procedures and few actors. Hence, the success story of environmental policy integration has stalled, and it is legislation, such as REACH, which will show whether the EU will remain one of the most advanced environmental policy regimes of the world.

### Civil society organisations in environmental policy[27]

Over at least the last thirty years, respect for the environment and the dangers of its destruction has become a 'societal concern' (Ruzza 2004: 58), very much triggered by the activities, constant pressure and the institutionalisation of environmental social movements (*ibid.*, Chapter 3). Thus, it is not surprising that, parallel to the growth of European environmental policy in the mid-1980s, environmentally oriented civil society actors recognised the potential importance of the EU level and the possibilities of collaborating with an administration seeking new competences.

In particular, the big four – the European Environmental Bureau (EEB), Greenpeace, the World Wide Fund for Nature (WWF) and Friends of the Earth (FoE) – have become important actors in Brussels. As Ruzza's extensive sociological research has shown, the environmental CSOs have, 'over the years ... undergone a process of institutionalisation' (*ibid.*: 69) in order to gain a reputation for 'expertise, reliability, and trust [which] are key resources in lobbying in Brussels as elsewhere' (Mazey and Richardson 2005: 106).

The landscape of CSOs in the environmental area is significantly different to that of the area of migration. While in the latter field human rights and other classic public interest organisations predominantly establish a relatively homogenous field with contestation only about certain confined issues (for instance, Christian organisations and the ILGA do not agree on same-sex partnerships), the field of the environment has mainly two camps, the classic environmental CSOs on the one hand, and business CSOs on the other.[28] Organisations that represent economic concerns, such as the European Chemical Industry Council (CEFIC), the European Association of Chemical Distributors (FECC) or BusinessEurope (the former UNICE) which had already been active at early stages of European integration, had to adapt to the increasing relevance of environmental concerns and were increasingly forced to frame their concerns in an environmentally friendly way.

Interestingly, the CEFIC has been characterised as 'one of the few really successful Euro-federations' (Mazey and Richardson 2005: 113) because the European chemical industry is dominated by some large manufacturers that makes the CEFIC more homogenous than others of its kind. However, this should not obscure the fact that, even within this strong umbrella organisation, national cleavages remain. According to Middlemas, 'the German chemical federation, VCI, opened its own Brussels office in 1993 to increase its weight in CEFIC *vis-à-vis* Britain and France, and to serve as a more suitable filter for information for German members less used to Brussels concepts' (Middlemas 1995: 747).

My interviews with CSO representatives, Commission staff and Member State representatives confirmed that the two camps of CSOs in environmental policy are largely separated in their participatory activities and informal attempts to make their concerns heard. While economic CSOs have good access and are well received in the Commission's economic Directorates-General, such as Enterprise and Industry, or Internal Market and Services, the environmental CSOs, by and large, focus on the Directorate-General on Environment.

This organisational segmentation has been lamented by some of the Commission staff members interviewed, but, in general, there dominates an affirmative perception of having close allies in their respective partners (see, similarly, Peters 2004b: 60). This state of affairs underlines that one should be careful not to treat the Commission as a unitary bloc, which it is not. The different departments have different interests and employ staff with different academic socialisations and perceptions of common problems and their solutions. In the REACH case, this became very evident.

Yet the strength of the different CSO camps varies. As one Member State representative stressed, the pressure on economic departments both at national and at EU level to justify any position that deviates from those of economic CSOs is much higher than to justify deviations from environmental CSOs. An environmental CSO representative expressed this situation by saying: 'We are the few – they are the many!' Another Member State representative explicitly expressed his view that this state of affairs was democratically problematical because the different concerns were not equally heard so that responsiveness was likely to be asymmetrical.

The segmentation of CSOs in environmental policy was also mirrored in the now closed CONECCS database. Here, 137 organisations were listed in the field of the environment,[29] of which only 12 predominantly deal with environmental concerns, the others being predominantly business associations. This segmentation has significantly increased with the new lobby register, in which 1,440 groups are registered under the classification of environment;[30] however, even among the 290 organisations that are listed as NGOs, the majority of them are associations that are only loosely working on environmental issues, such as the European Fashion Council, Terre des Hommes, or the German *Verband Privater Bauherren e.V.*

Today, the key environmentally oriented CSOs are very well established and co-ordinated as Green 10[31] at European level. According to the interviews with CSO representatives, this co-ordination works well. The CSOs join forces in their efforts to push forward common concerns and in order to distribute tasks among themselves according to special competences in order to make them visible to the public. In their contact with the EU institutions, they make use of their different fields of expertise and distribute tasks and co-ordinate action in order to compensate for their lack of resources when compared to business interests. In the REACH process, the environmentalist CSOs often co-authored their position papers and activities, including their contribution to the online consultation. With these co-operative structures, the environmental CSOs try to establish super-CSOs in order to meet the EU's tendency to favour quasi-corporatist structures, which is also particularly visible in the social policy field and in the regular meetings between the Commission, the upcoming Council presidencies and the Social Platform.

In addition to this, compared to CSOs in other policy fields, the environmental NGOs have a rather privileged position in the EU's financial system. For instance, in the EU's 'LIFE+ – the EU environmental protection programme',[32] CSOs have, since 1992, found multiple financial positions for which they are eligible (Council 1992). Furthermore, in the most recent LIFE+ regulation, CSOs are allowed to apply for annual operating grants, rather than only for grants for specific projects. Paragraph 12 of the regulation states:

> Non-governmental organisations (NGOs) contribute to the development and implementation of Community environmental policy and legislation. It is therefore appropriate for part of the LIFE+ budget to support the operations of a number of appropriately qualified environmental NGOs through the competitive and transparent awarding of annual operating grants. Such NGOs would need to be independent and non-profit-making and to pursue activities in at least three European countries, either alone or in the form of an association. (Council and European Parliament 2007)

Although, in principle, the same rules of the game, as previously discussed concerning the formal participatory rules, also apply to environmental policy CSOs, this policy area is, nevertheless, a special case for democratic participation in European policy-making, with potential impact beyond its policy scope. In particular, the wider transparency regime of the EU might be stimulated by developments in environmental policy. In 1990, as a result of the above-mentioned environmental action programmes, the Council had already decided upon a directive (Council 1990), which came into force in 1993, which aimed at regulating the access to information on the environmental affairs of all public authorities below the EU level, i.e. from the national to the local level, forcing all Member States to enact legislation on access to environmental information (Hallo 1997). The EU did not consider enacting measures that were special to one policy field, but relied on its general approach to transparency (see Chapter 4).

However, developments in the global sphere also pushed the EU forward by stimulating its environmental policy into becoming a forerunner for a participatory governance regime and the main battleground for the enhancement of participatory democracy. In 1992, Principle 10 of the Rio Declaration on Environment and Development highlighted three main features, namely: 1) access to environmental information; 2) informed and meaningful public participation; and 3) access to justice.[33] The United Nations Economic Commission for Europe (UNECE)[34] picked these three features up and succeeded, in 1998, in agreeing upon the Århus Convention on Access to Information, Public Participation in Decision-making and Access to Justice in Environmental Matters.[35]

The convention entered into force in 2001 after the first 16 signatories ratified it. Today, 41 European states are parties to the convention, including all the EU Member States, with the exception of Ireland, which has signed, but still not ratified, the convention. The convention expanded the definition of 'public authorities' in order to cover also regional organisations such as the institutions of the European Union. The implementation and ratification of the Århus Convention in the EU is an interesting, albeit not yet finished, case, which will possibly provide important stimuli for both environmental democracy and wider democratic participation in the EU's policy-making processes.[36]

In 2002/3, the European Commission issued the Århus Package, consisting of two planned directives for implementing each of the Århus Pillars, respectively. In 2003, two directives were agreed upon by the Council, implementing the first two Pillars on Transparency and Participation, thereby repealing the 1990 Directive on access to environmental information (Council and European Parliament 2003a, 2003b). The third planned Directive on access to justice has not been decided yet, so that the Århus Convention remains incompletely implemented at Member State level (European Commission 2003a). But since the EU itself is a signatory to the Convention, an independent step for ratification was necessary. In an interesting contradiction with its rhetoric on transparency and participation, it took the EU seven years to become a party to the Convention by ratifying it on 17 February 2005 (Council 2005). The following regulation that implements the Convention's provisions for the European institutions and bodies (Council and European Parliament 2006b) has some potential significance for both CSOs and the participatory regime of the EU, although, at the time of writing, it is too early to pronounce judgement on its influence. The potential importance has different sources: first, the regulation significantly extends the institutional scope of Directive 1049/2001 on Access to Information (see also Chapter 4), which only covers the three major European institutions, namely, the EP, the Council and the Commission, to all other community institutions and bodies.[37] Furthermore, the regulation opens a potential space for a true postnational application of participation rights, since it states in the Preamble, Point 6, that the Pillars of the Århus Convention 'are without discrimination as to citizenship, nationality or domicile' (*ibid.*). Yet, it remains to be seen to what extent this statement will be put into practice by the institutions, and, above all, whether if will find reflections in the ECJ's case law.

A first restriction is already inserted into the regulation, since only in

Title II of Access to Environmental Information is there explicit reference to this statement (Article 3). The third feature of the regulation with potential significance for CSOs concerns the issue of public participation. In Article 9(2), the community institutions and bodies are asked to strive for active inclusiveness, beyond mere financial support.[38] The fact that inclusion is to be achieved not only for those affected, but also for all those who have an interest in a pending decision of the EU is of some importance. This extension provides space for CSO activities which are rarely directly concerned with a Community act.

Upon the basis of this extension, the last potentially significant feature of the regulation also gains relevance, namely, access to justice. Title IV of the regulation (Articles 10–12) provides civil society organisations, for the first time, with a clear and explicit *locus standi*. CSOs which are non-profit-making organisations according to a Member State's law (Article 11(1)a) are entitled to: a) make a request for internal review; and b) institute proceedings before the ECJ, if the 'subject matter ... is covered by its objectives and activities' (Article. 11(1)d). In the case of a request for an internal review, a community institution or body is obliged to give reasons for its acts or administrative practices, thereby introducing an element of justification into the EU law.

In the process leading to this regulation, it was, in particular, the access to justice for CSOs that had been heavily contested between the two camps in the CSO field of the environment.[39] Economic groups such as CEFIC feared that NGOs would gain more rights for judicial review than companies, because of the clause that only non-profit organisations could gain access to internal review and to the Court. However, as I showed in Chapter 4, the first stage of participatory rights for non-state actors granted companies the right to go to the Court in cases in which they were directly affected by a Community act. Since companies, unlike CSOs, can fairly easily prove their concern, this *modus operandi* granted economic actors significant legal standing in the European legal system. Now, with the Århus regulation, non-state actors with so-called public interests are also given access to justice in the clearly defined policy area of environment, thus mitigating the disadvantage of public *versus* economic concerns.

To conclude, in the environmental policy area, both the intra-EU discourse on participatory governance and democracy, *and* the global developments on environmental democracy come together, thus making it a particularly interesting area for studying civil society organisations. In this lively context, the policy-making process that eventually led to the adoption of the REACH regulation took place, which will be analysed in the following section. The dual structure of the CSO field in the environmental area renders the analysis of responsiveness both more complicated and easier, because the need for justification is potentially higher for the public institutions as a means of defending their own positions in the light of the divergent input of CSOs.

*The content dimension: responsiveness in the case of REACH*[40]
This section turns again to the content dimension of responsiveness. The research rationale and its implementation was the same as in the case of family re-unification.

*The context and decision-making process of the empirical case*
*No data – no market.* This slogan, which was promoted by Greenpeace, succinctly sums up what the disputes on REACH (Regulation on Registration, Evaluation, Authorisation and Restriction of Chemicals) between environmental CSOs, economic CSOs and public institutions were all about. What it means is that only substances about which there is sufficient knowledge with regard to their characteristics, usefulness and risks should be placed on the market. Everybody unfamiliar with chemical policy would think that this principle would be the uncontested, existing principle for the marketing of chemicals; however, it is not. This means that we are all facing a situation in which there is a lack of profound knowledge about the long-term effects on human beings, on animals and on the wider environment of both the consumption and the exposure to the majority of the chemicals in the products that we use and consume

Only in the 1970s did a stronger environmental and consumer orientation, in many Member States, begin to demand some regulation of the use of chemicals (see Ronge and Körber 1994: 326ff). At European level, too, attempts were begun to regulate and harmonise chemical policies. Above all, the system based upon the implementation of the 1979 sixth amendment of Directive 67/548/EEC on the classification, packaging and labelling of dangerous substances was particularly important (Council 1979). The initial directive in 1967 was, above all, issued in order to facilitate trade among the then six Member States. Furthermore, it aimed to enhance health and safety at work – an important trigger of environmental policies throughout European integration – by strengthening worker protection against acute exposure to chemicals. However, no measures for a risk assessment of long-term exposure were introduced. This directive merely installed a committee for chemicals, which was obliged to list new chemicals that were to be placed on the market according to their known or suspected risks.

However, the information exchanges of this system proved to be ineffective, so that the sixth amendment of the original directive introduced the obligation for firms to carry out pre-market testing, hazard assessment and notification procedures; this, however, was only for new chemicals, i.e. post-1981, the date of the coming into force of the directive. Yet even this system did not remain uncontested and still possesses huge gaps. Currently, of about 100,000 listed substances in the European Inventory of Existing Commercial Substances, approximately 30,000 are of commercial significance. However, only about 2,500 chemicals were introduced on the market *after* 1981 and listed in the European List of Notified Chemical Substances.

This means that the majority of chemicals on the market have not yet undergone a registration and hazard assessment procedure, thereby violating the principle of *no data – no market*.[41] Moreover, the existing chemical regime in the EU, and the differences among the Member States, proved to be so complex that even the chemicals industry expressed an interest in establishing a comprehensive, harmonised European chemical regime which was seen to be necessary for the proper functioning of the internal market.

So far, advancement in European chemical policy has mainly been motivated by economic – in particular, trade – concerns, and only marginally by environmental or consumer protection (Lenschow 2005: 307). REACH is supposed to establish a coherent, integrated regime for European chemicals, and aims to find a new balance between economic and environmental concerns. Moreover, REACH expands the scope by including, next to the producers of a substance, also the so-called down-stream users, i.e. importers and exporters, manufacturers that process existing substances for their own products, etc.

Under pressure from Scandinavian countries and the Netherlands (Pesendorfer 2006), in December 1998 the EU Council publicly acknowledged the necessity to establish an integrated and coherent approach to the EU's chemicals policy, which adequately reflected the principles of precaution and sustainability. In June 1999, the Environment Council[42] took a step forward by giving a clear mandate to the Commission to take the appropriate measures. Consequently, on 24/25 February 1999, the Commission held a stakeholder brainstorming workshop entitled 'On the development of a future chemicals strategy for the European Union', in Brussels, and, in February 2001, it published a White Paper on the future of chemical policy (European Commission 2001d). In this White Paper, the following aims for a chemical regime were expressed:

- Protection of human health and the environment;
- Maintenance and enhancement of the competitiveness of the EU's chemicals industry;
- Prevention of fragmentation of the internal market;
- Increased transparency for both consumers and industry;
- Promotion of non-animal testing; and
- Conformity with EU international obligations under the WTO.

The White Paper tried to include all areas that could possibly be affected by chemical policy – without prioritising among the areas. Contestation and conflict was thus foreseeable. All (both existing and new) chemicals should be registered and evaluated, and an authorisation scheme should be established for chemicals of very high risk, such as carcinogenic, mutagenic or bioaccumulative substances. This authorisation scheme envisaged the possibility of the restriction and the substitution of chemicals.

In October 2003, after extensive consultations that encompassed an eight-week online consultation, several conferences and public hearings, and a series of impact assessments throughout the summer of 2003, the Commission published its draft proposal (European Commission 2003b) and passed it to the European Parliament. Two years later, after considerable procedural tactics and substantial contestation, the EP, under the co-decision procedure, agreed on a significantly amended draft version in its first reading in November 2005 (Council 2005). Just one month later, the Council arrived at a political agreement on REACH (European Parliament 2005). In June 2006, this common position was formally adopted by the Environment Council so that it could then serve as the basis for the second reading in the European Parliament. In between, the Commission published a Communication on the common position (European Commission 2006b). It took until early December 2006 for the EP and the Council finally to agree upon a final version of REACH. This agreement was endorsed at the EP's second reading (13 December 2006) and finally adopted at the Environment Council five days later (18 December 2006). REACH entered into force on 1 June 2007, but the new European Chemicals Agency in Helsinki, Finland, only became fully operational one year later.

In the REACH process, as Table 5.2 shows, the European institutions and the stakeholders were very actively engaged in numerous dialogical activities. Moreover, the Commission initiated the REACH Implementation Projects (RIPs), and – as proposed by CEFIC – launched the programme Strategic Partnerships on REACH Testing (SPORT) with industry, trade unions and the Member States. Besides these initiatives, CSOs such as the European Trade Union Confederation (ETUC) and the European Environmental Bureau (EEB) organised several major conferences to promote dialogue between all stakeholders, and countless smaller receptions, information meetings and other informal contacts also took place. Environmental groups sought to gain public visibility through international campaigns such as the World Wide Fund for Nature's DETOX-Campaign.[43]

All in all, although the informal contacts between the stakeholders and the decision-makers were of significance, one can also say that the Commission made an effort to render the formal policy formulation process open. In particular, the Internet consultation via the IPM Platform resulted in more than 6,300 contributions and, as the interviews revealed, influenced the first draft legislation – in favour of business concerns. The restrictive questionnaire that focused on technical questions was criticised as favouring business actors by avoiding a fundamental debate about the core principles and aims of REACH, such as the precautionary principle.

Despite the Commission's efforts to create an accessible, transparent and inclusive policy process, the REACH case shows how a mixture of formal – albeit technical – consultation exercises and informal policy-making practices has created asymmetric access to policy processes. It is resource intensive to

Table 5.2 Overview of key official participative activities during the
REACH process

| Date | Type of activity |
| --- | --- |
| 1999 | The European Commission organised a conference with 150 stakeholders. |
| 2001, 2 April | The European Commission organised a second stakeholder conference on the Chemicals White Paper. |
| 2003, 7 May–July 10 | The Commission published a very detailed document as reference document for the Internet consultation. Internet Consultation, 7 May until 10 July 2003. |
| 2003, 16 October | Stakeholders' briefing organised by the Commission on its impact assessment study. |
| 2005, 19 January | Joint public hearing on 'The new REACH legislation', organised by the EP's Committee on the Environment, Public Health and Food Safety, Committee on Industry, Research and Energy and Committee on Internal Market and Consumer Protection.[a] |

[a] The three parliamentary committees could not agree on a common programme for the hearing, so that, in the end, every committee organised its own panel with its own like-minded experts so that real dialogue between the different stakeholders was, by and large, avoided.

establish and maintain close contacts with the European institutions and to provide highly technical advice (personnel, financial, expertise, etc.), but even a strong environmental CSO, such as Greenpeace, cannot compete with the resources of business-oriented CSOs. Consequently, the former tend to focus on their natural allies in DG Environment and the Members of the EP's Environmental Committee, rather than attempting to convince the members of DG Industry.

Moreover, it is not only this resource asymmetry among the business and non-business CSOs in informal participatory patterns that accounts for the different strategies. While business CSOs try to be involved in policy-making without publicity, non-business concerns actively seek to increase their visibility by stimulating public debates. In addition, the public perception of the political salience of the different concerns of the various stakeholders is asymmetrically attributed, in that the echo of business concerns is considerably stronger in the policy process than environmental concerns, as the next section will show.

*The responsiveness to civil society arguments*
REACH affects industry, consumers, the health and safety of workers and the environment alike. It is a prime example for the disclosure of the enmeshment of a multitude of relevant concerns and thus shows the challenges for any institutionalisation of participatory democracy in modern complex societies.

Furthermore, REACH exposes the dependence of contemporary policy-making on scientific expertise by simultaneously revealing its limits, thus providing evidence of the fragile nature of the attempts to de-politicise in favour of exper-tocratic leadership. Given this complex situation, it is unsurprising that REACH has become, perhaps, the most actively lobbied policy decision in the EU's history – at least, this perception is omnipresent in many publications, leaflets, brochures and also in many of my conducted interviews.

Consequently, the coding scheme for the analysis had to accommodate this diversity of concerns. It was developed based upon the key concerns of the CSOs, as was visible in their contributions. The subsequent presentation of some elements of my extensive analysis is the result of a second run of the analysis. In the first run, I focused upon smaller instances, such as trans-parency requirements in the labelling of substances and products, or the sequence in which industry should be required to register and evaluate existing substances, but the analysis revealed that, during the years of the REACH process, the contributions of the CSOs became increasingly antago-nistic, hereby signifying a struggle for the major concepts whose definitions determine the overall character of REACH as either more industry-friendly or more environmentally friendly.

In order to substantiate this focus on the major concepts, in the following analysis of responsiveness, I have also included estimations and statements of the expert interviews which I conducted. This analytical approach proved useful in order to come to terms with the complicated issues of REACH, which often required advanced expertise in chemistry – however, the increas-ing antagonism of the contributions suggests that key issues that were contested and discussed throughout the seven years of the policy process were often of a political nature. My task was, thus, to identify the political messages behind the technical problems.

Thus, overall, the REACH case does not display fairly straightforward correspondence between general themes and individual articles, as was the case during the process of family re-unification. On the contrary, it is not only the general themes, but also the concrete issues, which are themselves aggre-gations of many different single propositions which are dispersed throughout the huge data file of the REACH regulation (the final regulation consists of 867 pages) and behind which their political messages lie. For the purpose of assessing the responsiveness of the REACH process, it is necessary to deal with the provisions at this aggregated level, because, more than the changes of single formulations in small articles, it is the change of the general spirit of the regulation which – possibly – mirrors responsiveness. This focus on the general topics was also the attitude of environmental CSOs, in particular:

> The least we can do, as stakeholders in this momentous event of the 're-designing' of European Chemicals Policy, is to make sure the basics are in place so that the greatest degree of protection will be afforded to future generations of wildlife and humans. (WWF 2001 (t2))

The final themes and codes on which I eventually focused the analysis are summarised in the Table 5.3; some of the issues and particular instances are shared by several of the general themes. Economic concerns centred particularly on the issues of competitiveness, innovation and trade. With regard to competitiveness, the costs of the REACH regime were disputed as well as the degree of transparency to which firms would be obliged. With a view to innovation, the extent to which highly dangerous substances should be substituted was a central issue which also had possible effects on competitiveness.

Furthermore, WTO compatibility and the non-discrimination of domestic enterprises *versus* importers was an issue of particular concern. Consumer and worker concerns and environmental concerns particularly focused on the insertion of the precautionary principle[44] into REACH and its specific definition. Occupational health and safety as well as the protection of consumers and the environment depend, among other things, on the

Table 5.3  Principles guiding the analysis of REACH

| General themes (code families) | Issues (issue codes) | Instances (coded quotes in the text) |
|---|---|---|
| Economic concerns | Competitiveness | i.a., costs involved; bureaucracy; transparency (duty of sharing and publishing data); scope of directive; risk-based approach |
|  | Innovation | i.a., authorisation: substitution of chemicals; loss of substances; R & D |
|  | Trade | i.a., WTO compatibility; relation domestic producers v. importers |
| Consumer and worker concerns | The precautionary principle | i.a., scope of directive; minimising exposure at workplace and at consumption; transparency (labelling of products); hazard-based approach; |
| Environmental concerns | Animal testing | Animal testing |
|  | The precautionary principle | see, above, authorisation regime |
| Procedural issues | Role of the agency | i.a., role of agency; burden of proof; degree of harmonisation; risk- v. volume-based approach; relation to existing legislation |

approach to risk management, i.e. whether a risk-based, a hazard-based or a volume-based approach would be installed.[45] Furthermore, environmental concerns included the effects of REACH on animal testing. REACH also shows that *procedural issues* are central to the final character of legislation.

The role of the soon-to-be-installed chemical agency,[46] for instance not only the question of whether the burden of proof lies on the part of the industry or the agency, but also the degree of harmonisation, were central issues for the participants of the process. REACH covers such a huge, complex area that I cannot even pretend to have followed every single thread that could be identified in the data. Nevertheless, I am confident that I have identified the central issues of REACH so that my analysis offers sufficient evidence to capture the responsiveness of the process as a whole.

As in the migration case, the purpose of this section cannot be to give a detailed account or an exegesis of the content of the directive,[47] or to inform about every step of the extensive analysis. Instead, it aims to present the core results of this analysis, focusing on the central elements of the general themes. Once more, I have divided the policy process into different stages, seven in all, starting from the 2001 White Paper, going on to the 2003 consultation document, accounting then for the changes in the official proposal by the Commission, then from 2003, reaching a peak with the Council's political agreement in December 2005, before the fine-graining took place in 2006, including the official adoption of the political agreement by the Environmental Council in June 2006, the successive Commission communication in July, and the second and final reading by the EP in September, a document which was then adopted by the Council in December 2006.

*Economic concerns I: competitiveness*
In the introduction of the 2001 White Paper, the Commission clearly stated its purpose of relating the issues of competitiveness with those of innovation and safety:

> It is ... essential to ensure the efficient functioning of the internal market and the competitiveness of the chemical industry. EU policy for chemicals should provide incentives for technical innovation and development of safer chemicals. (European Commission 2001d: 5)

Innovation should be triggered by emphasising the precautionary principle (see also below) and by introducing the mechanism of the substitution of highly dangerous substances. This, so the argument goes, would foster research and development efforts, and lead to innovations and thus increased competitiveness. Furthermore, the competitiveness of the European chemical industry is to be maintained by introducing a global approach that not only puts the burden of the testing costs of the substances onto the shoulders of intra-EU enterprises, but also imposed that:

> everyone who imports substances into the Community would make a fair contribution to these costs. (*Ibid.*: 15)

These two short quotations from the White Paper already show that the three issues which I have put under the heading of 'economic concerns' are very much related to each other, and not directly linked to individual clauses of the legislation, as was the case in the family re-unification case. Instead, they are concerned with the general direction of REACH and possible adverse future effects.

At a first glance, there appears to be consensus among the CSOs and the Commission: economic CSOs adopt a rhetoric that endorses the Commission's objective to mitigate the tension between economics and environment. The CEFIC, for instance, states that:

> [t]he chemical industry recognises its responsibilities and willingly accepts the challenges placed upon it to ensure the protection of human health and the environment while delivering good financial performance and meeting the expectations of society. (CEFIC 2000 [t1])

However, behind this rhetorical agreement, fierce divisions were visible, from the very outset, between the economic and the environmental CSOs, regarding which goals, market functioning and competitiveness, or the protection of human health and the environment, were the more important. In many statements, the economic CSOs doubted that the proposed provisions would guarantee competitiveness. One important strand of the discussion argued that particularly Small- and Medium-sized Enterprises (SMEs) would face an unbearable burden of high testing and registration costs, with the effect that the opposite of innovation would take place, namely, a de-selection of substances. A typical argument states that

> [t]he new EU Chemicals policy will bring about a very substantial change in the supply of chemicals. A supplier may not be willing to go through the expensive registration procedure when, in his view, the economic value of a substance bears no relation to the cost of its assessment. It has been estimated that the manufacturing industry could be faced with the de-selection of up to 50% of the substances currently available, most of them not because of their intrinsic risk but for economic reasons. This de-selection will in general lead to a dramatic increase of costs without contributing towards a healthier Europe. (Association of Downstream Users 2003 (t2))

Economic CSOs tend, in their arguments, to highlight a tension between the different goals of REACH, while many statements of environmental CSOs show attempts to counter these arguments by integrating the different goals. They stress the linkages and positive effects of the different goals, and try to make their case in the light of the arguments of the others. This means that the environmental CSOs made greater argumentative efforts in order to make their case.[48] A summary of the key arguments is given by the following quotation of the European Environmental Bureau:

> The costs estimated by industry, and by the Commission's business impact study,

ignore the potentially positive effects on innovation and competitiveness presented by REACH, for example:

- New markets for safer and more environmentally friendly products;
- Safer products will reduce the risk of future liability lawsuits, which can result in enormous costs (as has happened with asbestos);
- Increased trust among consumers, employees, local communities and investors, leading to a more positive business environment;
- Easier introduction of new chemicals onto the market will encourage development and innovation;
- A more predictable regulatory system will aid future long-term planning by industry; and
- Improved transparency and communication through the supply chain will lead to increased power and confidence for downstream users and SMEs. (EEB 2003: 1 (t2))

However, these kinds of future-oriented arguments face particular difficulties: they are hard to calculate and have a degree of uncertainty that does not appeal to economic actors. In the same document, the EEB argues desperately:

> Just because health and environmental benefits are difficult to quantify, it does not mean that they are unimportant – in reality they are the driving force behind the regulation of chemicals, so ignoring them is not acceptable. (*Ibid.*: 12)

However, as different interviews with state representatives, Commission civil servants and CSO members showed, even in cases of the availability of calculations, these numbers can be contested, used strategically or even ignored. The alleged cost-burden placed by REACH on SMEs, in particular, had such a high priority that several impact assessments by different institutions (such as Arthur D. Little, KPMG or the Commission's Joint Research Centre[49]) were undertaken in order to clarify the situation. The usages of these studies by many CSOs and some political actors were more strategic than based upon good arguments and reasoning. For instance, many interviewees agreed in their judgement about the serious methodological shortcomings of the influential study of the firm Arthur D. Little, which was issued by the German Association of Industries (BDI).

However, although the 'balloon has collapsed' (to quote an interviewed Member State representative) that SMEs, in particular, would suffer under REACH, the economic CSOs failed to repeat this point in many of their statements, so that a representative of the EP expressed his frustration by saying that 'du kannst denen Studien um den Kopf hauen, soviel du willst, sie wollen aber nicht zuhören ...' ('you can bash them on the head with impact assessments as much as you like, but they won't listen ...'). With 'they' the interviewee was referring to economic CSOs and the MEPs from economic committees.[50]

Hence, irrespective of the results of the various impact assessments, the

Commission's 2003 proposal for the REACH regulation (European Commission 2003b) tried to accommodate the concerns of the economic voices that were voiced in the online consultation which was undertaken in 2003. More than 6,400 contributions in the eight weeks of the consultation showed an enormous interest in REACH and the pressure on the Commission was considerable – particularly from the economic actors.

*Economic concerns II: innovation*
To become more concrete, it was, in particular, the link between competitiveness and innovation via application of substitution that was loosened in the Commission's proposal, and thus the scope of REACH was reduced in order to lessen the costs on enterprises.

Environmental CSOs put a lot of effort into emphasising the importance of the substitution mechanism in REACH. The following quotation explicates the general rule, proposed by these actors, that the safest substance should always be used. According to them, only this would guarantee compliance with the precautionary principle:

> There must be a general duty on all industries to use the safest available chemicals or techniques. Substitution is a crucial part of a precautionary regulatory approach, whereby chemicals with more hazardous properties are replaced by those with low hazard. (EEB *et al.* 2001 (t2))

In its White Paper, the Commission started off by encouraging substitution as the appropriate means both to stimulate innovation and to respect the precautionary principle. Two years later, however, in the 2003 proposal, attempts were made to reduce the costs for the industry in order not to endanger global competitiveness. The proposal states, among other things, that highly dangerous substances are not to be subject to the authorisation procedure (and thus exempted from being potentially subject to substitution requirements) if they are:

> solely for scientific research and development purposes or for product and process-orientated research and development purposes in quantities under 1 ton. (European Commission 2003b: 31)

With these restrictions, the Commission is confident of having found a better balance between economics and environment; it argues that:

> [w]hile the new legislation is designed to cover all those chemical substances that can lead to a certain exposure of citizens or the environment, great care has been taken to ensure that the new legislation does not overreach in terms of scope, costs and administrative burden. This is why the new legislation provides for a tiered approach for certain classes of chemical substances. This is in particular the case with regard to low tonnage substances or special uses (e.g., for research and development). At the same time this tiered approach

leads to a somewhat lighter regime in terms of cost and administrative burden from which SMEs will be able to benefit, without diminishing the protection of health and the environment. (*Ibid.*: 11)

For small and medium enterprises (SMEs), the following eased provisions are introduced:

For downstream users, the requirement to undertake chemical safety assessments and produce chemical safety reports has been strictly limited. Registration obligations were simplified for 1–10 tonnes (no chemical safety reports need be submitted; testing requirements were reduced). Polymers [are exempted from REACH]. (*Ibid.*: 10)

Thus, the REACH proposal has made a considerable development away from the strong emphasis on substitution in the White Paper to only a discretionary provision in the 2003 legislative proposal:

The application may include:
- a socio-economic analysis conducted in accordance with Annex XV;
- an analysis of the alternatives considering their risks and the technical and economic feasibility of substitution, where appropriate accompanied by a substitution plan, including research and development and a timetable for proposed actions by the applicant. (European Commission 2003b, explanatory note to Article 59)

Evidently, environmental CSOs were not content with this discretionary element, and they lamented the profound weakening of the authorisation, and thus substitution, scheme even more. Referring to the Commission's document, which was issued before the online consultation, environmental CSOs challenged, among other things, the following phrase:

The phrase 'however, the existence of an alternative is in itself insufficient grounds to refuse an authorisation' (Point 48 (3c)) is particularly unacceptable, as it clearly implies protection of the health and the environment is a secondary consideration. (4 Green NGO's 2003 submission to the online consultation [t2])

According to the argument of FoE and the WWF in a letter written to the permanent representatives, national ministries and the Council following the 2003 proposal, this provision would:

prevent regulators from acting against chemicals until serious harm has been caused – this is not compatible with a precautionary principle. (EEB *et al.* 2004b)

Thus, it is clear that the concerns of environmental CSOs with regard to authorisation and substitution were not responded to in the official documents.

In the final REACH regulation, the discretionary character of the authorisation provisions was reduced, at the surface, by using the word 'shall' instead of 'may'. But this change of wording does not signify a stronger reappearance of substitution. On the contrary, substitution was pushed aside even more. In the REACH regulation, very dangerous substances are able to receive authorisation for further use if the user can specify that the substances are adequately controlled. Thus, the application of adequate control as a central mechanism of the authorisation scheme was challenged by environmental CSOs:

> Even low concentrations and widely dispersed amounts of persistent, bioaccumulative substances can be re-concentrated by nature and accumulate in our bodies. In other words, 'adequate control' of these substances is all but impossible. (FoE 2003 (t3))

What an adequate control requires, and whether highly dangerous substances can successfully be adequately controlled, particularly in a long-term perspective with regard to their exposition, leaves significant room for the discretionary manoeuvring of the authorising authority, i.e. the Commission. Article 60 of the final regulation says:

> an authorisation shall be granted if the risk to human health or the environment from the use of a substance arising from the intrinsic properties specified in Annex XIV is adequately controlled in accordance with section 6.4 of Annex I and as documented in the applicant's chemical safety report, taking into account the opinion of the Committee for Risk Assessment referred to in Article 60 (4) (a). (Council 2006)

The course which the proposal has taken shows that, over the years of the REACH process, the provisions on authorisation and substitution in the official documents reflect the diminishing extent of the definition of substitution put forward by several environmental CSOs.

*Consumer, worker and environmental concerns: the precautionary principle*
Having presented the eventual downturn of the strong substitution requirement in REACH, much is already said with regard to the precautionary principle. However, the issue of substitution does not fully capture the concept of the precautionary principle. The way in which politics and (civil) society not only deals with the promises, but also the limits of scientific knowledge, and the extent to which political decisions can, and should, be based upon scientific expertise is also central to its application.

In the final REACH regulation, there is a formulation which says that authorisation may not be granted for substances:

> ... for which there is scientific evidence of probable serious effects to human health or the environment which give rise to an equivalent level of concern to those of other substances listed in points (a) to (e) and which are identified on a case-by-case basis in accordance with the procedure set out in Article 58. (Article 56 (f))

This means that the existence of scientific evidence, or at least strong scientific concern, is required for the authorisation of substances, which is

only the first step of its phasing-out *via* substitution. Thus, the public authorities eventually decided that sound knowledge should be the basis of their
legislation. They adopted a position that pursues risk prevention by following
a strategy of risk assessment and risk management, rather than precaution.
This decision is in line with calls by economic CSOs that had already been
issued in the run-up to the White Paper:

> risk assessment is not contrary to the precautionary principle; it is an essential
> requirement for its application along with cost/benefit analysis so as to avoid
> speculative precaution. (CEFIC 2000 (t1))

Greenpeace took a different stand on the precautionary principle. In a
study on the reforms of European chemical policy, issued in 1999, it said that:

> [t]he Precautionary Principle should provide an overarching paradigm to guide
> decision making even in the absence of certainty regarding the potential impacts
> of a chemical. This would convey the benefit of any doubt over effects on to the
> environment accepting that measures may, in some cases, be overprotective in
> the interests of avoiding harm, especially when uncertainties are large.
>
> In practical terms, the implementation of this principle would imply that
> action must be taken to avoid harm, or the threat of harm, before it occurs, even
> when firm evidence of cause-effect relationships is unavailable, that the 'burden
> of proof' is reversed, such that all chemicals are assumed hazardous, and
> regulated accordingly, until such time as sufficient evidence becomes available
> that the chemical presents no potential for hazards to ecosystems or human
> health ... (Greenpeace 1999: Section 3)

This statement reveals the awareness of the limits even of state-of-the-art
scientific knowledge and methods, and thus adopts an evolutionary approach
in which chemical substances are conceived of as harmful unless it is demonstrated that they are not. And, indeed, in its White Paper, the Commission
showed some awareness that a tension existed between the precautionary
principle and a strategy based upon risk assessment. It stated that:

> [t]he extent of testing required for detecting the intrinsic hazardous properties of
> a substance is often the subject of controversy. While, at first glance, it would
> seem reasonable to test chemicals until all hazardous properties (i.e. all adverse
> effects on all organisms at all potential doses) are known, theoretical and
> practical considerations reveal that it is neither possible nor desirable to meet this
> objective ... the available testing methodology has limitations, as demonstrated
> by the recent discussion on the identification of endocrine disrupters. The review
> and the development of our testing methodology must therefore be regarded as
> a continual challenge ... (European Commission 2001d: 11)

But, in the end, as I have already stated, the European institutions
decided to follow a risk assessment strategy. In so doing, REACH does not
reflect a substantial turn in the EU's approach to chemical policy, if one
follows the argument presented by FoE, which claims that the current regulation (prior to REACH) already considers risk assessment to be an objective

way of guaranteeing chemical safety, but continues to identify several limits
to this strategy:

> We know so little about pathways of exposure to many chemicals in the environ-
> ment that this crucial part of a risk assessment is often highly subjective.
>
> Risk assessments generally deal with individual chemicals, rather than
> mixtures of chemicals to which we are commonly exposed. The toxicity of such
> mixtures of chemicals is largely unknown.
>
> Establishing what is an 'acceptable risk' is a subjective decision and not an
> empirical scientific one. This is especially true in the case of carcinogenic,
> mutagenic and hormone-disrupting chemicals for which it may be considered
> that there is no 'safe dose' of exposure. As noted by professor vom Saal
> (University of Missouri): 'There are no safe doses of endocrine disruptors, just as
> there are no safe doses of carcinogens.'
>
> The use of risk assessment for the regulation of chemical releases is there-
> fore problematic and ineffective for environmental and health protection. A
> new way forward, which would be protective of the environment and human
> health from hazardous chemicals, (e.g., chemicals 'of very high concern'), would
> be to take action to prevent these chemicals at source. Steps should be taken
> to ensure the reduction and eventual elimination of hazardous chemicals from
> products, pipeline discharges, emissions to the atmosphere and losses from
> manufacturing processes and disposal operations. The new REACH proposal
> for chemical regulation should be used to help fulfil these safety goals and in
> so doing properly protect wildlife and human health from the health hazards
> posed by chemicals.
>
> Unless the current climate of reliance on standard risk assessment proce-
> dures is replaced with more precautionary approaches, it seems unlikely
> that, in practice, many authorisations will be refused. (EEB *et al.* 2004a:
> Section 2)

The struggles surrounding the inclusion and the definition of the precautionary principle in the REACH regulation point to a topic that goes beyond
the scope of this work. Namely, it shows that it is an ambiguous undertaking
to rely on such unspecific concepts in policy-making processes, and that
they can be used as a strategy to increase expertocracy and to add to the
de-politicisation of politics.[51]

*Procedural issues*
Besides these debates of the broad concepts that determine the main direction
of REACH, there was an intensive discussion about the different procedural
issues which concern the implementation and working of the regulation. But
it turned out that the procedural issues were not simply administrative
questions, but also decisive for the character of REACH. Below, I will discuss
some aspects of the role of the chemical agency.

The agency is particularly interesting because, to some extent, both
environmental *and* economic CSOs seemed to share opinions on its role.
Both groups of CSOs argued for a substantial degree of policy harmonisation

through a strong agency – however, the reasons behind this position differ. Economic CSOs usually issue the following argument:

> Leaving the implementation to national authorities is also associated to the risk that, at the end of such a process, the 'patchwork' will be even more pronounced than in the existing system. The consequences would be regulatory discrepancies (e.g., bans), which would enhance the competitive differences even in Europe. (EMCEF 2001 (t2))

This quotation states that a strong, centralised agency would be necessary in order to make the system more coherent, prevent different standards of application in different Member States, and thus reduce bureaucracy. Environmental CSOs, on the other hand, argue that:

> [t]o ensure that decisions are made with the intention to protect the environment and human health, and not only the economic benefit of shareholders, it has to be ensured that these decisions are being taken by independent bodies under the responsibility of the Member States or the European Commission. This, however, does not mean that the burden of proof of the hazardousness of a substance will lie with the latter. Industry should deliver data and should take responsibility and hold liability for the products they put on the market, and therefore prove that the substances they produce are the safest available for the purpose they intend to serve. Preliminary risk assessments should be carried out by industry; the results and data delivered should be independently checked through a Quality Assurance System, for example, by independent validation. (EEB 2001: 3 (t1))

Thus, these actors stress the control function of the agency in the implementation of REACH.

Although the environmental CSOs wanted to place the responsibility for assessing the hazards of substances and for providing the data on the shoulders of the industry, a public body should be in place to monitor the assessments of industry, and, if one recalls the discussion surrounding the substitution of substances, to deny authorisation, when necessary.

Hence, below the surface of the agreement on the need for a strong agency lies disagreement about substitution and authorisation as well as about a reversal of the burden of proof, often also dealt with in the REACH process under the heading of 'the duty of care'. Until REACH, it was either for the public authorities to undertake the risk assessments of substances (see also page 19 of the White Paper), or for injured parties to prove that a substance is dangerous and causes damage. Even in the run-up to the White Paper, the issue of the reversal of the burden of proof was already disputed between the two CSO camps. Economic CSOs argued that:

> [c]hemicals management should not be considered solely by consideration of inherent chemicals properties or a 'reversal of the burden of proof'. This approach is unacceptable to the chemical industry as it would jeopardise the competitive foundation of the industry and the benefits it brings to society. (CEFIC 2001: 2 (t1))

This statement shows that the associations close to the chemical industry see its capability for innovation and competitiveness endangered if the industry has to prove that its substances are *not* dangerous. On closer inspection, this statement reveals an opinion that puts the burden of proof not only on the public authorities, but also, to some degree, treats the public as a laboratory for substances about whose long-term effects the industry itself is unclear. Interestingly enough, some economic CSOs took a more defensive position, showing some awareness of this problem, so that calls for enhanced demonstration of self-responsibility were voiced:

> Enhanced Product Stewardship – development of an industry initiative to act on, and demonstrate that it is acting on, the principles of Product Stewardship. Key elements are: enhanced Product Stewardship management systems; improved customer support, particularly for SMEs; development of relevant Indicators of Performance. (CEFIC 1998)

The Commission, in its 2001 White Paper, seemed to share the position of the environmental CSOs and stated that the intention was one of:

> [m]aking industry responsible for safety: Responsibility to generate knowledge about chemicals should be placed on industry. Industry should also ensure that only chemicals that are safe for the intended uses are produced and/or placed on the market. The Commission proposes to shift responsibility to enterprises, for generating and assessing data and assessing the risks of the use of the substances. The enterprises should also provide adequate information to downstream users. (European Commission 2001a: 8)

In this initial statement, it becomes clear that it was the Commission's intention to force the chemical industry to guarantee the safety of its products. This position was re-iterated in the explanatory memorandum of the Commission's 2003 proposal:

> The allocation of responsibilities is inappropriate because the public authorities are responsible for the assessment instead of the enterprises that produce, import or use the substances. (European Commission 2003b: 7)

But, in the section on the general objectives of the planned regulation, one can observe a move to limit the scope of the burden of proof by connecting it with the concept of adequate control (see also above):

> The burden of proof is placed on the applicant to demonstrate that the risk from the use is adequately controlled or that the socio-economic benefits outweigh the risks. (European Commission 2003b: 1.7)

The final REACH regulation shows how the responsibility of the industry was further relaxed by simultaneously maintaining the burden of proof:

> The responsibility to assess the risks and hazards of substances should be given, in the first place, to the natural or legal persons that manufacture or import substances, but only when they do so in quantities exceeding a certain volume, to enable them to carry the associated burden. (Council 2006: Point 25).

*Conclusion*

This section has concentrated on the major tendencies of responsiveness of the REACH process towards the input of CSOs. By analysing the documents in more detail, it was striking to see that the discussion became more and more polarised. The same arguments were put forward again and again, and many indications suggest not only that the actors tended not to listen to each other, but also that they even tended not to pay attention to the results of the impact studies. In particular, the environmental NGOs made their claims visible, and their approach was based upon arguing and reason-giving.

However, the economic CSOs applied a mixed strategy: they engaged less openly in public discussions, and relied much more on their direct access to important official players in the process, placing significant trust in their lobbying capabilities. One part of the strategy of the business associations and conservative/liberal Members of the EP was to prolong the legislative process – with success. Due to this tactic, it was the newly elected EP that had to deal with REACH, which not only led to a further delay of one and a half years, but also to the watering-down of its measures, because the new EP was more conservative and business-friendly than the former.

Furthermore, the re-shuffle of competences in the EU institutions in favour of business concerns, which occurred in the course of the process, is mirrored in the responsiveness to different concerns. Economic CSOs profited from the procedural changes that strengthened business concerns both in the Commission and the Council. One can only speculate as to whether these changes were more important for shaping the directive's content than the argumentative input was. Environmental and consumer CSOs found themselves increasingly on the defensive, and some organisations seem to have given up on many issues, including, for example, the inclusion of lower tonnages for registration and the establishment of a hazard-based approach even in the registration and evaluation processes. Instead, they concentrated on key issues, such as on a quality criterion in the registration process, and, above all, on the authorisation scheme, which should, according to them, include the phasing out of chemicals of very high concern and their mandatory substitution.

Without this, they argued, the precautionary principle would not be respected at all and no substantial improvement in relation to the existing legislation would be achieved. Despite significant argumentative efforts for the precautionary principle, the opinions of the economic CSOs succeeded in avoiding a substantial application of this principle. Instead of a hazard-based approach to registration, a risk-based approach was introduced, and substitution was only made optional in the authorisation stage.

Altogether, the analysis reveals instances of responsiveness in the REACH legislation process. But it was also shown that the responsiveness was unequally distributed. At the beginning of the policy process, it was particular environmental CSOs that found responsiveness in the Commission. The majority of environmental civil society organisations expressed satisfaction with the early White Paper on Chemicals. Although economic CSOs welcomed the effort to establish a coherent chemical policy across the EU, they were disappointed by an imbalance between environmental and economic aspects. But this initial situation was reversed, as, for instance, the example of substitution clearly shows: the environmental CSOs' emphasis on this principle was strongly reflected in the White Paper, but it was significantly weakened in the 2003 proposal and in the final regulation. One can thus concede that responsiveness changed from an initial bias towards environmental CSOs, to a bias in favour of economic CSOs. The data suggest that short-term arguments are stronger than future-oriented arguments which, by nature, possess a higher degree of uncertainty.

## Notes

1 See Article 67 EC and the Protocol and Declaration on this article (Treaty of Nice) which required unanimous voting in the Council, mere consultation with the EP, and a shared right to policy initiation between the Commission and the Council (Alegre *et al.* 2005).
2 See http://www.europarl.europa.eu/summits/tam_en.htm#c (accessed 19 February 2010).
3 This was also the message of the interviewed CSOs.
4 One can observe this pattern also in European social policy, for instance. The case of the founding of the Social Platform is another example (see above).
5 See https://webgate.ec.europa.eu/transparency/regrin/consultation/search.do#search Result.
6 See http://www.statewatch.org/semdoc/ (accessed 19 February 2010).
7 The Green 10; Concord; the Social Platform.
8 See also e-mail communication with CCME (7 July 2005).
9 Interview at the German Permanent Representation.
10 See http://www.migpolgroup.org/projects_detail.php?id=43 (accessed 16 March 2010).
11 Council (2003).
12 It says there: 'No one shall be subjected to arbitrary interference with his privacy, family, home or correspondence, nor to attacks upon his honour and reputation. Everyone has the right to the protection of the law against such interference or attacks.'
13 '(1) Everyone has the right to respect for his private and family life, his home and his correspondence. (2) There shall be no interference by a public authority with the exercise of this right except such as is in accordance with the law and is necessary in a democratic society in the interests of national security, public safety or the economic well-being of the country, for the prevention of disorder or crime, for the protection of health or morals, or for the protection of the rights and freedoms of others.'
14 The EU's population growth depends largely on immigration, given a percentage increase of only 0.6 persons due to natural increase, but 3.6 persons because of net migration in 2006. It is since 1989 that net migration is the main source of the population increase in the EU (Niessen and Schibel 2005). For sources of the different data, see figures and publications available at:

http://epp.eurostat.ec.europa.eu/portal/page/portal/eurostat/home (accessed 22 February 2010).

15 I will not go into the directive in more detail, because its main issues will be covered subsequently by the discussion of the content analysis (for detailed legal analyses, see Guild 2004, Chapter 6; Oostrom-Staples 2007).

16 DG JHA has been renamed DG Freedom, Security and Justice.

17 Interview in the German Permanent Representation, June 2005.

18 The court argued that the provisions might, indeed, prove to be potentially problematical from a standpoint of fundamental rights. However, since the directive asks the Member States to act in respect of the international human rights conventions and jurisdiction, and since it does not stipulate the concrete implementation into national law, the directive itself was found not to counter human rights provisions. Although the Court dismissed the appeal, the ruling might nevertheless prove important. It is the first case in which the EP asked for the annulment of a directive for reasons of fundamental rights. The Court made explicit reference to the fundamental rights provisions of international law and to the European Charter of Fundamental Rights, making the latter a source of its jurisdiction despite the Charter's non-binding nature. With this decision, a development occurred in which the ECJ has increasingly expanded its traditional approach of referring to economic fundamental rights and to the constitutional provisions of the Member States; now, the ECJ found that it has the competence directly 'to decide whether a provision of a Community act respected fundamental rights' (European Court of Justice 2003a: 8), referring to the pan-European Human Rights court in Strasbourg, but not simply adopting its rulings. Thus, with the EP going to the Court, and with the way the ECJ dealt with this case, we might have witnessed the beginning of a new dynamic of fundamental rights protection in Europe, with EU institutions now claiming competencies for urging the community legislation and the Member States to respect fundamental rights.

19 Note that, in particular, papers written by Christian organisations, such as the CCME, were partly signed by more than the authorising organisations. Therefore, the number of CSOs represented by these documents is actually higher than 14.

20 As I underlined in the methods section of Chapter 4, this research approach cannot identify causal effects, but instead relies on the plausibilisation of potential associations in the data.

21 I make extensive use of direct quotations from the analysed documents. These quotations are used if and when the expressed position is typical for the totality of documents. The identification of typical quotations was fairly straightforward because the CSOs, albeit with different emphasis on certain points, usually shared the understanding of key points. In the REACH case, however, I will show that, although there existed two opposing camps of CSOs, it was nonetheless possible to identify typical arguments within each camp, respectively.

22 See, in particular, Council (1968b) on the Freedom of Movement of Workers and, amending the old directive and summarising dispersed rules for EU citizens, and Council and European Parliament (2004) on the Right of Citizens of the Union and their Family Members to move and reside freely within the Territory of the Member States.

23 The immigration prevention effects of integration requirements are, for instance, visible in Germany. As the quality newspaper *Frankfurter Rundschau* reports (16 February 2008), the numbers of married partners that received permission to immigrate to Germany in order to be re-united with their partners decreased by about 60% in 2007, after pre-migration language tests were made obligatory.

24 The draft proposals of the EU are more than just the simple new articles. Instead, the proposals consist of a general introduction and comments on the changes of each

article. Thus, they are fairly transparent and, to some extent, reasonably argued documents. However, the final document lacks this justificatory moment.

25  See also Bell (2004) on the problems for the new Member States in the area of environmental policy and the potential impact, with a particular focus on the challenges posed by the new European arena to the local environmental civil society organisations. For the latter aspect and the standing of Eastern European CSOs in Brussels, see also Hallstrom (2004).

26  In March 2000, the European Council pronounced the aim to becoming 'the most dynamic and competitive knowledge-based economy in the world capable of sustainable economic growth with more and better jobs and greater social cohesion, and respect for the environment by 2010'. See the Presidency Conclusions at: http://www.consilium.europa.eu/ueDocs/cms_Data/docs/pressData/en/ec/00100–r1.en0.htm (accessed 19 February 2010).

27  REACH is predominantly discussed as belonging to the environmental policy area. However, it is clear that it also severely affects industrial policies, policies for health and safety in the workplace, and consumer policies. In the subsequent analysis, I also considered the CSOs involved in these areas.

28  Please recall the broad definition of CSOs put forward in this study, which recognises business interests as legitimate concerns of civil society. Thus, it encompasses business associations as long as they themselves do not engage in profit-making businesses.

29  These data stem from summer 2006.

30  See https://webgate.ec.europa.eu/transparency/regrin/consultation/search.do#searchResult (accessed 19 March 2010).

31  Many members of the Green 10 receive Commission funding to secure their operations.

32  See http://ec.europa.eu/environment/life/index.htm (accessed 19 February 2010).

33  Principle 10 of the Rio Declaration on Environment and Development says: 'Environmental issues are best handled with the participation of all concerned citizens, at the relevant level. At the national level, each individual shall have appropriate access to information concerning the environment that is held by public authorities, including information on hazardous materials and activities in their communities, and the opportunity to participate in decision-making processes. States shall facilitate and encourage public awareness and participation by making information widely available. Effective access to judicial and administrative proceedings, including redress and remedy, shall be provided'; see http://www.un.org/documents/ga/conf151/aconf15126–1annex1.htm (accessed 19 February 2010).

34  UNECE is one of the five regional economic commissions of the UN. It was founded in 1947 by the UN Economic and Social Committee, which aimed at fostering the economic co-operation of its Member States. Today, 56 states are members in UNECE, all European states (including Turkey and Israel), all non-European former Soviet states, and the USA and Canada.

35  See http://www.unece.org/env/pp/ (accessed 19 February 2010).

36  For the transnational character of the administrative law of the Århus Convention and the problems of the interlegality of international, European and national law, see, in particular, Fischer-Lescano (2008).

37  Article 2(c) of the regulation says: 'Community institution or body means any public institution, body, office or agency established by, or on the basis of, the Treaty …'.

38  Article 9(2) says that 'Community institutions and bodies shall identify the public affected or likely to be affected by, or having an interest in, a plan or programme of the type referred to in paragraph 1, taking into account the objectives of this Regulation'.

39   This dispute is, inter alia, documented in a letter of the Green 10 of January 13 to the members of the EP before its second reading on the regulation.

40   Initially, REACH consists of two regulations that together establish the new chemicals regime, one focusing on the core of REACH, the other on the establishment of a European Chemicals Agency. The final regulation combines these two documents (Council and European Parliament 2006a).

41   According to the Commission, 'existing substances amount to more than 99% of the total volume of all substances on the market, and are not subject to the same testing requirements'. See the preamble of the European Commission (2003b), that is to establish a European Chemicals Agency and amending Council and European Parliament (1999) and Regulation (EC) COM (2003) 644 final as the 'new' substances. However, numbers vary in documents, which show the insufficient data available.

42   During the Italian Presidency (in the latter half of 2003), and – according to interviews – apparently not debated beforehand by Prime Minister Berlusconi, the Competitiveness Council became responsible for REACH, instead of the Environmental Council. However, Germany and Denmark decided to send their Environmental Ministers to Council meetings on REACH. Moreover, within the other European institutions, responsibility for REACH was contested. In the Commission, DG Environment was originally responsible, and produced the White Paper in 2001, although it also shares responsibility with DG Enterprise and Industry. Moreover, after a fierce battle in the EP, the Environmental Committee remained the leading committee, while the other committees, such as the Competitiveness Committee, received the right to bring their own amendments to the plenary sessions. For a useful description of the early stages of the REACH process, see Pesendorfer (2006) and Hey *et al.* (2006).

43   See http://panda.org/detox (accessed 22 February 2010).

44   The precautionary principle is a central element of modern risk-management. It acknowledges that natural-scientific experiments are also based upon data gaps, decisions to weigh different variables, etc., thus, that risk-assessment based upon scientific information is always incomplete and based upon the then scientific state of the art. As was the case with the Århus Convention, the introduction of the precautionary principle into environmental policy also had a global source. The Rio Declaration, issued at the United Nations Conference on Environment and Development (Rio de Janeiro, 3 to 14 June 1992), emphasised in its Principle 15 that: '[i]n order to protect the environment, the precautionary approach shall be widely applied by States according to their capabilities. Where there are threats of serious or irreversible damage, lack of full scientific certainty shall not be used as a reason for postponing cost-effective measures to prevent environmental degradation' (see www.unep.org/Documents.Multilingual/Default.asp?DocumentID=78&ArticleID =1163, accessed 19 February 2010). The European Commission published a Communication from the Commission on the precautionary principle (European Commission 2000c), specifying the application of this principle in the EU. It spelled out that the application of the precautionary principle pre-supposes the 'identification of potentially negative effects resulting from a phenomenon, product or process; [and] a scientific evaluation of the risk which because of the insufficiency of the data, their inconclusive or imprecise nature, makes it impossible to determine with sufficient certainty the risk in question' (p. 15) and that the principles of risk management have to be applied, namely, proportionality, non-discrimination, consistency, examination of the benefits and costs of action or lack of action and examination of scientific developments.

45   The industry's risk-based approach implies a tiered approach to registration and risk

assessment. This means that there are different stages of assessment intensity according to the risk of the chemical – and not according to the substance's intrinsic hazards or the volume of yearly production (volume-based approach) – CEFIC argues that this minimises animal testing (it will do so) because it would make the tests of non-risky substances superfluous. However, environmental and consumer CSOs have consistently asked how one knows the risks of substances before comprehensive testing. A hazard-based approach would be more appropriate to the precautionary principle.

46    The European Chemicals Agency started working on 1 June 2007 in Helsinki. See http://echa.europa.eu/ (accessed 22 February 2010).

47    In fact, this would exceed my competencies: as a political scientist, I am not in the position to judge, let us say, the pros and cons of certain test methods over others. Nor can I myself conduct an impact assessment study about, for instance, the cost-burden of REACH for downstream users. For these technical issues, I simply have to rely on the judgements of the experts that authored the different analysed documents as well as on my conducted interviews.

48    One can assume, and some interviews support this hunch, that environmental CSOs need to make greater argumentative efforts in order to be heard against a mainstream that is economically dominated, particularly in the context of the Lisbon Strategy's focus on competitiveness.

49    See http://ec.europa.eu/dgs/jrc/index.cfm (accessed 19 February 2010).

50    This interviewee revealed interesting insider information about the network connections of the chemical industry with certain MEPs and it could convincingly be shown how these connections delayed REACH and led to a trimming down of its scope.

51    Such principles have some (at least to me) intuitive appeal, although their subsequent application is difficult: upon which basis should policy-making take place – on an intuitive basis or a rational basis? Scientific knowledge, which is allegedly rational, is questioned with regard to its appropriateness to provide a stable basis for policy-making; at least if used as the main basis for decisions, because scientific expertise is more ambiguous than perhaps wished for by policy-makers. For instance, the focus on certainly necessary impact assessments in the REACH process did not prevent political decisions, which, at the end of the day, are necessarily also influenced by the values of the decision-takers. Scientific objectivity is a myth and policy-making procedures need to accommodate this.

# PART III

Democratising participatory governance in the European Union – the institutional perspective

# Introduction

Having specified the instrumental and normative roles of participation in democratic theory in general, and the potential of collective actors to contribute to the democratisation of policy-making processes through participation in particular (Part I), and having, furthermore, portrayed the formal participatory regime of the EU as well as assessed its responsiveness to participatory practices in selected policy processes (Part II), this last part of the book draws together the conceptual reflections and the empirical insights gained in the previous chapters.

It represents the third element of the triad of normative reflections, empirical analysis and institutional considerations, as unfolded in the introductory chapter. It formulates answers to the guiding research question introduced at the very beginning, namely, whether the participation of non-governmental collective actors brings about democratising effects on policy-making processes in the EU, and aims to give empirically founded and normatively informed proposals for feasible institutional improvements.

In a first step, the empirical insights will be put together in order to reflect upon the results in the light of the normative conditions spelled out earlier. In doing so, I will identify the democratic pathologies of the existing participatory regime of the EU. This diagnosis is then taken up in order to conceptualise a model of deliberative participation and to propose its institutionalisation in a regulated model of participatory governance. In the concluding remarks, I will extend the perspective beyond the immediate scope of this study, and reflect upon some of the wider implications of my findings for the future of democracy at large in a globalising context.

# 6

# Deliberative participation in EU policy-making

## Making sense of participatory governance in the EU

The purpose of this section is to lay the grounds for the envisaged institutional reflections in the second part of this chapter. Consequently, it characterises the participatory regime of the EU in order to identify its strengths and weaknesses in making use of the democratising potential of the participation of civil society organisations. For this, I will first summarise the main findings of the two previous empirical chapters in order to illustrate the democratic deficiencies of the existing system.

### The contours of the EU's participatory regime

In line with the democratic theory considerations of Chapter 2, one can distinguish three ideal-type models of participation. These models differ in their instrumental or normative understanding of participation and in their respective regulative logic. The first model purports the instrumental understanding of participation, and relies on a logic of voluntarism and *laissez-faire*. Following this logic, participatory activities are conceptualised as taking place on a market-place of competing, aggregated interests in which public institutions select participants according to their own needs for expertise and societal allies. In contrast, the third model follows the normative understanding of participation, relying on a rights-based logic. Regulated participation is deemed necessary here in order to foster the equality of interests on the market-place and to encourage public institutions to offer participatory avenues to the existing variety of voices.

In between these antagonistic models, a *mixed model* exists, which attempts to combine these two understandings of participation. It tries to organise the interests of the market-place better, structuring it in a functional logic according to policy segments. Accordingly, each policy area should deal with a circumscribed set of participants, which are not only instrumental to the decision-makers, but also represent the spectrum of voices within this specific area. In line with its more modest normative aspirations, the model's regulative logic does not follow a strong rights-based approach, but, instead, draws upon softer forms of governance arrangements alongside such means as codes of conduct, action plans or broad initiatives, as well as the self-organisation of associations.

Table 6.1 Contours of the EU's participatory regime

|  |  | Understanding of participation | Regulative logic |
|---|---|---|---|
| | Transparency | Fairly normative | Rule-based |
| Procedural dimension | Access | Instrumental with normative rhetoric | Soft governance |
| | Inclusion | Predominantly instrumental | Predominantly *laissez-faire* |
| Content dimension | REACH | | Family re-unification |
| | Responsiveness | Observable (but biased) | Not observable |

With these ideal-type models in mind, one can summarise the findings of the empirical chapters in Table 6.1. The table shows that the results of the empirical analysis resist an easy categorisation, but call for a nuanced approach, instead. The contours of the EU's participatory regime are far from following one of the ideal-type models coherently, but meander among pluralist, associative and deliberative characteristics. Each of the four evaluative conditions possesses different attributes, as I will elaborate below. Moreover, the analysis has made it clear that this picture is only a snapshot because the participatory regime is a moving target which is still in the making. Nevertheless, the analysis has revealed certain tendencies that allow for the identification of the current regime's democratic deficiencies and the specification of starting points for institutional enhancements.

*The procedural dimension*
The historical overview (Chapter 4) of the participatory rights and the subsequent detailed analysis of the third phase (*vis-à-vis* the three aspects of transparency, access and inclusion) revealed a remarkably dynamic, two-sided development. Initially, participatory rights were requested by, and designed for, only a limited scope of actors, namely, firms and enterprises. Over time, participatory provisions have been broadened in scope, expanding first to the social partners and today encompassing both special interest and public interest organisations.

However, this expansion in scope has been paralleled by decreasing regulative breadth. While firms have gained hard participatory rights in instances in which they are directly concerned, the social dialogue is organised in a mixture of clear rules with a treaty-base and several accompanying unconditional sectoral dialogue processes. To date, the system of participation for civil society organisations remains encased in soft and lofty language, full of normative exuberance but with little substantial provisions. In addition, the more actors have, at least potentially, gained access to EU policy-making processes, the less explicit the rules for participation have become – so that, at the end of the day, it is hard to distinguish empirically between participation and lobbying. The European Transparency Initiative has invigorated this fuzziness and the new Lobby Register pushes the participation language backwards, suggesting that the high tide of the participatory democracy talk might be over.

The examination of the most recent phase of the EU's formal participatory provisions, in the procedural dimension, has confirmed the evolving of this duality of widening actors' scope and shrinking regulatory rigour, but it has also added elements to the overall picture that are important from a democratic theory perspective. Most importantly, the analysis shows that the current participatory regime in the EU is not a coherent set of rules, but, on the contrary, that it is composed of fairly independent sub-regimes which follow different regulative logics which purport different understandings of participation.

It is, above all, the aspect of transparency that has undergone the most substantial development towards a coherent transparency regime and towards being conducive to the democratisation of the EU's policy processes. In the early 1990s, reacting to a ruling of the ECJ as well as to calls for the improvement of democratic legitimacy, the three main European institutions started to implement individual information strategies which were eventually pooled into a first set of common rules in Regulation 1049/2001. What is particularly important here is that the multi-level reality of EU policy processes has, to some extent, been respected by extending the scope of the regulation to the relevant documents of the Member States.

However, the ongoing discussions in the context of the European Transparency Initiative about a revision of this regulation reveal that considerable limits to coherence still remain in the transparency regime. Consequently, it is still the responsibility of each individual institution to implement the transparency rules so that discretionary practices no longer result in unequal access to information. Such effects could possibly be mitigated by the establishment of a single access point of transparency. So, evidently, the dominant regulative logic of the transparency regime is rule-based, and the understanding of participation is increasingly influenced by considerations of democracy. However, there is no coherent plan to bring the transparency regime consistently in line with democratic requirements.

With regard to access and inclusion, the existing rules and practices are only loosely coupled, if at all – and thus one can hardly speak of regimes. The findings of the historical overview concerning the duality of the expansion in the scope of actors, on the one hand, and decreasing binding force of rules, on the other, have shown that inclusion was widened but the rules of access had been softened, particularly for the more recent types of actor. The recently introduced access provisions for CSOs mainly focus on e-governance mechanisms, such as online consultations and online databases, and thus complement more traditional forms of consultations, such as public hearings and conferences. But overall, there remains a huge gap between these findings and the intensive rhetoric on access, participation and democracy, i.e. between the reality of instrumental participation and the discussion on normative participation.

The sketchy landscape of participatory access mechanisms and provisions provides evidence of a regulative logic which is based upon mainly soft governance mechanisms. A similar situation presents itself with regard to inclusion, as only in a few selected policy areas, such as social policy, are some explicit efforts made to include a variety of CSOs into the policy processes actively. The overall picture is dominated by a *laissez-faire* approach and an instrumental understanding of participation, in which only the CSOs that promised helpful expertise for the respective public institution were actively included.

*The content dimension*
The analysis of the content dimension, with its focus on responsiveness, by and large confirms the above picture of the rather indistinct shape of the formal participatory regime in the EU. There is no coherent approach among the EU institutions about how to organise their responsiveness to civil society concerns jointly. Despite the fact that both policy areas are, in principle, subject to the same formal rules, the case studies show a similarity in its general pattern, but could disclose important differences in the practice of participation between the two examined policy fields. In the early stages of the policy processes, the European Commission tried to act inclusively by inviting stakeholders to discussions on the prospective legislation. However, as soon as the official legislative process between the EU institutions started, the cases began to deviate from each other. These differences mirror the criteria for the initial case selection.

In legal migration policy, where the inter-governmental rules of unanimity prevailed, Member States showed no willingness to listen to civil society. The moment the Council entered the stage, it dominated the process and the efforts of CSOs to make themselves heard remained peripheral to the process. The policy of secrecy that has always dominated migration questions was able to prevail because migration issues remain within the scope of unanimity rules. In the REACH case, too, it was the Council, in the shape of its Working Group on Chemicals, which led the final negotiating of the legislative drafts. However, under the co-decision procedure, the Council could not shut the doors completely. Consequently, the EP's role was more important and provided a greater opportunity for CSOs to be heard. One reason for this is that the Members of Parliament are far less equipped with expertise than the Council, because they do not have huge bureaucracies at their disposal and thus have greater need for external expertise.

In addition to these institutional influences, policy field specific characteristics also affected the participation of CSOs. For the migration case, the data provide strong grounds to suggest that the securitisation of migration policies has increased since the attacks of 11 September 2001, overshadowing the possible needs for economic migration (beyond high-skilled labour) and human rights concerns. Apparently, this development has shifted the balance of power even more to the disadvantage of most CSO priority issues, which are pre-dominantly led by human rights concerns, rather than by economic considerations.

In contrast to migration, environmental policy is an established policy area in the EU's supranational First Pillar and the general political will for its integration is undisputed. However, the current dominance of economic perspectives in the EU again favours the already dominant economic voices to the disadvantage of other concerns. Yet in contrast with the migration case, where the shift away from human rights concerns apparently contributed to diminishing the possibility for CSOs to be heard, the CSOs in the REACH process were better able to accommodate the frame of economic dominance. Arguably, the greater divergence among CSO concerns facilitated overall coping. This diversity among CSOs in the REACH process is also reflected in the different strategies to obtain access to the policy process. Economic CSOs apply both public and more secretive strategies, while human rights, environmental and consumer CSOs tend to rely more on argumentative efforts and to strive for publicity.

*Conclusion*

The results generally suggest that primarily the relatively restricted number of well-organised CSOs have benefited from the partial opening-up of policy processes. Put differently, European policy-making processes *do* rely on instrumental participation, but make only limited use of the normative potential of CSOs. In general, the EU's participatory regime is interested in the participatory objective of stability, rather than democratisation, as was spelled out above (Table 6.1).

However, deviating from this general statement, the area of environmental policy suggests that hard law policy processes have not been totally unaffected by the lively discourse on CSO participation in recent years. The means of e-governance which are in use contribute to a partial de-territorialisation of consultation and participation, without, however, having (to date) the ability to balance the disadvantages of silent concerns, such as environmental issues *vis-à-vis* economic interests. On-line consultations, it becomes evident, are not an adequate substitute for active efforts to support the equal inclusion of weaker concerns.

The EU's participatory regime approaches a shape that McCormick calls

'*Sektoralstaat*' (McCormick 2007, Chapter 6), in which bureaucrats, experts and those most affected by a concrete decision consult each other. But these 'deliberations in the microspheres of transnational policymaking' (*ibid.*: 235) are fairly unconnected to the general public sphere, so that their democratic characters have to be further specified.

All in all, the development of a participatory infrastructure has not kept up with the pace of the participation discourse. Currently, the participation of CSOs in the EU's policy-making processes depends on three major factors: first, the legal basis of the issue area in question, and thus the respective involvement of the EU institutions (the role of the Commission is stronger in First Pillar issues than in Second or Third Pillar issues, for instance); second, the coincidence of CSOs meeting interested civil servants in either the Commission and/or in the national executives; and third, the general *volonté politique* of the Member States to integrate the respective policy area and to abandon their tradition of secrecy.

The findings are in line with the previous empirical results that the European Commission, in particular, has shown some 'procedural ambition ... to achieve a more stable (though possibly informal) set of policy actor relationships' (Mazey and Richardson 2005). Civil society policy dialogue, though, should not just be maintained within the European Commission. It would be equally important to extend this dialogue to the other European institutions. However, there is still no sign of an outspoken formal procedural framework that would establish a 'right to be heard' (Bignami 2003: 3) in which truly 'participation can be exercised which would entail a considerable expansion of existing *locus standi* rules both in terms of input into the process and control *ex post facto*' (Curtin 2003: 71), and which would replace the current largely discretionary system of grace and favour.

Consequently, European participatory governance is hard to distinguish from classical lobbying, whose political objective 'is not to change legislators' minds but to assist natural allies in achieving their own, coincident objectives' (Hall and Deardorff 2006: 69). It remains to be seen whether the renewed debates in the context of the European Transparency Initiative on revised lobbying regulation will make a significant difference. This recent initiative does, at least, bear the risk that attention will shift from the necessity of public institutions to increase their democratic legitimacy, to civil society organisations being compelled to prove their representativeness and democratic character.

In the light of these results, one must doubt whether practicable civil society participation is truly the goal of the technocrats in the European Commission, and of the executive in the Council and in many Member States, despite the many rhetorical declarations. It could be shown that expertise, above all, serves as a gate-opener for CSOs – a finding which finds support in previous research on EU lobbying. Thus, we can, at best, observe expertocratic participation, although to what extent this helps democratising EU policy-making remains rather questionable.

### The democratic deficiencies in the existing participatory regime

The previous synopsis of the key results of the empirical analysis has demonstrated that the existing participatory regime of the EU should not be pictured as an integrated regime, but rather as an inconsistent system of different rules and often informal practices which resembles, as was shown, the features of a 'Sektoralstaat' (McCormick 2007, Chapter 6).

This result suggests that there are limits to the democratic character of the currently observable participatory practices. It is now necessary to substantiate these findings in order to highlight to what extent participatory governance in the EU predominantly serves instrumental purposes and stabilises the existing policy-making structures, whether it directly adds to their democratisation, or whether it fails to provide for democratic participation and thus even weakens their (potential) democratic character. As I will demonstrate in this section, it is the last alternative which dominates participatory governance practices in the EU. I will show that the current regime is democratically deficient both from the instrumental *and* from the normative perspective, hereby, once more, concentrating on the four democratic standards.

For an instrumental model of participation to be democratically neutral, the existence of some provisions of transparency and access is necessary, in so far as they enable all the divergent groups to participate and thus to influence the political institutions. Such provisions are important because they render the interest of the market-place aggregation functional along the lines developed by classical American pluralism. This approach emphasises that a fair and equal competition between different groups – as well as access to the policy processes – must be given (for details, see Chapter 2). If one takes this as a proximate description of the instrumental model of democratic participation, one has to concede that the EU's participatory regime partly fails to deliver democratic instrumental participation.

On the positive side, fairly advanced transparency provisions exist, which enable all interested actors to gain access to much of the relevant information. Furthermore, in particular, the European Commission's rejection of strong regulation stems from the wish to prevent hurdles that could hinder the activities of many different associative actors from being erected. In addition, an unregulated market of interests diminishes one of the most important perils of participation, namely, the danger of co-optation. Apparently, the less participatory practices are subject to concrete conditions, the more freely interest groups can act according to their own preferences. The EU *does* leave enough space for political contestation in order for CSOs to avoid blatant co-optation (see, similarly, Hunold 2005: 326) as can be demonstrated in the case of REACH.

On the negative side, though, the costs of this *laissez-faire* attitude in terms of access partially outweigh these benefits, above all, with regard to political equality. The observable unregulated approach to participation coincides with the growing importance of governance mechanisms which help to open up the institutional paths of policy-making. One could argue that one can observe a de-formalisation of policy-making, aggravated by informal participatory structures that are not contained by rules. One result of *laissez-faire* participation is an inclusion of voices by grace and favour, i.e. one that depends on the discretion of individual persons, and consequently violates the principle of equality of access.

In addition, the principle of self-determination is endangered by this practice, because informality and discretion support an asymmetrical relationship between the participant and the receiving institution: the former has either to beg for access or be able to offer specific goods, above all, expertise. Such practices potentially cause civil society participants to end up as 'an instrument of co-optation' (Kaufman 1969b: 211). These problems go together with a transparency regime that does not directly address the accountability of the policy processes, but, instead, fosters a tendency for informal authority in the EU. The availability of information is one thing, but the ability to track the succession and the sources of the different positions throughout a policy process is another, and would be beneficial for the accountability of the process.

Besides transparency and access, a normative model of democratic participation, in which participation contributes to the democratisation of policy-making, requires inclusion and equal responsiveness. Inclusiveness, however, cannot be achieved in informal, non-transparent and discretionary structures which do not seek to strive for equal pluralism, but, to the contrary, favour elitism and technocracy. To some extent, this non-conditional access regime is not an impediment to equal pluralism; again, however, it is questionable whether *laissez-faire* has not (perhaps unintended) asymmetrical tendencies, in that the stronger CSOs are better able to participate. The instances of responsiveness which were detectable by means of the content analysis were considerably biased towards certain voices.

This finding would be less problematical if the adoption of certain, and thus the rejection of other, arguments was openly justified by the receiving EU institutions. However, the European Commission did not systematically summarise the most frequent of the arguments put forward in the REACH online consultation (or the reactions to the Green Paper on the ETI); it only issued summaries that did not further justify or balance its reasons for adopting certain issues and not others. The findings of the responsiveness-analysis could not refute the expected outcome of bias. In addition to this, there are the very limited efforts by EU institutions to provide empowering mechanisms for weaker CSOs. Furthermore, instances such as the civil dialogue are confined to limited policy-areas and are predominantly aimed at the super-CSOs, i.e. at the highest networks which often have other European and/or national level networks as members.[1]

Altogether, it is striking that the existing EU participatory regime not only falls short of providing satisfying opportunities for democratic partici-pation in the normative understanding of participation, but also in the instrumental understanding of participation. This means that the EU's practices of participation and consultation might be instrumentally necessary for effective governance, but that they not only fail to make use of the democ-ratising potential of CSO participation, but even weaken the existing democratic character of its parliamentarian system.

The EU's participatory regime is dominated by an understanding of classical pluralist participation based upon *laissez-faire* and informality – *ergo* one can speak about classical lobbying dominating the practice of EU partici-patory governance beyond the rhetorical veil. The rhetoric obscures the EU's tendency to confuse 'die Öffentlichkeit ohnehin immer mit *public relations* [...] und bei *private consulting* ihr Heil gesucht und verloren [zu] haben' ('confuse *transparency* with *public relations* and take persistent refuge in private consultation') (Brunkhorst 2007: 15). Put differently, a sceptic's view about the future of democracy, in particular, Colin Crouch's rather polemical appraisal of consultative practices as the 'maximisation of minimal participa-tion' (Crouch 2004: 112) under the discursive umbrella of participation, practices which he perceives as being biased towards economic interests, corresponds fairly well with the current EU's participatory regime.

The resulting participatory practices are, hence, not sufficiently able, from a democratic theory perspective, to contain lobbying democratically by setting provisions in place to tackle the democratic perils of lobbying, as explicated in the critique on classical pluralism. What is needed, therefore, are mechanisms that tackle, in particular, these deficiencies of *laissez-faire*, or, to put it differently, practices that transform lobbying into democratic participation.

## Institutionalising deliberative participation as a contribution to a democratically governed Europe

The discussion above has particularly highlighted two deficiencies of the EU's participatory governance practices which must be contained if one seeks to transform the participation of civil society organisations into a productive means of democratising EU policy-making processes. The two deficiencies are, first, the *laissez-faire* and the often informal character of the participatory practices, and, second, the asymmetrical pattern of responsiveness. One could easily stop with this diagnosis and come to a conclusion about the exagger-ated normative promises that had been connected to the participation of civil society organisations in European policy-making. However, this would confuse the normative potential of these participatory activities with their insufficient implementation. The democratic benefit of civil society partici-pation is no automatism, but needs to be actively nurtured (Scholte 2002:

281) also by the selfsame institution that seeks to strengthen its very own democratic legitimacy.

Consequently, this section is dedicated to reflections on how to institutionalise the participation of civil society organisation better in order to make better use of its normative potential. I will develop the argument that a procedural framework of both the right *and* the duty to justify one's own position reciprocally in the light of the positions of the others should be institutionalised in order to mitigate both deficiencies of the EU's current participatory regime. This model would, if implemented, improve these practices, without claiming to solve all the democratic problems that the EU might have from different theoretical perspectives. Instead, it would be a theoretically founded partial solution to the main democratic problems of European participatory governance.

Building upon the insights of the theoretical discussion of Chapter 2, I will make the case for the establishment of a regulated model of deliberative participation that is capable of meeting the above-mentioned democratic challenges. Such a model would make use of the normative value of both deliberation and associative participation. After developing the productive guidance of the theories on democratic participation, I will introduce the concept of deliberative participation and reflect upon the role of law for a procedural strengthening of democracy. I will then move on to some more concrete proposals on how to institutionalise deliberative participation. I will propose a two-stage model of regulated deliberative participation, and show that the empirical findings have revealed some positive starting points for the realisation of this model. This exercise demonstrates that democratic theory entails practical relevance.

### Productive guidance of the theories on democratic participation

In Chapter 2, I discussed three contemporary democratic theories which are, albeit to different degrees, concerned with the participation of non-state collective actors (pluralism, associative democracy, and deliberative democracy). From there, I extracted four, shared, key democratic conditions as evaluative guidance for the empirical analysis. I will now ask the three approaches – without repeating the earlier theoretical discussion – to what extent they also offer productive guidance for an institutional enhancement of the EU's participatory regime; the aim is to tackle, in particular, the problems connected with *laissez-faire* and informality as well as those connected with asymmetrical responsiveness. The usage of the democratic theoretical approaches as practical guidance does not imply the claim that these approaches offer immediate and/or coherent proposals for institutional implementation (see, similarly, Wolf 2000: 214). Nevertheless, they do offer intuitions about what institutions should look like if they are to tackle and to mitigate the specific democratic deficiencies of the EU's participatory regime.

Classical American pluralism offers the least productive guidance for democratically improving the EU's participatory regime, although its basic assumptions could be transposed from a national to a postnational context. An important normative claim of pluralist theory is that interest groups compete with each other on a marketplace of interests, and that this competition, if left undistorted by regulation and state intervention, leads to equal representation of interests, thus strengthening political equality. This claim, evidently, only works provided that basic freedoms, such as the freedoms of speech and of association, are given. Now, there seems to be – in principle – no obstacle that would hinder the emergence of a trans-European 'pluralists' bazaar' (Gerstenberg 1997: 85), thereby possibly establishing the contours of a plural (democratic) society. In fact, the empirical findings, to some degree, sketch a European market of ideas which fails to generate equality, as the analysis of responsiveness, in particular, has shown.

The pluralist image of an equilibrium among the plurality of existing interest groups is no more plausible beyond the nation state than it was within the nation state. The findings illustrate the considerable diversity of groups and the significant asymmetries in their ability to access the policy process; thus, the problems of factionalism, of asymmetry and of the dominance of particular groups, which have been criticised at national level, are reproduced at supranational level. Nevertheless, what should be borne in mind for the institutional proposals is the pluralists' emphasis that the existence of interest groups is a vital ingredient for democratic political processes. According to the pluralists' claim, the interests of minorities are more capable of demanding responsiveness from the decision-takers by both using and strengthening the channels for voice, rather than by mere voting activities. At the very least, the institutional frame needs to illuminate the shadowy corners of the 'pluralists' bazaar'; at best, it is capable of enhancing political equality within unregulated interest representation and lobbying practices.

Irrespective of their differences, the approaches of associative democracy provide, in at least two respects, guidance for institutional innovation. First of all, both in Cohen and Rogers' (1992) and in Hirst's (1994, Chapter 2) conception, the role of law as a procedural framework for the participatory activities of secondary associations is emphasised. As was elaborated earlier, the associative democrats' call for the regulation of associational life by state action can, to some degree, be interpreted as a reaction to the pluralists' failure to achieve political equality. State action should provide a legal framework in order to establish equal rules and – particularly in the interpretation of Cohen and Rogers – to stimulate actively the emergence of the *encompassing associations* which are supposed to possess the capacity to integrate and to amplify the weaker concerns that would remain unheard on the pluralists' competitive marketplace. To some extent, the development of super-NGOs at EU level, together with the financial support of the European Commission, can be interpreted as cautious steps towards more encompassing, Europe-wide NGOs.

The second aspect is the emphasis on the value of associative participation itself. The encompassing associations are an attempt to come to terms with the reality of diversity, which purports the idea that, within the institutionalised environment of these associations, the plurality and asymmetry of concerns are contained, and the forces for societal self-governance are bundled. This should counter governmental elitist technocracy. Furthermore, the encompassing associations serve as condensed spaces in the public sphere, capable of better transporting societal concerns into the governmental realm. Thus, they can be interpreted as increasing inclusiveness by offering an agency dimension to societal concerns.

Deliberative democracy's particularly productive contribution in the present context is its conceptualisation of justification as a mechanism of democratic legitimacy (Cohen 1996: 99). This vision implies that the democratic burden of policy-making can be shifted, at least partially, on to de-personalised procedures of reciprocal justification both in the strong and the weak public sphere (see, again, Baynes 2002; and Fraser 1992). The justificatory procedure, which neither necessitates a territorial dimension, nor prescribes concrete institutional forms, possesses normative quality – so the basic claim goes – if it is based upon fair, public and reciprocal communication processes. Justification is more than a simple exchange of (diverging) standpoints; instead, it is 'a matter of offering reasons for alternatives' (Cohen and Rogers 2003: 241). With regard to political equality, the idea is that it is the power of the arguments, rather than the material power, which should ultimately count. This epistemic conception of achieving democratic legitimacy through reciprocal justificatory processes makes it particularly adaptable to the complexity of a postnational context. It rationalises the political process by stressing the possibility of learning effects, which, in turn, entails the reversibility of political decisions.

Although deliberative democracy, as an ideal theory, does not make concrete institutional proposals, its institutional implementation requires a framework based upon formal rules. Particularly in the Habermasian tradition of deliberative democracy, an inherent relationship between law and democracy is developed, as it is suggested that rules contain the capacity both to enhance and to enforce democratic practices (see, amongst others, Gerstenberg 1997, Part II; Habermas 1992, Chapter III; 1995). Clear rules seem necessary to institutionalise rights for participation in inclusionary communicative processes.

This brief reminder of the three basic theories illustrates the different potentials for productively guiding institutional innovation. Pluralism offers the least productive guidance, because the basic freedoms which are necessary for both the emergence and the existence of a pluralist landscape can be taken for granted throughout the EU. The contours of the current EU participatory regime already fit quite well with a pluralist understanding of interest group participation, including the qualifications with regard to political equality.

Thus, with my institutional intention in mind, it seems most promising to consider the associative and deliberative offers for productive guidance.

The productive contribution for the institutional innovation of associative democracy lies, in particular, in the emphasis on the necessity of appropriate regulation in order to empower and structure the participation of associations. The most productive element of deliberative democracy is the conceptual elaboration of the normative quality of reciprocal justification and reason-giving as a constitutive component of democratic policy-making processes. In the following, I will develop a concept of deliberative participation, which integrates these different productive elements. However, it must be admitted that this integrative approach may be attacked by theoretical purists, and it will certainly not do full justice to both the richness and the differences of the respective theories. However, I believe that both associative and deliberative democracy have enough ground in common – above all, the emphasis on non-aggregative forms of democratic legitimacy – to be compatible with each other, at least, if the final interest is to find stimuli for institutional innovation, rather than the development of a new theory of democracy.

### Conceptualising regulated deliberative participation

The theories of the democratic participation of collective actors suggest three elements – associative participation, reciprocal justification, and a regulative frame – that productively guide the subsequent proposal of a participatory model which would, in itself, be more democratic and, in being so, thereby contribute to the democratisation of the EU policy-making processes. I argue now that these elements can, and, indeed, should, be integrated into a model of regulated deliberative participation. The particular challenge for deliberative participation is to propose suitable institutions that avoid 'reproduzieren ... den Effekt strukturell bedingter Sprachlosigkeit' (reproducing ... the effect of structurally induced voicelessness') (Gerstenberg 1997: 72f). It has to show that a procedural combination of associative participation with justificatory requirements mitigates the problems of the political (in-)equality of the existing EU's participatory regimes.

I will discuss this challenge by turning to the three productive elements, showing that each of them adds a specific normative and practical contribution, while an independent institutionalisation would lack normative significance, but that the integration of them within the concept of deliberative participation renders them fully functional. The circular model of deliberative participation, as pictured in Figure 6.1 below, illustrates that the strengths of associative participation and justification mutually re-inforce each other by tackling the weaknesses of the other.

The inclusion of associative participation into the model of deliberative participation follows the conviction that participation is an essential part of any model of democracy (see Part I and Buchstein and Jörke 2003: 486ff).

Associative participation offers an agency structure for the articulation of societal concerns to the policy-making agenda, particularly in political sites above the nation state. Furthermore, the associationalists' emphasis on the subsidiarity and multi-level structures of public policy-making could be easily accommodated in the European context.

However, associative participation has some significant weaknesses that make it clear why a democratic participatory regime cannot rely on it predominantly. Above all, associative participation is not capable of overcoming the asymmetrical problems of pluralism. The more encompassing that European super-CSOs become, and the more they are included in corporatist-like structures, the more their own requirement for (democratic) legitimacy will grow (Beisheim 2001), thereby duplicating the legitimacy problems of international organisations.

Furthermore, in the multi-level and multi-polar structure of the EU, the question of where, and at which level, the creation of these encompassing associations should be based remains unanswered. It is doubtful whether such associations would, themselves, be able to do justice to the complexity and diversity of the different levels of the EU polity. Certainly, the inclusion of CSOs as diverse as possible, as agents of associative participation, does not offer a guarantee that equal respect for *all* the different viewpoints will be achieved. In fact, the empirical findings suggest caution against expectations that are too optimistic in this regard. An exclusively actor-centred conceptualisation of participation would fall short of inclusiveness, and thus of political equality, because of the evident structural problems and asymmetries of the variety of concerns.

Therefore, participation cannot rely on the normative value of associational participation alone, but should, instead, be combined with the deliberative democratic principle of mutual justification. If the public institutions are compelled to justify their positions and decisions in the light of the ideally inclusive arguments put forward by diverse CSOs, the unjustified unequal treatment of the different concerns becomes visible and can be publicly scandalised.[2]

The link of associative participation with justification has to be established by the introduction of legal rules. A legal framework systematically integrates and relates both elements to each other. In doing so, I try to take the productive element of deliberative democracy on board, which is its communicative core, without losing sight of my understanding of democracy as a participatory practice. In relating the justificatory moment of deliberative democracy to associative participation, I argue that the process would be more capable of coming to terms with the existing cultural and normative plurality without reproducing the structural inequalities. Instead, their existence would be made public.

Again, the role of law is crucial because of its inherent demand for symmetry and equality. The condition would be that all participants in a policy process would be required to make their case in the light of the arguments of the others, thereby opening 'a space of interpretation' (Benhabib 2007: 455) and contestation within (and outside) the process. The idea is that, through the introduction of reciprocal justificatory obligations, a process of 'democratic iteration' (Benhabib 2004, Chapter 5) would be initiated, which would condense 'the interplay between formal processes of law-making and informal processes of opinion- and will-formation' (Benhabib 2007: 456). Within the iterative communication processes, the power of the arguments would be strengthened at the cost of the asymmetrical material power of the participants.

The associative participatory moment increases the equal diversity of arguments through institutionalised avenues for the physical participation of the bearers of as many arguments as possible. The particular value of including associative participation into this model is that it offers a more applied approach to the deliberative democratic necessity of equal inclusiveness towards persons, themes and reasons (Gerstenberg 1997: 25), than the reliance on rather anonymous discourses in the public sphere does.[3] Associations are even more important as a (probably insufficient) substitute for an almost non-existent European public sphere.

This reconciliatory exercise within a procedural framework seems necessary if one wants to avoid 'deliberation without democracy' (Niesen 2006). This combination opens up spaces for containing the structural inequalities of actors and interests, without claiming that it would be feasible to avoid them totally. It strives for equality of arguments by establishing a reinforcing, iterative circle of inclusiveness between associative participation and justificatory requirements. The model's circular shape does not suggest a closure to non-included participants, but offers the constant possibility for new actors and arguments to enter the circle. It aims to offer an institutional response to the prominent claim of (Habermasian) deliberative democracy that a policy outcome may only become legitimate 'if all those possibly affected by it could consent to it after participating in rational discourses'

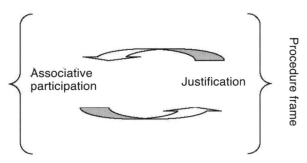

Figure 6.1 The circular model of deliberative participation

(Habermas 1995: 16). By emphasising both associative participation and justificatory requirements, the model aims to offer a practicable way of bringing this abstract principle closer to political reality. With its participatory moment, it increases the potential inclusiveness of actors and themes, and by accentuating the reciprocal justificatory moment, it seeks to enhance the rationality of the policy process.

The emphasis on reciprocal justification pre-supposes a high degree of personal and situational rationality, against which an objection of naivety and of impossibility can be made. It would be naive to believe that, in concrete social situations, something akin to an ideal speech situation would be possible, in which real-world asymmetries do not count (on this objection, see Cohen and Rogers 2003). Furthermore, even if one accepts that it would be possible to identify the best argument – and thus to achieve consensus – under real-world conditions, arguments are laden with diverse needs, preferences and value-backgrounds which make consensus hard to achieve, and make politics both necessary and possible in the first place. Both kinds of objections find support in the current functioning of the EU's participatory regime, as characterised above.

However, such objections tend to neglect the fact that deliberative democracy is an ideal theory. Its epistemic accentuation implies the fallibility of political decisions and therefore demands their potential reversibility; this, in turn, is a pure democratic demand. Furthermore, as was convincingly argued by Lafont (2006), the requirement for reciprocal justification – the author speaks of the condition of 'mutual justifiability' (Lafont 2006: 7) – does not imply unanimous consensus. Instead, it seeks those decisions that are agreeable to most of the participants.[4] A regulative framework that holds both elements together would seem to be necessary, in order to establish an institutional setting that both enables associative participation and instigates justification on a level playing-field. The essential purpose of this frame is the approximation towards an ideal of complete inclusion, as this is inherent to the demands for the symmetry of the structure of law.

Associative participation and reciprocal justification need a mechanism that relates both elements to each other. Deliberative participation proposes an institutional frame based upon a system of rights as the appropriate means for this integration. It suggests a procedural frame in order to empower and guarantee all the participants of a policy process the right and the duty to give and take reasons, and thus to institutionalise a discursive arrangement based upon rights. It is inclusive to a variety of actors and offers space for expressing contestation in a regulated manner. But why, one could object, should a procedural right and duty to justification for all the participants of a policy process be able to mitigate asymmetries which are based upon material inequalities? Inequality in both power and resources is inevitable in our complex world, and this inequality becomes politically problematical if it is deliberately used to the disadvantage of others. If one accepts this more narrow focus on political, rather than material, equality, the task would not be to overcome inequalities in material terms, but to find procedures in which these inequalities are not translated into political power. Hence, a procedural framework for the politics of non-domination and self-containment is required (see Offe 1989: 745).[5]

Non-domination intends to contain the abuse of power and thus serves, in a liberal tradition, the function of limiting authority. In order to be democratic, a positive element of constituting autonomy is also required. Non-domination, which is a concept that stresses the liberal emphasis of constraining public authority through law, needs to be coupled with entitlements to participate in the communicative processes of reciprocal justification, thereby underlining the role of law in constituting democratic public authority (Meisterhans 2007: 132ff). Deliberative participation seeks to realise this combination of controlling authority and enabling autonomy. Such a framework can be realised through the encouragement of all the participants of a policy process to engage in deliberative processes by obliging them to justify their arguments in the light of the arguments of the other participants.

If a procedural framework succeeds in establishing rules for reciprocal justification, one would have procedures that encourage self-containment and discourage domination because everyone would be obliged to contextualise their own arguments, i.e. not to disregard the existence of other positions or their specific reasons. Reciprocal justification thus provokes an obligation to 'die eigenen Gründe und die der anderen auf rationale und offen, faire Weise verstehen und bedenken' (understand and reflect on one's own reasons and on those of the others in a rational, open and fair manner) (Forst 2007: 254). This procedural justificatory conception of deliberative democracy neither necessarily leads to consensus, nor implies preference changes; on the contrary, it leaves space for agonistic moments and continuous contestation.[6] It procedurally secures that the arguments of the others do not restrict one's own ability to participate in argumentative and justificatory processes (Forst 2007: 254f) so that nobody's deliberative capability is restricted by procedural constraints.

Through a procedural approach that fosters this kind of fairness of deliberation by demanding self-containment and non-domination, a considerably higher degree of political equality could be achieved even without intervening directly in the material sources of inequality. However, I do not claim that all the problems of inequality can be accommodated by this framework. Different capabilities to express concerns still remain and would certainly influence the deliberative process. However, the model offers an opportunity structure for the equal participation of CSOs, since it partially adopts the shift of the normative burden away from concrete actors on to justificatory, i.e. communicative, processes. Thus, 'Überzeugung als Waffe der Schwachen' ('Persuasion as the weapon of the weak') (Deitelhoff 2006, Chapter 8.4.2) becomes potentially sharpened and made operational.

Furthermore, the legitimacy of civil society organisations to raise matters for disadvantaged groups or for *voiceless* concerns in participatory processes is increased, because the requirement of representativeness is loosened through the enhanced publicity of reflexive justification. Through the public deliberative interactions, the self-assigned representativeness of CSOs comes under public scrutiny as the potential aim of contestation.[7]

The participation of CSOs serves as the actor-basis for the communicative processes in the strong public sphere, even if deliberative participation fails to offer complete participatory equality. At the very least, deliberative participation strengthens 'the kind of equality necessary to force closed organizations to limit or justify the costs they impose on others' (Warren 2002: 697).

From a theoretical perspective, one particular difficulty of applying Forst's model of a right to justification in the context of this study is due to the fact that Forst elaborates a highly abstract conception of the right to justification as a basic human right at the level of the individual.[8] Is such a conception easily transferable to the level of collective actors? It is not my intention to suggest that civil society organisations or other collective actors could easily be treated as if they were unitary actors, and I do not want to claim that civil society organisations could, or should, be granted something akin to a basic associational right of reciprocal justification in every respect, either. Instead, I start from institutional intuitions of the theories and argue that it is possible to implement suitable mechanisms, through the instigation of law, in a concrete context of participatory governance; these mechanisms would then possess legal grounding. The establishment of a right and a duty to reciprocal justification within a model of deliberative participation would improve the normative quality of participatory practices.

Deliberative participation thus emphasises the importance of legal rules for enhancing democratic policy-making. The regulated model of deliberative participation can be understood as an attempt to stimulate a catch-up development of democratic policy-making in the EU. With a similar intention, Hitzel-Cassanges speaks about both 'provisory rights' and 'provisory institutions' (2006), so that the model of deliberative participation could be understood as attempt to propose a concrete vision for institutionalising such a double provisional arrangement.[9]

The particular democratic value of provisory deliberative participation is twofold: it empowers associative participation by granting equal access rights, and it provides the rules of the game for reciprocal justification. It thus opens the perspective for the approximation towards democratic ideals without claiming to be, in itself, already fully democratic. This model has to include a judicial component if the individual participants feel that they are structurally disadvantaged and/or if other participants persistently fail to realise their justificatory obligations. It proposes to institutionalise better the interface between political system and civil society by creating participatory forums of deliberation (Gerstenberg 1997: 126), because it would be normatively unsatisfactory simply to tolerate deliberative participatory elements without providing a regulated framework.

Overall, deliberative participation is a model that promises to improve incrementally the democratic quality of European policy-making in its multi-level context. The model would democratically enhance the micro-mechanics of the EU's participatory regime by a better linkage of the political institutions with CSOs, *via* the introduction of regulated, reciprocal justificatory mechanisms, without aiming to overcome the regime's character of a '*Sektoralstaat*'. The model's ultimate aim is to institutionally entangle argumentative and strategic reasoning with each other (see Habermas 1999: 285) in order to establish structures of 'responsive democracy' (Kuper 2004).

### Institutionalising regulated deliberative participation

The model of deliberative participation has to fulfil both a minimum and a maximum objective: the minimum objective is to propose an institutional setting that allows for some optimism that the EU's current participatory practice will be brought into line with the instrumental understanding of democratic participation. In the maximum objective, these institutions should even be capable of transforming the participatory practices towards democracy-enhancing practices. Thus, deliberative participation should, first, contribute to transform lobbying into instrumental democratic participation, and, second, open spaces for reciprocal justification. These two objectives, I argue, require a two-stage model of deliberative participation. In this section, I will sketch out the general principles of this institutionalisation and will then argue that the empirical findings show some concrete starting points for the realisation of such a project.

### The reformist stage one

The starting point for the first stage of deliberative participation is the existing participatory regime of the EU. Its aim is to prevent the abuse – by the current practice – of the aggregative forms of participation on purely instrumental grounds, void of considerations of equality, by tackling its *laissez-faire* approach and bringing light into the shadows of its informality. Hence, the key mechanisms of the reform strategy of regulated participation are to introduce a legal framework that fosters both the publicity and the formality of associative participation. It proposes improvements that remain within a liberal tradition in which the enhancement of equal opportunities *via* the allocation of rights and duties is seen as adequate for enhancing political equality.

The empirical analysis suggests that the informal character of the lobbying practices, irrespective of the few formal consultative mechanisms, obscures both the number and the intensity of the contacts between the public institutions and the private actors. The great differences among the civil society organisations, which are reflected in the grace and favour approach through which the public institutions offer (often informal) access to policy-makers, violates the principle of political equality. Thus, a legalised interest group system would seem to be necessary in order to counterbalance some aspects of the asymmetrical capabilities of different organisations and to stimulate the public institutions towards a more egalitarian approach. Such a legal framework would offer all the CSOs that wish to partake in a dialogue equal rights for participation. Moreover, it would also provide them with access rights to some judicial mechanisms in cases of neglect. This could, in a first step, become part of the Ombudsman's tasks, but, ultimately, access rights to the European Court of Justice would seem to be necessary.

The legal framework would, on the other hand, oblige the EU to establish these equal rights of participation for all civil society organisations. It would further compel the European institutions to be transparent about their formal and informal consultations and require the CS organisations to make all their lobbying activities public. It would ask the EU institutions to systematise their efforts in funding civil society organisations in order to come closer to the equal inclusion of all voices. Such an enhanced regulatory character of participatory governance would increase the transparency of classic interest representation, would cast light into the shadowy corners of lobbying, and would thus increase the overall accountability of European decision-making.

If implemented, such a framework would establish a coherent access and transparency regime for the participation of associations in EU policy-making processes. It would tackle the key problems that make the current practices partially democratically deficient, even when considered from the normatively more modest standpoint of instrumental democratic participation. This liberal reform strategy would certainly be an improvement on the current situation, but it would, nonetheless, fail to accommodate the problem of asymmetrical responsiveness. The thin proceduralism of this first stage needs to be complemented by thicker proceduralism in a second stage, namely, the obligation for reciprocal justification.

*The transformative stage two*
The second stage of this model goes beyond these rather managerial efforts in order to improve the administration of participation in the reformist stage. The aim would be to strengthen the democratic fabric of the policy-making processes by introducing the epistemic element of reciprocal justification as a complement to associative participation. Arguably, the discursive dimension of justification and reason-giving is apt to tackle more directly the inequalities that remain even if equal rights *are* assigned, thereby ultimately transforming instrumental practices of participation into normative participation, which is constitutive to the strengthening of democracy. What this stage would need to accomplish would be to support argumentative processes that were based upon reciprocity and publicity – beyond the first stage's guarantee of equal inclusion

and access. Thus, it would be necessary to stimulate 'Formen reflexive[r] Selbstkorrektur- und Einspruchsmöglichkeiten' ('elements of a reflexive self-correction and the right to mutual contestation') (Forst 2007: 259).

The transformative stage allocates rights and duties to all the participants of a policy process, both the public institutions and the CSOs. Above all, it would oblige all actors to justify their own positions clearly with regard to the positions of the others. The public institutions, as the ultimate decision-takers, would have the duty of justifying both their positions and the final decision by transparent reason-giving of why Option A, instead of Option B, succeeded, or why a new Option C was created. Hereby, the epistemic quality of publicly made arguments ideally replaces the influential quality of secretly made claims. Evidently, stronger associations with more resources would be better able to pay more experts and thus come up with more elaborated justifications, but the reciprocity requirement of this stage forces all the participating actors to make their case in the light of the reasons of the others. Thus, the CSOs would also be obliged to engage in reciprocal justificatory processes, rather than simply ignoring the arguments of others and repeatedly making the same points all over again, as was the case in the REACH process. Thus, every actor has the duty to give reasons, but also has the right to receive reasons, thereby extending the requirement of responsiveness beyond the public institutions.

If implemented, this transformative stage would have significant consequences for both types of actors, public and private. It would be an attempt to limit the 'rent-seeking account of interest group activity' (Mansbridge, 1992: 496–7) by obliging all interests to consider their positions in a broader context. It would be a means of ending the secrecy of policy-making behind close doors in the ludicrous universe of expert committees, and would encourage dominant actors to contextualise their own interests. The obligation for justification might change the preferences of the participants, enrich the process with new information, generate innovative ideas, and enhance inclusiveness. Its publicity would be an important contribution to the strengthening of the capabilities of disadvantaged groups by offering them the opportunity to scandalise unequal treatment publicly.

Clearly, these reflections describe ideal situations. From a pragmatic perspective, the introduction of extensive reciprocal justification comes at the price of prolonging the decision-making processes. Certainly, there is a potential tension between the speed of decisions and their deliberative quality. But practical concerns are not viable reasons to stop thinking about democratic reform strategies. From a pragmatic perspective that seeks not to overload policy processes with too many reflexive loops, one could envisage a two-step online consultation model and some public events in between the two stages.

The first step would resemble the current practices of online consultations in which everybody would be given the opportunity to make their own case. In the second stage, the Commission would prepare key summaries of the main arguments (as it already does today), more clearly elaborate the key disagreements, respond to them, and would then ask everybody to react explicitly to these disagreements in new public statements. Finally, the European institutions would need to analyse these argumentative statements and would be required to place the final decision within this context. Together with the achievements of the reformist stage one, the model of deliberative participation thus conceived would achieve a practicable and significant democratic improvement of the EU's participatory regime.

Sceptics will, of course, immediately argue that this model is overly unrealistic and that it would bring about an insurmountable burden of bureaucracy. However, I argue that this not the case, and that the empirical analysis has revealed several starting points at which both the reformist and the transformative stages could be tied.

With regard to deliberative participation's reformist stage, the currently ongoing European Transparency Initiative would be a window of opportunity for a real reform of the EU's participatory regime. However, as I explained in some detail in Chapter 4, although the direction that the ETI will finally take is still unclear, it seems realistic to expect only a one-sided reform in which it is the interest groups and civil society organisations that will have to comply with more regulation. This would establish an important step forward, but it would also fall short of obliging the European institutions to upgrade their own practices substantially. It might, however, be the global level that will serve as trigger for substantial improvements within the administrative logic of the first stage. The Århus Convention on access to information, public participation in decision-making and access to justice in environmental matters, which was agreed to by the United Nations Economic Commission for Europe (UNECE), foresees access to information, public participation in decision-making, and justice in environmental matters – all of which, I believe, are very important for democratic participation in all policy areas. However, the EU is apparently divided about which way to go in its participatory regime, as the EU's 2005 ratification of a watered-down version shows (see Chapter 4).

For the model's second transformative sage, there are less concrete starting points for institutional innovation. However, in the context of the ETI, a Code of Conduct of Good Participation between the EU institutions and the participating organisations would seem to be achievable in order to introduce an appropriate, not overly ambitious, tool that could establish norms of arguing, reasoning and justification. The proposed Code of Conduct would not expect miracles from the subscribers and would be based upon the familiar sanctions of soft law, above all naming and shaming. Although there is no such code in sight in the near future, the European Commission recently began the practice of offering responses to on-line consultations on the IPM, in order to summarise the main arguments put forward and even to comment partly on its own positions in the light of these arguments, which shows that the Commission practices show cautious steps towards more public reflexivity.

Although the EU's current participatory regime is not coherently structured according to democratic requirements, some recent developments provide room for cautious optimism. As social scientists, we will need some patience in the coming years to observe whether, and, if so, to what extent, the intensive discourse on participation and democracy in Europe will leave the stage of rhetoric and enter the phase of realisation. Unfortunately, even the Reform Treaty of Lisbon does not boost such expectations. In its new Article 8, the mention of the principle of participatory democracy, as originally envisaged in the Constitutional Treaty, was deleted. In doing so, the EU has not grasped the opportunity to make itself, even in the (not only, but also) symbolic realm of constitutional language, more accessible to the peoples and their various participatory activities. However, since the wording of Article 8 has survived, by and large, unscathed, there might be some legal leverage for further developing a regulated model of deliberative participation in the EU.

## Notes

1  The EU's efforts to foster the construction of super-NGOs could, perhaps, be interpreted as an instance of the artifactual nature of encompassing organisations, as emphasised by Cohen and Rogers (1992; see also Chapter 2). If one were to follow this argumentation, then, the need for internal democratic legitimacy of such encompassing organisations would be growing.

2  Concerns that are not taken up by any CSO are, according to this view, in danger of being excluded altogether. However, the openness that is achieved by public justification, and the characterisation of political deliberation as an ongoing process which is punctuated by decision-taking moments (Lafont 2006), makes it likely that attentive observers will spot potentially missing relevant arguments and urge their consideration.

3  An exclusive focus on the epistemic quality of deliberative democracy would push the concept of participation too far aside, and would be in danger of resulting in empty proceduralism. However, the equal inclusion of CSOs that point to concrete problems and propose concrete solutions introduces a substantial element into the justificatory procedure. Evidently, this element evades the thick substantive concerns of, for instance, material equality and justice, but possesses, nevertheless, significant substantial content by being based upon the principle of equality.

4  Lafont continues that minorities are then willing to consent to a decision which they did not agree to if the decision-making process was deliberative in nature, i.e. if they had the opportunity to make their case but failed to convince the others.

5  Claus Offe argues that the Habermasian discourse ethics inherently entail a 'procedure of self-containment' (Offe 1989: 745).

6  This proposed procedural framework of deliberative participation also helps to overcome problems that one encounters by relating aspects of deliberative democracy with associative participation. Traditionally, deliberative democracy's emphasis on the changeability of preferences through deliberation is made at an individual level.

At the level of collective actors, where individuals are only delegates and/or representatives, the issue of changing preferences is much trickier. A delegate of an organisation is usually less free, if enabled at all, to change the position of his or her organisation if it becomes clear throughout a deliberation process that the original position is not viable in the light of other arguments. In such a situation, the deliberation process would have to be interrupted until each organisation newly adopted its position. This certainly important step could not, however, be endlessly repeated, otherwise a policy process would become extremely prolonged and ineffective. But, as I showed above, deliberative participation does not have to lead to consensus, and disagreement can remain. It does not require preference changes, but accommodates the practical problems of interacting collective actors.

7　For the power of NGOs to construct the identities of their constituency, see Hahn (2008).

8　Forst's right to justification entails 'ein qualifiziertes Vetorecht gegen all die Normen und Praktiken, die nicht allgemein-reziprok gerechtfertigt werden können, oder … gegen Normen, die mit reziproken allgemeinen Gründen zurückgewiesen werden können. Dies ist das basale moralische Recht von Personen, das in einem gegebenen Gerechtigkeitskontext substantielle Formen annimmt und zu institutionalisieren ist. Es bildet die Grundlage für eine Konzeption von Menschenrechten wie auch für die Rechtfertigung einer konkreten gesellschaftlichen Struktur' (Forst 2002: 225, cited in Meisterhans 2007: 18).

9　The picture of provisory institutions underlines the idea that there is no unique way of institutionalising democracy. Instead, political institutions should be understood as necessarily flawed attempts to approach a normative ideal. A prominent conception of this provisory idea is Dahl's notion of polyarchy. By using this term, Dahl recognises that political institutions fall short of the normative ideal without implying that they are normatively condemnable, for this reason. On the contrary, for Dahl, a polyarchy is 'one of the most extraordinary of all human artefacts' (see, i.a., Dahl 1989: 223) and 'a handy way of referring to a modern representative democracy with universal suffrage […] More precisely, a polyarchical democracy is a political system with … six democratic institutions' (Dahl 1998: 90), namely, elected representatives, free, fair and frequent elections, freedom of expression, alternative information, associational democracy, and inclusive citizenship.

# 7

# Concluding remarks

So far, I have focused on both the formal and the operational shape of the European Union's participatory regime, which I examined in the light of the evaluative insights gained from democratic theory reflections on the normative value of the participation of non-state collective actors. Following from this juxtaposition of normative insights and empirical results, I conceptualised a model of deliberative participation and proposed its institutionalisation in a regulated model of participatory governance. This final chapter seeks to extend this perspective by reflecting upon some of the wider implications of my findings.

In order to do so, let me briefly recall the scope of this study. With the help of Bernhard Peter's reminder that democracy 'is often used in two different senses' (2004a: 3), namely, referring either to democracy at large or to specific institutional contexts, the scope of this study was limited in order to focus on the political institutions that either hinder or facilitate political participation. However, this limited and more modest scope is clearly nested within the study's broader concern about the future of democracy in a globalising world, as was developed at the very beginning of this study. This concern was, ultimately, the driving force behind this research.

This concluding section shows that the second sense of democracy at large is inscribed into the specific findings of this study. I demonstrate this in the following (1) by starting from rather concrete considerations about both the promises and the limits of the proposed model of deliberative participation. Then, I argue (2) that my empirical observations suggest that the looming Third Transformation of Democracy should not only be understood as a repetition of the Second Transformation writ large as yet another spatial extension, but also that democratic practices are challenged by a qualitative change in globalising politics. Thus, I gradually extend my focus from the specific realm of this study towards (3) some thoughts about the future of democracy at large.

(1) In order to avoid any misunderstanding, it is important to stress that the proposed model of regulated deliberative participation neither claims to possess the capacity to solve all the democratic problems of EU policy-making, nor is it able to solve all the democratic problems that are related to

the participation of collective actors. Instead, it is the result of a research endeavour that has sought to identify the 'serious and systematic democratic deficits' (Fung 2006: 670) of the existing governance practices with the aim 'of devising appropriate institutional remedies' (ibid.). Standing alone, deliberative participation would not be able to bear the democratic burden of governance beyond the nation state. Instead, it should be perceived as an addendum to the democratisation of policy-making processes beyond the nation state by enhancing their participatory and deliberative character alike. It offers some theoretically founded guidance on the well-known institutional challenges of democratic governance, as succinctly summarised by Johan P. Olsen:

> How to make political leaders responsive to public opinion and avoid shallow populism? How to use neutral experts and secure professional integrity and avoid technocracy? How to secure the rule of law without excessive formalism? How to ensure that specifically affected interests are heard without giving privileges to strongly organized interests? (Olsen 2003: 94)

Deliberative participation should not be confused with democracy as such; it is a model that improves the equality of the participants of a policy process, that enhances public accountability by obliging public justification, and which speaks to the concept of self-determination by diminishing the dependence of participatory activities from their social and economical status. It claims to be a worthy attempt to strengthen participatory democracy by de-stabilising 'entrenched forms of authority – starting with, but not limited to, technocratic authority – in ways that may clear the way for an eventual reconstruction of democracy' (Sabel and Zeitlin 2006). Deliberative participation is thus about institutionalising the principle of mutual recognition and respect by means of introducing the obligation for reflexivity, without which no peaceful co-operation and democracy in complex and diverse societies would be possible.

Nevertheless, deliberative participation does not aim to rescue democracy at large, but remains within the modest scope of this research undertaking. Deliberative participation is not about decisions on the moral fibre or constitutional fundamentals of a political society, but tries to extend the application of deliberation 'to very concrete matters' (Fung and Wright 2003a: 15), such as chemicals regulation or family migration, and to (re-)integrate deliberation with the participatory practices of both individuals and associative actors (*ibid.*). Deliberative participation thus pursues a similar programme to that of the authors who developed a model of empowered participatory governance (Fung and Wright 2003b), namely, to follow 'real-world experiments' (Fung and Wright 2003a: 5) which aim to elucidate a re-design of democratic institutions in order to adapt them better to the contemporary challenges for democracy. It shares – with empowered participatory governance – the conviction that public institutions are a crucial part of democratic participatory governance, and that participatory processes should be organised non-voluntaristically, i.e. according to a rights-based approach (Fung and Wright 2003a: 22). But it also extends this approach, in that it proposes to institutionalise participatory governance in political contexts beyond the nation state in a way that is conducive to the democratisation of its policy processes.[1]

Deliberative participation is a project that subscribes to the view that 'the cure of the ills of democracy is more democracy' (Bohman 1995: 101). The implication that it does not strive to disavow other forms of democratic procedures, but, instead, to complement them, seems to be an important notion of caution in order to prevent any misunderstandings about the model. One should avoid overloading it with normative expectations which it cannot fulfil in the struggles of practical policy-making. Thus, some sort of safeguard about overloading deliberative participation seems advisable (similarly, Wolf 2000: 215). Above all, decision-rights should remain in the hands of the European institutions along the lines stipulated by its constitutional frame as laid down in the treaties. It is their responsibility to end the deliberative participatory process and to come to a decision, which is then, however, the result of a well-argued, transparent and thus accountable process in which many different positions and options are publicly laid on the table.

(2) The empirical observations about the participatory practices in EU policy-making point to the challenges for finding a straightforward institutional solution for improving participatory democracy. As the case studies suggest, the nature of postnational policy-making is characterised by a tremendous plurality of governmental and non-governmental agents and by a diffusion of the political onto multiple sites and arenas that are embedded in a complex multi-level structure. Postnational policy-making is situated in a hybrid institutional environment in which pluralisation and diffusion are virulent. Administrative bodies possess both executive and legislative functions, such as the European Commission, for example; there are, furthermore, strong remnants of diplomacy contained in intergovernmental structures; and the 'rise of the unelected' (Vibert 2007) technical agencies also play a role.[2] This hybrid context suggests that a Third Transformation of Democracy is, indeed, necessary, and that it is not simply a second transformation writ large. Clearly, there is a danger of losing sight of the people in the multiplicity of formal and informal networks between the multiple institutional centres if lobbying and consultation are all too easily glorified as democratic participation within these structures.

Altogether, if such an interpretation of the nature of postnational policy-making is accepted, it seems plausible that deliberative participation will avoid the problems of cosmopolitan visions that make a strong case for extending the political institutions of national democracies on to the global scale (see, amongst others Archibugi, Held and Köhler 1998; Held 1995). There is no a 'one size fits all' solution to the problem of transforming democracy, and there cannot be one. Democracy is an ideal, not a formula for institutional design. It is inclusive to different types of actors and practices, rather than exclusively focused on prescribed techniques, such as the electoral participation of individuals.

This means that one has to find practices for democratic participation that are realisable at different spatial levels of action, and that are sensitive for the new quality of postnational policy-making. This is precisely the aim of the proposed model of regulated deliberative participation. With regard to the spatial demands on democratic participation, against the background of my findings and such models as the empowered participatory governance (Fung and Wright 2003b), it seems reasonable to suggest that the lower the level, the more participation by individuals is possible. And, the other way round, the higher the spatial level, the more important the participation of collective actors becomes, if it is complemented with communicative rules of procedure along the lines sketched out above.

From this, it follows that modern politics, in order to be democratic, must actively seek to transform multi-level governance into multi-level participatory governance, and thus regulate participation according to the fundamental democratic requirement of equality. The course of this study has shown that it is no easy undertaking to rescue the participatory principle, and that it has to be re-interpreted as containing democratic legitimacy if it is to realise reciprocal justification. The key is to find procedures that seek to combine the participatory activities of the individual and as diverse as possible collective actors with the communicative demands of reciprocal justification, thereby grappling with the new quality of postnational policy-making.

Justification is a means of self-constraint in order to achieve non-domination in the hybrid context of globalising politics. Its institutionalisation has to strive for rules that are tailored for the weaker groups, in order to tackle asymmetries and hinder all too easy domination. More powerful groups possess the capacity for agency in a *laissez-faire* context, but less powerful groups do not. Thus, participatory procedures have to disadvantage the advantaged groups. Thus, it is not about directly interfering with the roots of the asymmetries – this is impossible both for EU institutions and at international level, and, even in strong national welfare states, inequalities remain – but it is important to determine the conditions in which self-constraints are institutionalised and domination discouraged by the publicity of justification. The public institutions are bound by requirements of non-domination until it comes to the final decision-taking moment. Here, we reach the limits of deliberative participation. Deliberative participation contributes to the democratisation of policy-processes by strengthening public, fair and reciprocal justificatory processes, but does not establish a new decision-taking method. For this, participatory governance based upon the model of a regulated deliberative participation has to be linked with other forms of democratically legitimate mechanisms.

The institutional setting of the EU offers some potential for improvements by a better realised separation of power (see among other things the confusion of the executive and legislative powers of the Commission, and the still incomplete supervisory role of the EP). The institutions of traditional government, or their supranational complements, delineate the boundaries of participatory governance – boundaries which are dynamic and constantly changing as the shift from a national centre to supranational, international, subnational and/or transnational levels and actors goes on. Deliberative participation is necessary to render participatory governance operational in a democratic manner, or, at least, in a way that aims at democratisation by increasing the performance of the four evaluative aspects that guided the empirical analysis. It not only re-conceptualises the state–society relationship within a postnational context, but also offers more space for societal self-organisation. What deliberative participation promises is to link, better and more equally, the wishes and needs of the people to concrete public policy-making.

(3) What, however, and hereby expanding the modest ambition of this study, are the consequences of the insights presented here for reflections on the future of democracy in a globalising world? I am not able to present, in this final section, a comprehensive vision of democracy, which I have deliberately avoided aiming at throughout this study. Nevertheless, I believe that there are some aspects that further research should take into account.

It is important to underline that this study – without claiming that it is the first to do so – tries to encourage political observers and commentators to overcome the idealisation of the modern nation state as the quasi-ideal institutionalisation of democracy. This adherence to the nation state is explainable, though, as a consequence of insecurity. We are insecure about the future course of global politics, whether it will be peaceful, stable and prosperous, or the opposite. This insecurity provokes us to look at the nation state's institutions through rose-coloured spectacles, forgetting much of the critique about their insufficiencies, their alleged diminishing steering capacities, etc. As I tried to show with the help of authors such as Robert Dahl, David Held and others, the lessons of history offer some grounds for turning the head optimistically away from the (now perceived) cosiness of the national past towards the uncertainties of a postnational future.

Since its emergence, the practices of democracy have undergone substantial transformations which, by the same token, also transform our key democratic concepts, such as self-determination or political equality. Nevertheless, democracy has survived as both an idea and as a political ideal that stimulates much thought, political action and conflict. These historical lessons can offer us some optimism about our ability to find ways to substantiate democracy even in a context of hybridisation and complexity. There is no 'one and only' procedure of how to create democracy; what is important, though, is to scrutinise constantly the existing institutions and practices with regard to their capacity to empower equally the expression of as many concerns as possible throughout all stages of policy-making processes. Regulated deliberative participation is an attempt to offer some guidance to such efforts by opening up the possibility of establishing structures of participatory and deliberative experimentalism.

In addition, and, perhaps, even more important than this, another effect of deliberative participation is particularly valuable for the survival and the strengthening of democracy. It is the widely spread perception of inevitability, of the absence of political options, of the determinacy through economic constraints that feeds into the source of much democratic scepticism, discontent and talk on the democratic deficits of the EU, not only of the systems of global governance, but also of nation states alike. Beyond the concrete proposals to alter, and the potentially practical implications in altering, policy-making practices, the obligation to public and reciprocal justification tackles this 'apprehension before a decline of the political' (Rosanvallon 2006: 218).

If implemented properly, the participatory dimension of deliberative participation offers a stable and durable institutional infrastructure for a widening of participatory activities, transforming the EU's talk about empowerment into practical opportunities. The justificatory dimension encourages a transformation of the political practices, potentially alters the habits of policy-makers, and thus brings the political and the civil spheres closer together. Public justification not only illuminates the dark chambers of lobbying, but also unmasks the invisible structures of the hybrid institutional environment which disguises the political roots of every (non-)decision. There is always an option to deviate, but one has to know about it. And knowledge about different political options and the origins of political decisions are at the roots of the people's trust in politics – and trust, in turn, is a condition for democracy and democratic participation to flourish. Here, the quotation by Woodrow Wilson, which I put at the very beginning of this book, becomes clear in its full meaning: 'Light is the only thing that can sweeten our political atmosphere', and deliberative participation is a contribution to this enterprise.

### Notes

1  Many attempts to consider practical institutional solutions for enhancing democracy beyond voting mechanisms remain in national contexts; see, for instance, Smith's (2005) compendium on 57 democratic innovations around the world. Similarly, discussions about forms of non-electoral representation also stress that deliberative

participation is essentially integrated into a system of existing representative institutions (Lafont 2006; Urbinati and Warren 2008), thereby essentially not moving beyond the Habermasian two-track model (see Chapter 2 above). Even where Urbinati and Warren do leave the national realm, their discussion of the representativity of NGOs at global level remains lofty and insufficiently institutionally contained, a critique which this book attempts to overcome.

2   Evidently, agencies did not play a role in the previously analysed cases, although it was also about the founding of a new (chemical) agency; however, see additionally Geradin and Petit (2004).

# *B*IBLIOGRAPHY

## Primary documents

Association of Downstream Users (COTANCE, EURATEX, INTERGRAF, ECMA, FPE, BLIC, CITPA, UEA, TIE) 2003, 'New European Chemicals Strategy', Brussels.

Christian Organisations (CARITAS Europa, CCME, COMECE, ICMC) 2000a, 'Position on EU Commission Proposal for a Council Directive on the right to family reunification' [COM (1999) 638 final], Brussels.

Christian Organisations (CARITAS Europa, CCME, COMECE, ICMC, JRS) 2000b, 'Position on the Amended EU Commission Proposal for a Council Directive on the right to family reunification', [COM (2000) 624 final], Brussels.

Christian Organisations (CARITAS Europa, CCME, COMECE, ICMC) 2002, 'Position on the Amended EU Commission Proposal for a Council Directive on the right to family reunification' [COM(2002) 225 final], Brussels.

CEFIC 1998, 'Letter to the Safety of Chemicals Committee', New Approach-Chemicals Management, Brussels.

CEFIC 2000, 'Chemicals Management 2000+ "Confidence in Chemicals". The view of the European Chemical Industry on future European chemicals policy', Brussels.

CEFIC 2001, 'Thought starter on REACH. An initial proposal for translating the REACH system into practice. A practicable decision making procedure for the implementation of the REACH system'.

Committee of the Regions 2002, 'Opinion of the Committee of the Regions on the "Amended Proposal for a Council Directive on the Right to Family Reunification"', *Official Journal of the European Union* (127), 16–19.

Coordeurop 2002, 5. 'Observations & commentary on the proposed Directive on Family Reunification', Brussels.

Council and European Parliament 1999, 'Directive 1999/45/EC of the European Parliament and of the Council of 31 May 1999 concerning the approximation of the laws, regulations and administrative provisions of the Member States relating to the classification, packaging and labelling of dangerous preparations'.

Council and European Parliament 2001, 'Regulation (EC) No. 1049/2001 of the European Parliament and of the Council of 30 May 2001 regarding public access to European Parliament, Council and Commission documents'.

Council and European Parliament 2001, 'Regulation (EC) No. 1049/2001 of the European Parliament and of the Council of 30 May 2001 regarding public access to European Parliament, Council and Commission documents'.

Council and European Parliament 2003a, 'Directive 2003/4/EC of the European Parliament and of the Council of 28 January 2003 on public access to environmental information and repealing Council Directive 90/313/EEC'.

Council and European Parliament 2003b, 'Directive 2003/35/EC of the European Parliament and of the Council of 26 May 2003 providing for public participation in respect of the drawing up of certain plans and programmes relating to the environment and amending with regard to public participation and access to justice'.

Council and European Parliament 2004, 'Council Directive 2004/38/EC of the European Parliament and of the Council of 28 April 2004 on the right of citizens of the Union and their family members to move and reside freely within the territory of the Member States.

Council and European Parliament 2006a, 'Regulation (EC) No. 1907/2006 of the European Parliament and of the Council of 18 December 2006 concerning the Registration, Evaluation, Authorisation and Restriction of Chemicals (REACH), establishing a European Chemicals Agency, amending Directive 1999/45/EC and repealing Council Regulation (EEC) No. 793/93 and Commission Regulation (EC) No. 1488/94 as well as Council Directive 76/769/EEC and Commission Directives 91/155/EEC, 93/67/EEC, 93/105/EC and 2000/21/EC'.

Council and European Parliament 2006b, 'Regulation 1367/2006/EC of the European Parliament and of the Council of 6th September 2006 concerning environment: access to information and justice, public participation, application of the Århus Convention'.

Council and European Parliament 2007, 'Regulation (EC) No. 614/2007 of the European Parliament and of the Council of 23 May 2007 concerning the Financial Instrument for the Environment (LIFE+)'.

Council 1968a, 'Regulation (EEC) No. 1612/68 of the Council of 15 October 1968 on freedom of movement for workers within the Community'.

Council 1968b, 'Council Directive 68/360/EEC of 15 October 1968 on the abolition of restrictions on movement and residence within the Community for workers of Member States and their families'.

Council 1979, 'Council Directive 79/831/EEC of 18 September 1979 amending for the sixth time Directive 67/548/EEC on the approximation of the laws, regulations and administrative provisions relating to the classification, packaging and labelling of dangerous substances'.

Council 1990, 'Council Directive 90/313/EEC of 7 June 1990 on the freedom of access to information on the environment'.

Council 1992, 'Council Regulation (EEC) No. 1973/92 of 21 May 1992 establishing a financial instrument for the environment (LIFE)'.

Council 1993, 'Council Decision 93/73/EC of 20 December 1993 on public access to Council documents'.

Council 1994, 'Council Directive 94/45/EC of 22 September 1994 on the establishment of a European Works Council or a procedure in Community-scale undertakings and Community-scale groups of undertakings for the purposes of informing and consulting employees'.

Council 1996, 'Council Directive 96/34/EC of 3 June 1996 on the framework agreement on parental leave concluded by UNICE, CEEP and the ETUC'.

Council 1997, 'Council Directive 97/81/EC of 15 December 1997 concerning the Framework Agreement on part-time work concluded by UNICE, CEEP and the ETUC – Annex: Framework agreement on part-time work'.

Council 1999, 'Council Directive 1999/70/EC of 28 June 1999 concerning the framework agreement on fixed-term work concluded by ETUC, UNICE and CEEP'.

Council 2000, 'Council Decision 2000/527/EC of 14 August 2000 amending Decision 93/731/EC on public access to Council documents and Council Decision 2000/23/EC on the improvement of information on the Council's legislative activities and the public register of Council documents'.

Council 2002, 'Council Regulation (EC, Euratom) No. 1605/2002 on the Financial Regulation applicable to the general budget of the European Communities'.

Council 2003, 'Council Directive 2003/86/EC of 22 September 2003 on the right to family reunification'.

Council 2005, 'Council Decision 2005/370/EC of 17 February 2005 on the conclusion, on behalf of the European Community, of the convention on access to information, public participation in decision-making and access to justice in environmental matters'.

Council 2006, 'Common position adopted by the Council with a view to the adoption of a Regulation of the European Parliament and of the Council concerning the Registration, Evaluation, Authorisation and Restriction of Chemicals (REACH), establishing a European Chemicals Agency, amending Directive 1999/45/EC of the European Parliament and of the Council and repealing Council Regulation (EEC) No. 793/93 and Commission Regulation (EC) No. 1488/94 as well as Council Directive 76/769/EEC and Commission Directives 91/155/EEC, 93/67/EEC, 93/105/EC and 2000/2 1/EC, 2003/0256 (COD)'.

ECRE 1999, 'Position on the integration of refugees in Europe', Brussels.

ECRE 2000, 'Position on refugee family reunification', Brussels.

ECRE, ENAR, MPG 1999, 'Guarding standards–shaping the agenda, analysis of the Treaty of Amsterdam and present EU policy on migration, asylum and anti-Discrimination', Brussels.

EEB 2001, 'EEB first comments to the White Paper on the future EU Chemicals Policy, input to the stakeholder conference on the chemicals White Paper', Brussels.

EEB 2003, 'EEB Position on Commission proposal for a regulation on REACH', Brussels.

EEB, Eurogroup for Animal Welfare, FoE, WWF 2001, 'A new EU chemicals policy – some key arguments', Brussels.

EEB, FoE, Greenpeace, WWF 2003, 'Act now for a safer future! A citizen's guide to responding to the Commission's consultation on a new chemicals policy', Brussels.

EEB, EEN, FoE, Greenpeace 2004a, 'Chemicals beyond control. Ensuring EU chemicals policy protects human health and the environment', Brussels.

EEB, EEN, FoE, Greenpeace 2004b, 'Letter to: environment, economy, industry and trade ministers of the European Union/Representations; CC: permanent representations', Brussels.

EMCEF 2001, 'Position paper of 2 April 2001'.

ENAR 2002, 'ENAR position paper, regarding the amended proposal for a Council Directive on the right to family reunion presented by the Commission, COM (2002) 22', Brussels.

ENAR, ILPA, MPG 2000, 'The Amsterdam Proposals or how to influence policy debates on asylum and immigration', Brussels.

European Commission 1992a, 'Communication on an open and structured dialogue between the Commission and special interest groups' (COM (1992) 2271 final).

European Commission 1992b, 'Communication on increased transparency in the work of the Commission' (SEC (1992) 2274 final).

European Commission 1993a, 'Public access to the institutions' documents. Communication to the Council, the Parliament and the Economic and Social Committee' (COM (1993) 191 final).

European Commission 1993b, 'Openness in the Community. Communication from the Commission to the Council and the Parliament and the Economic and Social Committee' (COM (1993) 258 final).

European Commission 1994, 'Commission decision 94/90/EC on access to information'.

European Commission 1997, 'Promoting the role of voluntary organisations and foundations in Europe. Communication from the Commission' (COM (1997) 241 final).

European Commission 1999, 'Proposal for a Council Directive on the right to family reunification' (COM (1999) 638 final).

European Commission 2000a, 'The Commission and non-governmental organisations: building a stronger partnership' (COM (2000) 11 final).

European Commission 2000b, 'Amended proposal for a Council directive on the right to family reunification' (COM (2000) 624 final).

European Commission 2000c, 'Communication from the Commission on the precautionary principle' (COM (2000) 1 final).

European Commission 2001a, 'European Governance. A White Paper' (COM (2001) 428 final).

European Commission 2001b, 'Communication from the Commission to the Council, the European Parliament, the Economic and Social Committee and the Committee of the Regions on certain legal aspects relating to cinematographic and other audiovisual works' (COM (2001) 428 final).

European Commission 2001c, 'Communication from the Commission to the Council and the European Parliament on an open method of coordination for the community immigration policy' (COM/2001/0387 final).

European Commission 2001d, 'White Paper – strategy for a future chemicals policy' (COM (2001) 88 final).

European Commission 2002a, 'Communication from the Commission towards a reinforced culture of consultation and dialogue – general principles and minimum standards for consultation of interested parties by the Commission' (COM (2002) 704 final).

European Commission 2002b, 'Commission Regulation (EC, Euratom) No. 2342/2002 laying down detailed rules for the implementation of Council Regulation (EC, Euratom) No. 1605/2002 on the Financial Regulation applicable to the general budget of the European Communities'.

European Commission 2002c, 'Amended proposal for a Council Directive on the right to family reunification' (COM (2002) 225 final).

European Commission 2003a, 'Proposal for a Directive of the European Parliament and of the Council on access to justice in environmental matters' (COM (2003) 624 final).

European Commission 2003b, Proposal for a Regulation of the European Parliament and of the Council concerning the Registration, Evaluation, Authorisation and Restriction of Chemicals (REACH), establishing a European Chemicals Agency and amending Directive 1999/45/EC and Regulation (EC) on persistent organic pollutants' (COM (2003) 644 final).

European Commission 2006a, 'Green Paper – European transparency initiative' (COM (2006) 194 final).

European Commission 2006b, 'Communication from the Commission to the European Parliament pursuant to the second subparagraph of Article 251(2) of the EC Treaty concerning the common position of the Council on the adoption of a Regulation of the European Parliament and of the Council concerning the Registration, Evaluation, Authorisation and Restriction of Chemicals' (COM (2006) 375 final).

European Commission 2007a, 'Green Paper on public access to documents held by institutions of the European Community – a review' (COM (2007) 185 final).

European Commission 2007b, 'Communication from the Commission – follow-up to the Green Paper 'european Transparency Initiative' (COM (2007) 127 final).

European Council 1992, 'Birmingham Declaration, annexed to the Presidency Conclusions of the European Council summit in Birmingham', 16 October 1992.

European Council 1999, 'Tampere European Council Presidency Conclusions', 15 and 16 October 1999.

European Council 2005, 'The Hague Programme: strengthening freedom, security and justice in the European Union' (OJ C 53/2005).

European Court of Justice 1996, 'Urteil des Gerichtshofes vom 30. April 1996. – Königreich der Niederlande gegen Rat der Europäischen Union. – Nichtigkeitsklage – Regelung über den Zugang der Öffentlichkeit zu Ratsdokumenten', (C-58/94).

European Court of Justice 2003a, 'Klage des Europäischen Parlaments gegen den Rat der Europäischen Union, eingereicht am 22. Dezember 2003' (C-540/03).

European Court of Justice 2003b, 'Urteil des Gerichts erster Instanz (Vierte Kammer) vom 9. April 2003. – Forum des migrants de l'Union européenne gegen Kommission der

Europäischen Gemeinschaften. – Finanzielle Unterstützung durch die Gemeinschaft – Verwaltungskosten – Entscheidung, die finanzielle Unterstützung zu beenden – Grundsatz der Wirtschaftlichkeit der Haushaltsführung – Auslegung der Bedingungen für die Unterstützung – Verteidigungsrechte – Vertrauensschutz' (T-217/01).

European Economic and Social Committee 1999, 'Stellungnahme des Wirtschafts- und Sozialausschusses zum Thema "Die Rolle und der Beitrag der organisierten Zivilgesellschaft zum europäischen Einigungswerk"', (OJ 1999/C 329/10).

European Ombudsman 2007, 'Speech by the European Ombudsman to the Civil Liberties Committee of the European Parliament' (29.11.2007).

European Parliament 1992, 'Proposals for the enlarged bureau with a view to laying down rules governing the representation of special interest groups at the European Parliament (the "Galle-Report")' (PE 200.405/final).

European Parliament 1997, 'European Parliament Decision 97/632/EC of 10 July 1997 on public access to European Parliament documents'.

European Parliament 2000, 'Report on the proposal for a Council directive on the right to family reunification' (COM (1999) 638 – C5-0077/2000 – 1999/0258(CNS)), Committee on Citizens' Freedoms and Rights, Justice and Home Affairs, Brussels.

European Parliament 2003, 'Report on the amended proposal for a Council directive on the right to family reunification' (COM (2002) 225 – C5-0220/2002 – 1999/0258 (CNS)), (renewed consultation), Committee on Citizens' Freedoms and Rights, Justice and Home Affairs, Brussels.

European Parliament 2005, 'Legislative resolution on the proposal for a regulation of the European Parliament and of the Council on the Registration, Evaluation, Authorisation and Restriction of Chemicals (REACH), establishing a European Chemicals Agency and amending Directive 1999/45/EC and Regulation (EC) No. …/… [on Persistent Organic Pollutants]' (COM (2003) 0644 – C5-0530/2003 – 2003/0256 (COD)).

Governance Team of the European Commission 2001, 'Report to the Commission on Consultations conducted for the preparation of the White Paper on Democratic European Governance' (SG/8533/01)

Greenpeace 1999, 'The way forward out of the chemicals crisis, an alternative, precautionary approach to the regulation of the manufacturing, marketing and use of chemicals in Europe', Brussels.

ILGA 2001, 'Position paper on the proposal for a Council Directive on the right to family reunification', Brussels.

Save the Children 2003, 'Separated children and EU asylum and immigration policy', Stockholm, PartnerPrint.

Sutherland 1992, 'The internal market after 1992 – meeting the challenge (Sutherland Report), Report to the EEC Commission by the High Level Group on the Operation of Internal Market', SEC (92) 2044.

UNHCR 2002, 'UNHCR's comments on the amended proposal of the European Commission for a council directive on the right to family reunification' (COM (2002) 225 final, 2 May 2002).

United Nations Economic Commission for Europe 1998, 'Convention on access to information, public participation in decision-making and access to justice in environmental matters' (Århus Convention).

WWF 2001, 'Elizabeth Salter Green, Director WWF European Toxics Programme. A stakeholders' conference on the Chemicals White Paper', 2 April 2001, Brussels.

## Academic Publications

Abromeit, H. 2002, *Wozu braucht man Demokratie?*, Leske & Budrich, Opladen.

Adamson, W.L. 1989, 'Convergences in Recent Democratic Theory', *Theory and Society*, vol. 18, no. 1, pp. 125–42.

Alegre, S., M. den Boer, G. Callovi, S. Peers and C. Pineda Polo 2005, *The Hague Programme. Strengthening Freedom, Security and Justice in the EU*, EPC Working Paper, no. 15, European Policy Centre, Brussels.

Alhadeff, G., S. Wilson and G. Forwood 2002, *European Civil Society Coming of Age*, Platform of European Social NGOs, Brussels.

Almond, G.A. 1991, 'Capitalism and Democracy', *Political Science and Politics*, vol. 24, no. 3, pp. 467–74.

Anheier, H., E. Priller and A. Zimmer 2000, 'Zur zivilgesellschaftlichen Dimension des Dritten Sektors', in H.-D. Klingemann and F. Neidhardt (eds), *Die Zukunft der Demokratie. Herausforderungen im Zeitalter der Globalisierung*, Edition Sigma, Berlin, pp. 71–98.

Archibugi, D., D. Held and M. Köhler (eds) 1998, *Re-imagining Political Community. Studies in Cosmopolitan Democracy*, Polity Press, Cambridge.

Armstrong, K.A. 2002, 'Rediscovering Civil Society: The European Union and the White Paper on Governance', *European Law Journal*, vol. 8, no. 1, pp. 102–32.

Bader, V. 2001a, 'Introduction', in P.Q. Hirst and V. Bader (eds), *Associative Democracy: The Real Third Way*, Frank Cass, London, Portland, pp. 1–14.

Bader, V. 2001b, 'Problems and Prospects of Associative Democracy: Cohen and Rogers Revisited', in P.Q. Hirst and V. Bader (eds), *Associative Democracy: The Real Third Way*, Frank Cass, London, Portland, pp. 31–70.

Bailey, M. and D. Braybrooke 2003, 'Robert A. Dahl's Philosophy of Democracy, Exhibited in his Essays', *Annual Review of Political Science*, vol. 6, pp. 99–118.

Barber, B. 2003, *Strong Democracy. Participatory Politics for a New Age*, 3rd edn, University of California Press, Berkeley, Los Angeles, London.

Baynes, K. 2002, 'A Critical Theory Perspective on Civil Society and the State', in N. Rosenblum and R.C. Post (eds), *Civil Society and Government*, Princeton University Press, Princeton, Oxford, pp. 123–45.

Beisheim, M. 2001, 'Demokratisierung einer klimapolitischen Global Governance durch NGOs? Chancen und Probleme des Legitimationspotentials von NGOs', in A. Brunnengräber, A. Klein and H. Walk (eds), *NGOs als Legitimationsressource: Zivilgesellschaftliche Partizipationsformen im Globalisierungsprozess*, Leske & Budrich, Opladen, pp. 115-36.

Bell, R.G. 2004, 'Further up the Learning Curve: NGOs from Transition to Brussels', *Environmental Politics*, vol. 13, no. 1, pp. 194–215.

Bellamy, R. and D. Castiglione 2003, 'Legitimizing the Euro-"polity" and its "Regime": The Normative Turn in EU Studies', *European Journal of Political Theory*, vol. 2, no. 1, pp. 7–34.

Benhabib, S. 1996a, 'Toward a Deliberative Model of Democratic Legitimacy', in S. Benhabib (ed.), *Democracy and Difference. Contesting the Boundaries of the Political*, Princeton University Press, Princeton, pp. 67–94.

Benhabib, S. (ed.) 1996b, *Democracy and Difference. Contesting the Boundaries of the Political*, Princeton University Press, Princeton.

Benhabib, S. 2004, *The Rights of Others: Aliens, Residents and Citizens*, Cambridge, Cambridge University Press.

Benhabib, S. 2007, 'Democratic Exclusions and Democratic Iterations: Delemmas of "Just Membership" and Prospects of Cosmopolitan Federalism', *European Journal of Political Theory* vol. 6, no. 4, pp. 445–62.

Bevir, M. 2006, 'Democratic Governance: Systems and Radical Perspectives', *Public Administration Review*, vol. 66, no. 3, pp. 426–36.

Bignami, F. 2003, *Three Generations of Participation Rights in European Administrative Proceedings*, Jean Monnet Working Paper 11/03, NYU School of Law, New York.

Birch, A.H. 1993, *The Concepts and Theories of Modern Democracy*, Routledge, London, New York.

Blühdorn, I. 2006, 'The Third Transformation of Democracy: The Post-Democratic Revolution and the Simulative Regeneration of Democratic Beliefs', *Paper presented at 'Postdemokratie'. Gemeinsame Tagung der Sektionen 'Politische Theorien und Ideengeschichte' und 'Staatslehre und Politische Verwaltung' in Verbindung mit dem Sonderforschungsbereich 597 'Staatlichkeit im Wandel'*, University of Bremen.

Blühdorn, I. 2007, 'The Participatory Revolution: New Social Movements and Civil Society', in K. Larres (ed.), *A Companion to Europe Since 1945*, Blackwell, London.

Boeles, P. 2001, 'Directive on Family Reunification: Are the Dilemmas Resolved?', *European Journal of Migration and Law*, vol. 3, no. 1, pp. 61–71.

Bogner, A., B. Littig and W. Menz (eds) 2002, *Das Experteninterview. Theorie, Methode, Anwendung*, Leske & Budrich, Opladen.

Bohman, J. 1995, 'The Democratic Minimum: Is Democracy a Means to Global Justice?', *Ethics & International Affairs*, vol. 19, no. 1, pp. 101–16.

Bouwen, P. 2002, 'A Comparative Study of Business Lobbying in the European Parliament, the European Commission and the Council of Ministers', MPIfG Discussion Paper 02/7, Max Planck Institute for the Study of Societies, Cologne.

Bouwen, P. 2007, 'Competing for Consultation: Civil Society and Conflict between the European Commission and the European Parliament', *West European Politics*, vol. 30, no. 2, pp. 265–84.

Brunkhorst, H. 2006, 'Die Legitimationskrise der Weltgesellschaft. Global Rule of Law, Global Constitutionalism und Weltstaatlichkeit', *Workshop 'Verfassung und Recht der Weltgesellschaft'*, University of Bremen, 8–9 December 2006.

Brunkhorst, H. 2007, 'Unbezähmbare Öffentlichkeit – Europa zwischen transnationaler Klassenherrschaft und egalitärer Konstitutionalisierung', *Leviathan*, vol. 35, no. 1, pp. 12–29.

Buchstein, H. and D. Jörke 2003, 'Das Unbehagen an der Demokratietheorie', *Leviathan*, vol. 35, no. 1, vol. 31, no. 4, pp. 470–95.

Butt Philip, A. 1985, *Pressure Groups in the European Community*, UACES Occasional Papers, no 3.

Carmel, E. 1999, 'Concepts, Context and Dicsourse in a Comparative Study', *International Journal of Social Research Methodology. Theory & Praxis*, vol. 2, no. 2, pp. 141–50.

Carter, A. and G. Stokes 2002, 'Introduction', in A. Carter and G. Stokes (eds), *Democratic Theory Today. Challenges for the 21st Century*, Polity Press, Cambridge, pp. 1–19.

Chabanet, D. 2007, 'The Regulation of Interest Groups in the European Union', paper presented to the *Connex Thematic Conference on Accountability*, Florence, 29–30 June 2007.

Chambers, S. 2003, 'Deliberative Democratic Theory', *Annual Review of Political Science*, vol. 6, pp. 307–26.

Chambers, S. and J. Kopstein 2001, 'Bad Civil Society', *Political Theory*, vol. 29, no. 6, pp. 837–65.

Christiano, T. 1996, *The Rule of the Many. Fundamental Issues in Democratic Theory*, Westview Press, Boulder.

Christiano, T. 2003, 'An Argument for Democratic Equality', in T. Christiano (ed.), *Philosophy & Democracy. An Anthology*, Oxford University Press, Oxford, pp. 39–67.

Chryssochoou, D.N. 2000, 'Meta-Theory and the Study of the European Union: Capturing the Normative Turn', *European Integration*, vol. 22, pp. 123–44.

Clays, P., C. Gobin, I. Smets and P. Winand (eds) 1998, *Pluralism, Lobbying and European Unity/Pluralism, Lobbyisme et Construction européenne*, European Interuniversity Press, Brussels.

Cohen, J. 1996, 'Procedure and Substance in Deliberative Democracy', in S. Benhabib (ed.), *Democracy and Difference. Contesting the Boundaries of the Political*, Princeton University Press, Princeton, pp. 95–119.

Cohen, J. and J. Rogers 1992, 'Secondary Associations and Democratic Governance', *Politics & Society*, vol. 20, no. 4, pp. 393–472.

Cohen, J. and J. Rogers 1994, 'Solidarity, Democracy, Association', in W. Streeck (ed.), *Staat und Verbände*, Westdeutscher Verlag, Opladen, pp. 136–59.

Cohen, J. and J. Rogers 2003, 'Power and Reason', in A. Fung and E.O. Wright (eds), *Deepening Democracy. Institutional Innovation in Empowered Participatory Governance*, Verso, London, New York, pp. 237–55.

Connolly, W.E. 1969a, 'The Challenge to Pluralist Theory', in W.E. Connolly (ed.), *The Bias of Pluralism*, Atherton Press, New York, pp. 3–34.

Connolly, W.E. (ed.) 1969b, *The Bias of Pluralism*, Atherton Press, New York.

Cram, L. 1997, *Policy-Making in the European Union: Conceptual Lenses and European Integration*, Routledge, London.

Crouch, C. 2004, *Post-Democracy*, Polity Press, Cambridge.

Crouch, C. 2006, 'Neo-corporatism and democracy', in C. Crouch and W. Streeck (eds), *The Diversity of Democracy. Corporatism, Social Order and Political Conflict*, Edward Elgar, Cheltenham, Northampton, MA, pp. 46–70.

Cullen, P.P. 2005, 'Revisiting the Civil Dialogue: EU NGOs, Ratification of the Constitutional Treaty and Participatory Democracy', paper presented to the *EUSA Biennial Conference*, Austin, Texas

Curtin, D.M. 1996, 'Betwixt and Between: Democracy and Transparency in the Governance of the European Union', in J.A. Winter, D.M. Curtin, A.E. Kellermann and B. De Witte (eds), *Reforming the Treaty of the European Union. The Legal Debate*, Kluwer Law International, The Hague, pp. 95-121.

Curtin, D.M. 2003, 'Private Interest Representation or Civil Society Deliberation? A Contemporary Dilemma for European Union Governance', *Social & Legal Studies*, vol. 12, no. 1, pp. 55–75.

Dahl, R.A. 1956, *A Preface to Democratic Theory*, Chicago, IL.

Dahl, R.A. 1966, 'Further Reflections on 'The Elitist Theory of Democracy'', *American Political Science Review*, vol. 60, no. 2, pp. 296–305.

Dahl, R.A. 1971, *Polyarchy. Participation and Opposition*, Yale University Press, New Haven, London.

Dahl, R.A. 1982, *Dilemmas of Pluralist Democracy. Autonomy vs. Control*, Yale University Press, New Haven, London.

Dahl, R.A. 1985, *A Preface to Economic Democracy*, Polity Press, Cambridge.

Dahl, R.A. 1989, *Democracy and its Critics*, Yale University Press, New Haven, London.

Dahl, R.A. 1991, 'A Rejoinder', *Journal of Politics*, vol. 53, no. 1, pp. 226–31.

Dahl, R.A. 1994, 'A Democratic Dilemma: System Effectiveness versus Citizen Participation', *Political Science Quarterly*, vol. 109, no. 1, pp. 23–34.

Dahl, R.A. 1998, *On Democracy*, Yale University Press, New Haven, London.

Davis, R.W. 1999, 'Public Access to Community Documents: A Fundamental Right?', *European Integration Online Papers (EIoP)*, vol. 3, no. 8.

De la Porte, C. and P. Nanz 2004, 'OMC – A Deliberative-Democratic Mode of Governance? The Cases of Employment and Pensions', *Journal of European Public Policy*, vol. 11, no. 2.

De la Porte, C. and P. Pochet 2005, 'Participation in the Open Method of Co-ordination. The Cases of Employment and Social Inclusion', in J. Zeitlin, P. Pochet and L.

Magnusson (eds), *The Open Method of Co-ordination. The European Employment and Social Inclusion Strategies*, P.I.E.–Peter Lang, Brussels, pp. 353–90.

De Schutter, O. 2002, 'Europe in Search of its Civil Society', *European Law Journal*, vol. 8, no. 2, pp. 198–217.

Deitelhoff, N. 2006, Überzeugung in der Politik. Grundzüge einer Diskurstheorie internationalen Regierens, Suhrkamp, Frankfurt a. M.

Downs, A. 1968, Ökonomische Theorie der Demokratie, Mohr, Tübingen.

Eichener, V. and H. Voelzkow 1994, 'Europäische Integration und verbandliche Interessenvermittlung. Ko-Evolution von politisch-administrativem System und Verbändelandschaft', in V. Eichener and H. Voelzkow (eds), *Europäische Integration und verbandliche Interessenvermittlung*, Metropolis-Verlag, Marburg, pp. 9–25.

EIRR 1991, *European Industrial Relations Review* no. 207.

EIRR 1994, *European Industrial Relations Review* no. 245.

Eising, R. and B. Kohler-Koch (eds) 2005, *Interessenpolitik in Europa*, Nomos, Baden-Baden.

Elster, J. 1998, 'Introduction', in J. Elster (ed.), *Deliberative Democracy*, Cambridge University Press, Cambridge, New York, pp. 1–18.

European Citizen Action Service 2004, *The Financial Relationship between NGOs and the European Commission*, ECAS, Brussels.

Falkner, G. 1996, 'European Works Councils and the Maastricht Social Agreement: Towards a New Policy Style?', *Journal of European Public Policy*, vol. 3, no. 2, pp. 192–208.

Falkner, G. 1998, *EU Social Policy in the 1990s. Towards a Corporatist Policy Community*, Routledge, London, New York.

Falkner, G. 2006, 'Collective Participation in the European Union: The "Euro Corporatism" Debate', in C. Crouch and W. Streeck (eds), *The Diversity of Democracy. Corporatism, Social Order and Political Conflict*, Edward Elgar, Cheltenham, Northampton, MA, pp. 223–42.

Farrelly, C. 2004, *An Introduction to Contemporary Political Theory*, Sage, London, Thousand Oaks, New Delhi.

Favell, A. 1998, 'Introduction', *Journal of Ethnic and Migration Studies*, vol. 24, no. 4, pp. 605-11.

Favell, A. and R. Hansen 2002, 'Markets Against Politics: Migration, EU Enlargement and the Idea of Europe', *Journal of Ethnic and Migration Studies*, vol. 28, no. 4, pp. 581–601.

Ferguson, J. 2003, *Improving Citizens' Access to Documents: ECAS Recommendations to the European Commission and Other Institutions*, ECAS, Brussels.

Fischer-Lescano, A. 2008, 'Transnationales Verwaltungsrecht. Privatverwaltungsrecht, Verbandsklage und Kollisionsrecht nach der Århus-Konvention', *Juristen Zeitung*, vol. 63, pp. 373–424.

Follesdal, A. and S. Hix 2006, 'Why There is a Democratic Deficit in the EU: A Response to Majone and Moravcsik', *Journal of Common Market Studies*, vol. 44, no. 3, pp. 533–62.

Forst, R. 2001, 'The Rule of Reasons. Three Models of Deliberative Democracy', *Ratio Juris*, vol. 14, no. 4, pp. 345–78.

Forst, R. 2002, 'Eine Theorie transnationaler Gerechtigkeit', in R. Schmücker and U. Steinvorth (eds), *Gerechtigkeit und Politik: Philosophische Perspektiven*, Akademie Verlag, Berlin, pp. 185–232.

Forst, R. 2007, *Das Recht auf Rechtfertigung. Elemente einer konstruktivistischen Theorie der Gerechtigkeit*, Suhrkamp, Frankfurt a. M.

Fraser, N. 1992, 'Rethinking the Public Sphere. A Contribution to the Critique of Actually Existing Democracy', in C. Calhoun (ed.), *Habermas and the Public Sphere*, MIT Press, Cambridge, MA, pp. 109–43.

Fraser, N. 2007, 'Die Transnationalisierung der Öffentlichkeit. Legitimität und Effektivität der öffentlichen Meinung in einer postwestfälischen Welt', in P. Niesen and B. Herborth (eds), *Anarchie der kommunikativen Freiheit. Jürgen Habemas und die Theorie der internationalen Politik*, Suhrkamp, Frankfurt a. M., pp. 224–53.

Freise, M. (ed.) 2008, *European Civil Society on the Road to Success?*, Nomos, Baden-Baden.

Friedrich, D. 2006, 'Policy Process, Governance and Democracy in the EU: The Case of the Open Method of Co-ordination on Social Inclusion in Germany', *Policy & Politics*, vol. 34, no. 2, pp. 367–83.

Friedrich, D. 2007, 'Democratic Aspiration Meets Political Reality: Participation of Organized Civil Society in Selected European Policy Processes', in J. Steffek, C. Kissling and P. Nanz (eds), *Civil Society Participation in European and Global Governance: A Cure for the Democratic Deficit?*, Palgrave, Basingstoke, pp. 141–65.

Friedrich, D. 2008, 'Actual and Potential Contributions of Civil Society Organisations to Democratic EU Governance', in M. Freise (ed.), *European Civil Society on the Road to Success?*, Nomos, Baden-Baden, pp. 67–86.

Friedrich, D. and P. Nanz 2007, 'Europe's Civil Society from a Normative-Democratic Point of View: The Case of the EU's Migration Policy', in C. Ruzza and V. Della Sala (eds), *Governance and Civil Society*, Manchester University Press, Manchester, pp. 113–33.

Fung, A. 2003, 'Associations and Democracy: Between Theories, Hopes and Realities', *Annual Review of Sociology*, vol. 29, pp. 515–39.

Fung, A. 2006, 'Democratizing the Policy Process', in M. Moran, M. Rein and R.E. Goodin (eds), *The Oxford Handbook of Public Policy*, Oxford University Press, Oxford, New York, pp. 669–85.

Fung, A. and E.O. Wright 2003a, 'Thinking about Empowered Participatory Governance', in A. Fung and E.O. Wright (eds), *Deepening Democracy. Institutional Innovation in Empowered Participatory Governance*, Verso, London, New York, pp. 3–42.

Fung, A. and E.O. Wright (eds) 2003b, *Deepening Democracy. Institutional Innovation in Empowered Participatory Governance*, Verso, London, New York.

Geddes, A. 1998, 'The Representation of "Migrants' interests" in the European Union', *Journal of Ethnic and Migration Studies*, vol. 24, no. 4, pp. 695–713.

Geddes, A. 2000, 'Lobbying for Migrant Inclusion in the European Union: New Opportunities for Transnational Advocacy?', *Journal of European Public Policy*, vol. 7, no. 4, pp. 632–49.

Geddes, A. 2003, *The Politics of Migration and Immigration in Europe*, Sage, London, Thousand Oaks, New Delhi.

Geradin, D. and N. Petit 2004, *The Development of Agencies at EU and National Levels: Conceptual Analysis and Proposals for Reform*, Jean Monnet Working Paper, no 01/04, New York.

Gerhards, J. 2002, 'Das Öffentlichkeitsdefizit der EU im Horizont normativer Öffentlichkeitstheorien', in H. Kaelble, M. Kirsch and A. Schmidt-Gernig (eds), *Transnationale Öffentlichkeiten und Identitäten im 20. Jahrhundert*, Campus, Frankfurt, New York, pp. 135–58.

Gerring, J. 2001, *Social Science Methodology: A Criterial Framework*, Cambridge University Press, Cambridge.

Gerring, J. 2004, 'What Is a Case Study and What Is It Good for?', *American Political Science Review*, vol. 98, no. 2, pp. 341–54.

Gerstenberg, O. 1997, *Bürgerrechte und deliberative Demokratie. Elemente einer pluralistischen Verfassungstheorie*, Suhrkamp, Frankfurt a. M.

Glaser, B.G. and A.L. Strauss 1980, *The Discovery of Grounded Theory. Strategies for Qualitative Research*, 11th edn, Aldine Publisher, New York.

Greenwood, J. 1997, *Representing Interests in the European Union*, MacMillan Press Ltd., Houndmills.

Greenwood, J. 2003, *Interest Representation in the European Union*, Palgrave, Houndmills.

Greenwood, J. 2007, 'Review Article: Organized Civil Society and Democratic Legitimacy in the European Union', *British Journal of Political Science*, vol. 37, no. 2, pp. 333–57.

Greenwood, J. and D. Halpin 2005, 'The Public Governance of Interest Groups in the European Union: Does Regulating Groups for "Representativeness" Strengthen Input Legitimacy?', *Paper prepared for the ECPR conference*, Budapest.

Greenwood, J., M. Knodt and C. Quittkat (eds) 2011, 'Territorial and Functional Interest Representation in EU-Governance', *Journal of European Integration*, Special Issue, Vol. 33 (2011).

Greven, M.T. 2005, 'The Informalization of Transnational Governance: A Threat to Democratic Government', in E. Grande and L.W. Pauly (eds), *Complex Sovereignty: Reconstituting Political Authority in the Twenty-first Century*, University of Toronto Press, Toronto, Buffalo, London, pp. 261–84.

Greven, M.T. 2007, 'Some Considerations on Participation in "Participatory Governance"', in B. Kohler-Koch and B. Rittberger (eds), *Debating the Democratic Legitimacy of the EU*, Rowman & Littlefield, Lanham, pp. 372–96.

Grote, J.R. and B. Gbikpi 2002, *Participatory Governance. Political and Societal Implications*, Leske & Budrich, Opladen.

Guild, E. 2004, The Legal Elements of European Identity. EU Citizenship and Migration Law, Kluwer Law International, The Hague.

Guiraudon, V. 1998, 'International Human Rights Norms and their incorporation: The Protection of Aliens in Europe', EUI Working Papers, 98/4, European University Institute.

Guiraudon, V. 2000, 'European Integration and Migration Policy: Vertical Policy-making as Venue Shopping', *Journal of Common Market Studies*, vol. 38, no. 2, pp. 251–71.

Guiraudon, V. 2001a, 'Seeking New Venues: The Europeanization of Migration-Related Policies', *Schweizerische Zeitschrift für Politikwissenschaft*, vol. 7, no. 3, pp. 100–6.

Guiraudon, V. 2001b, 'Weak Weapons of the Weak? Transnational Mobilization around Migration in the European Union', in D. Imig and S. Tarrow (eds), *Contentious Europeans. Protest and Politics in an Emerging Polity*, Rowman & Littlefield, Lanham, Boulder, New York, Oxford, pp. 163–83.

Guiraudon, V. 2003, 'The Constitution of a European Immigration Policy Domain: A Political Sociology Approach', *Journal of European Public Policy*, vol. 10, no. 2, pp. 263–82.

Habermas, J. 1992, *Faktizität und Geltung. Beiträge zur Diskurstheorie des Rechts und des demokratischen Rechtsstaats*, Suhrkamp, Frankfurt a. M.

Habermas, J. 1995, 'On the Internal Relation Between the Rule of Law and Democracy', *European Journal of Philosophy*, vol. 3, no. 1, pp. 12–20.

Habermas, J. 1996a, *Between Facts and Norms*, Polity Press, Cambridge, Malden.

Habermas, J. 1996b, 'Three Normative Models of Democracy', in S. Benhabib (ed.), *Democracy and Difference. Contesting the Boundaries of the Political*, Princeton University Press, Princeton, pp. 21–30.

Habermas, J. 1998, *Die postnationale Konstellation. Politische Essays*, Suhrkamp, Frankfurt a. M.

Habermas, J. 1999, *Die Einbeziehung des Anderen. Studien zur politischen Theorie*, Suhrkamp, Frankfurt a. M.

Habermas, J., L.V. Friedeburg, C. Oehler and F. Weltz 1961, *Student und Politik. Eine soziologische Untersuchung zum politischen Bewußtsein Frankfurter Studenten*, Hermann Luchterhand Verlag, Neuwied.

Hahn, K. 2008, 'NGOs' Power of Definition. Identity Production in Counter Human Trafficking Discourses and the Debates on the UN Protocol', PhD thesis, University of Bremen.

Hall, M. 1992, 'Behind the European Works Councils Directive: The European Commission's Legislative Strategy', *British Journal of Industrial Relations*, vol. 30, no. 4, pp. 547–67.

Hall, R.L. and A.V. Deardorff 2006, 'Lobbying as Legislative Subsidy', *American Political Science Review*, vol. 100, no. 1, pp. 69–84.

Hallo, R.E. 1997, *Public Access to Environmental Information*, European Environmental Agency.

Hallstrom, L.K. 2004, 'Eurocratising Enlargement? EU Elites and NGO Participation in European Environmental Policy', *Environmental Politics*, vol. 13, no. 1, pp. 175–93.

Hamilton, A., J. Madison and J. Jay 2003, *The Federalist with Letters of 'Brutus'*, Cambridge University Press, Cambridge, New York.

Hantrais, L. 2000, *Social Policy in the European Union*, 2nd edn, Macmillan, Houndmills.

Harden, I. 2002, *Openness and Data Protection in the European Union*, Queen's Papers on Europeanisation no. 9, Queen's University, Belfast.

Hardy, C., B. Harley and N. Phillips 2004, 'Discourse Analysis and Content Analysis: Two Solitudes?', *Qualitative Methods*, vol. 4, no. 1, pp. 19–22.

Hauptmann, E. 2001, 'Can Less Be More? Leftist Deliberative Democrats' Critique of Participatory Democracy', *Polity*, vol. 33, no. 3, pp. 397–421.

Heinelt, H. 2003, 'Participatory Governance and European Democracy. Bringing Empirical Evidence to a Theoretical Debate', *the conference on 'Debating the Democratic Legitimacy of the European Union'*, Mannheim University.

Heinelt, H., P. Getimis, G. Kafkalas, R. Smith and E. Swyngedouw (eds) 2002, *Participaptory Governance in Multi-Level Context. Concepts and Experience*, Leske & Budrich, Opladen.

Held, D. 1995, *Democracy and the Global Order. From the Modern State to Cosmopolitan Governance*, Polity Press, Cambridge.

Held, D. 2006, *Models of Democracy*, 3rd edn, Polity Press, Cambridge, Oxford.

Hendriks, C.M. 2006, 'Integrated Deliberation: Reconciling Civil Society's Dual Role in Deliberative Democracy', *Political Studies*, vol. 54, pp. 486–508.

Héritier, A. 1999, *Policy-Making and Diversity in Europe. Escape from the Deadlock*, Cambridge University Press, Cambridge.

Hey, C., K. Jacob and A. Volkery 2006, 'Better Regulation by New Governance Hybrids? Governance Models and the Reform of European Chemicals Policy', in F.-r. 02–2006 (ed.), FFU-report 02–2006, Environmental Policy Research Centre, Berlin.

Hildebrand, P.M. 2005, 'The European Community's Environmental Policy, 1957 to '1992': From Incidental Measures to an International Regime?', in A. Jordan (ed.), *Environmental Policy in the European Union*, Earthscan, London, Sterling, pp. 19–41.

Hilmer, J.D. 2010, 'The State of *Participatory* Democratic Theory', *New Political Science*, vol. 32, no. 1, pp. 43–63.

Hirst, P.Q. 1992, 'Comments on "Secondary Associations and Democratic Governance"', *Politics & Society*, vol. 20, no. 4, pp. 473–80.

Hirst, P.Q. 1994, *Associative Democracy. New Forms of Economic and Social Governance*, Polity Press, Cambridge.

Hirst, P.Q. and V. Bader (eds) 2001, *Associative Democracy: The Real Third Way*, Frank Cass, London, Portland.

Hitzel-Cassagnes, T. 2006, 'Demokratisches Recht ohne Staat?', *presentation at the Workshop 'Verfassung und Recht der Weltgesellschaft'*, University of Bremen, 8–9 December 2006.

Hix, S. 2005, *The Political System of the European Union*, Macmillan, Houndmills.

Hix, S., A.G. Noury and G. Roland 2007, *Democratic Politics in the European Parliament*, Cambridge University Press, Cambridge.

Howlett, M. and M. Ramesh 1995, *Studying Public Policy. Policy Cycles and Policy Subsystems*, Oxford University Press, Oxford, New York.

Hunold, C. 2005, 'Green Political Theory and the European Union: The Case for a Non-integrated Civil Society', *Environmental Politics*, vol. 14, no. 3, pp. 324–43.

Huster, S. 2008, *Europapolitik aus dem Ausschuss. Innenansichten des Ausschusswesens der EU*, VS Verlag für Sozialwissenschaften, Wiesbaden.

Huysmans, J. 2000, 'The European Union and the Securitization of Migration', *Journal of Common Market Studies*, vol. 38, no. 5, pp. 751–77.

ILR 1995, 'European Works Councils: Social Partners Anticipate a Directive', *International Labour Review*, vol. 134, no. 1, pp. 91–103.

Jachtenfuchs, M. 1997, 'Democracy and Governance in the European Union', *European Integration Online Papers (EIoP)*, vol. 1, no. 2.

Jensen, T. 2009, 'The Democratic Deficit of the European Union', *Living Reviews in Democracy*, vol. 1, no. 4.

Joerges, C. and J. Neyer 1997, 'From Intergovernmental Bargaining to Deliberative Political Processes: The Constitutionalisation of Comitology', *European Law Journal*, vol. 3, no. 3, pp. 272–99.

Johnson, A. 2005, *European Welfare States and Supranational Governance of Social Policy*, Palgrave Macmillan, Houndmills.

Jordan, A. 2005, 'Introduction: European Union Environmental Policy – Actors. Institutions and Policy Processes', in A. Jordan (ed.), *Environmental Policy in the European Union*, Earthscan, London, Sterling, pp. 1–18.

Kastoryano, R. 1998, *Transnational Participation an Citizenship: Immigrants in the European Union*, Centre d'Etudes et de Recherches Internationales, WPTC-98-12.

Kastoryano, R. 2003, 'Transnational Networks and Political Participation. The Place of Immigration in the European Union', in M. Berezin and M. Schain (eds), *Europe without Borders. Remapping Territory, Citizenship and Identity in a Transnational Age*, The Johns Hopkins University Press, Baltimore, London, pp. 64–85.

Kaufman, A.S. 1969a, 'Human Nature and Participatory Democracy', in W.E. Connolly (ed.), *The Bias of Pluralism*, Atherton Press, New York, pp. 178–200.

Kaufman, A.S. 1969b, 'Participatory Democracy: 10 Years Later', in W.E. Connolly (ed.), *The Bias of Pluralism*, Atherton Press, New York, pp. 201–12.

Keller, R. 2004, *Diskursforschung. Eine Einführung für SozialwissenschaftlerInnen*, VS Verlag für Sozialwissenschaften, Wiesbaden.

Kendall, J. and H. Anheier 1999, 'The Third Sector and the European Union Policy Process: an Initial Evaluation', *Journal of European Public Policy*, vol. 6, no. 2, pp. 283–307.

Kneip, S. 2006, 'Demokratieimmanente Grenzen der Verfassungsgerichtsbarkeit', in M. Becker and R. Zimmerling (eds), *Politik und Recht. PVS-Sonderheft 36*, VS Verlag für Sozialwissenschaften, Opladen, pp. 259–81.

Knodt, M. 2005, *Regieren im erweiterten europäischen Mehrebenensystem. Internationale Einbettung der EU in die WTO*, Nomos, Baden-Baden.

Knodt, M. and B. Finke (eds) 2005, *Europäische der Zivilgesellschaft: Konzepte, Akteure, Strategien*, VS Verlag für Sozialwissenschaften, Wiesbaden.

Kohler-Koch, B. 1992, *Interesen und Integration. die Rolle organisierter Interessen im westeuropäsichen Integrationsprozeß*, MZES Working Papers, AB III, No. 1, Mannheim Centre for European Social Research, Mannheim.

Kohler-Koch, B. 1997, 'Organized Interests in European Integration: The Evolution of a New Type of Governance?', in H. Wallace and A.R. Young (eds), *Participation and Policy-Making in the European Union*, Clarendon Press, Oxford, pp. 42–68.

Kohler-Koch, B. and B. Rittberger 2007a, 'Charting Crowded Territory: Debating the Democratic Legitimacy of the European Union', in B. Kohler-Koch and B. Rittberger (eds), *Debating the Democratic Legitimacy of the European Union*, Rowman & Littlefield, Lanham, Boulder, New York, Toronto, Plymouth, pp. 1–29.

Kohler-Koch, B. and B. Rittberger (eds) 2007b, *Debating the Democratic Legitimacy of the European Union*, Rowman & Littlefield, Lanham, Boulder, New York, Toronto, Plymouth.

Korpi, W. 1983, *The Democratic Class Struggle*, Routledge & Kegan Paul, London, Boston, Melbourne, Henley.

Kowalsky, W. 1999, *Europäische Sozialpolitik. Ausgangsbedingungen, Antriebskräfte und Entwickungspotentiale*, Leske & Budrich, Opladen.

Kratochwil, F. 2006, 'On Legitimacy', *International Relations*, vol. 20, no. 3, pp. 302–8.

Kuper, A. 2004, *Democracy Beyond Borders: Justice and Representation in Global Institutions*, Oxford University Press, Oxford.

Kuper, B.-O. 1997, 'Für ein soziales Europa. Die freie Wohlfahrtspflege und die europäische Einigung – die "Economie Sociale" als europäische Rechtsform', *Blätter der Wohlfahrtspflege – Deutsche Zeitschrift für Sozialarbeit*, vol. 7/8, pp. 157–59.

Lafont, C. 2006, 'Is the Ideal of a Deliberative Democracy Coherent?', in S. Besson, J.L. Martí and V. Seiler (eds), *Deliberative Democracy and its Discontents*, Ashgate, Aldershot, pp. 3–26.

Lahusen, C. 2004, 'Joining the Cocktail Circuit: Social Movement Organizations at the European Union', *Mobilization*, vol. 9, no. 1, pp. 55–71.

Leibfried, S. and P. Pierson (eds) 1998, *Standort Europa: Europäische Sozialpolitik*, Suhrkamp, Frankfurt a. M.

Leibfried, S. and M. Zürn (eds) 2006, *Transformationen des Staates?*, Suhrkamp, Frankfurt a. M.

Lenschow, A. 2005, 'Environmental Policy. Contending Dynamics of Policy Change', in H. Wallace, W. Wallace and M.A. Pollack (eds), *Policy-making in the European Union*, Oxford University Press, Oxford, pp. 305–27.

Lodge, M. 2001, *From Varieties of the Welfare State to Convergence of the Regulatory State? The 'Europeanisation' of Regulatory Transparency*, Queen's Papers on Europeanisation, no. 10, Queen's University, Belfast.

Lord, C. 2004, *A Democratic Audit of the European Union*, Palgrave, Houndmills.

Lowi, T. 1969, 'The Public Philosophy: Interest-Group Liberalism', in W.E. Connolly (ed.), *The Bias of Pluralism*, Atherton Press, New York, pp. 81–122.

Magnette, P. 2003, 'European Governance and Civic Participation: Beyond Elitist Citizenship?', *Political Studies*, vol. 51, pp. 144–60.

Majone, G. 1998, 'Europe's "Democratic Deficit": The Question of Standards', *European Law Journal*, vol. 4, no. 1, pp. 5–28.

Majone, G. 1999, 'The Regulatory State and its Legitimacy Problems', *West European Politics*, vol. 22, no. 1, pp. 1–24.

Manin, B. 1987, 'On Legitimacy and Political Deliberation', *Political Theory*, vol. 15, no. 3, pp. 338–68.

Manley, J.F. 1983, 'Neo-Pluralism: A Class Analysis of Pluralism I and Pluralism II', *American Political Science Review*, vol. 77, no. 2, pp. 368–83.

Mansbridge, J. 1992, 'A Deliberative Perspective on Neocorporatism', *Politics & Society*, vol. 20, no. 4, pp. 493–505.

Mansbridge, J. 1995, 'Does Participation Make Better Citizens?', *PEGS Conference*.

Mansbridge, J. 2003, 'Practice-Thought-Practice', in A. Fung and E.O. Wright (eds), *Deepening Democracy. Institutional Innovation in Empowered Participatory Governance*, Verso, London, New York, pp. 175–99.

Martens, K. 2002, 'Alte und neue Players – eine Begriffsbestimmung', in C. Frantz and A. Zimmer (eds), *Zivilgesellschaft international. Alte und neue NGOs*, Leske & Budrich, Opladen, pp. 25–50.

Mazey, S. and J. Richardson 2005, 'Environmental Groups and the European Community: Challenges and Opportunities', in A. Jordan (ed.), *Environmental Policy in the European*

*Union*, Earthscan, London, Sterling, pp. 106–21.

McCormick, J.P. 2007, *Weber, Habermas, and Transformations of the European State*, Cambridge University Press, Cambridge.

McGrew, A. 1997, 'Globalization and Territorial Democracy: An Introduction', in A. McGrew (ed.), *The Transformation of Democracy? Globalization and Territorial Democracy*, Polity Press, Open University Press, Cambridge, pp. 1–24.

Medding, P.Y. 1969, ''Elitist' Democracy: An Unsuccessful Critique of a Misunderstood Theory', *Journal of Politics*, vol. 31, no. 3, pp. 641–54.

Meisterhans, N. 2007, 'Eine weltbürgerliche Verfassung für die Weltgesellschaft? Zur herrschaftsbegründenden Konstitutionalisierung von Menschenrechten', PhD thesis, University of Bremen.

Middlemas, K. 1995, *Orchestrating Europe. The Informal Politics of the European Union 1973–95*, Fontana Press, London.

Migration Policy Group 2002, *Engaging Stakeholders in the Emerging EU debates on Migration*, Brussels.

Moravcsik, A. 2002, 'In Defence of the "Democratic Deficit": Reassessing Legitimacy in the European Union', *Journal of Common Market Studies*, vol. 40, no. 5, pp. 603–24.

Moravcsik, A. 2004, 'Is there a "Democratic Deficit" in World Politics? A Framework for Analysis', *Government and Opposition*, vol. 39, no. 2, pp. 336–63.

Moravcsik, A. 2008, 'The Myth of Europe's "Democratic Deficit"', *Intereconomics: Review of European Economic Policy*, vol. 43, no. 2, pp. 331–40.

Mutz, D. 2008, 'Is Deliberative Democracy a Falsifiable Theory?', *Annual Review of Political Science*, vol. 11, pp. 521–38.

Nanz, P. 2001, 'Europolis. Constitutional Patriotism beyond the Nation-State', PhD thesis, European University Institute, Florence.

Nanz, P. 2006, *Europolis. Constitutional Patriotism Beyond the Nation-State*, Manchester University Press, Manchester.

Nanz, P. and J. Steffek 2004, 'Global Governance, Participation and the Public Sphere', *Government and Opposition*, vol. 39, no. 2, pp. 314–35.

Nanz, P. and J. Steffek 2005, 'Assessing the Democratic Quality of Deliberation in International Governance – Criteria and Research Strategies', *Acta Politica*, vol. 40, no. 3, pp. 368–83.

Niesen, P. 2006, 'Deliberation ohne Demokratie? Zur Konstruktion von Legitimität jenseits des Nationalstaats', *paper presented at the workshop 'Staatlichkeit ohne Staat? Chancen und Aporien von Demokratie, Verfassung und Recht auf europäischer und globaler Ebene'*, 13–14 October 2006, University of Bremen.

Niessen, J. 2001, 'Overlapping Interests and Conflicting Agendas: The Knocking into Shape of EU Immigration Policies', *European Journal of Migration and Law*, vol. 3, no. 4, pp. 419–34.

Niessen, J. 2002, 'Consultations on Immigration Policies in the European Union', *European Journal of Migration and Law*, vol. 4, no. 1, pp. 79–83.

Niessen, J. and Y. Schibel (eds) 2005, *Immigration as a Labour Market Strategy – European and North American Perspectives*, Migration Policy Group, Brussels.

Nohlen, D. 2000, *Wahlrecht und Parteiensystem*, 3rd edn, Leske & Budrich, Opladen.

Öberg, U. 1998, 'Public Access to Documents After the Entry into Force of the Amsterdam Treaty: Much Ado About Nothing?', *European Integration Online Papers (EIoP)*, vol. 2, no. 8.

Obradovic, D. 2005, *Civil and the Social Dialogue in European Governance*, Integrated Project 'NewGov – New Modes of Governance', coordinated by the European University Institute, Florence.

Offe, C. 1989, 'Bindung, Fessel, Bremse. Die Unübersichtlichkeit von Selbstbeschränkungsformeln', in A. Honneth, T. McCarthy, C. Offe and A. Wellmer (eds), *Zwischenbetrachtungen. Im Prozeß der Aufklärung. Jürgen Habermas zum 60. Geburtstag*, Suhrkamp, Frankfurt a. M., pp. 739–74.

Offe, C. and U.K. Preuss 2006, 'The Problem of Legitimacy in the European Polity. Is Democratization the Answer?', Constitutional Webpapers no. 6, Mannheim.

Olsen, J.P. 2003, 'What is a Legitimate Role for Euro-citizens?', *Comparative European Politics*, vol. 1, no. 1, pp. 91–110.

Oostrom-Staples, H. 2007, 'The Family Reunficiation Directive: a Tool Preserving Member State Interest or Conducive to Family Unity?', in A. Baldaccini, E. Guild and H. Toner (eds), *Whose Freedom, Security and Justice? EU Immigration and Asylum Law and Policy*, Hart Publishing, Oxford, Portland, pp. 451–88.

Pateman, C. 1970, *Participation and Democratic Theory*, Cambridge University Press, Cambridge.

Pedersen, J. 2009, 'Habermas and the Political Sciences: The Relationship Between', *Philosophy of the Social Sciences*, vol. 39, no. 3, pp. 381–407.

Peers, S. 2002a, 'Key Legislative Developments on Migration in the European Union', *European Journal of Migration and Law*, vol. 4, no. 3, pp. 339–67.

Peers, S. 2002b, 'Key Legislative Developments on Migration in the European Union', *European Journal of Migration and Law*, vol. 4, no. 1, pp. 85–126.

Peers, S. 2003, 'Key Legislative Developments on Migration in the European Union', *European Journal of Migration and Law*, vol. 5, no. 3, pp. 387–410.

Peers, S. 2004, 'Key Legislative Developments on Migration in the European Union', *European Journal of Migration and Law*, vol. 6, no. 3, pp. 243–67.

Peers, S. 2005, 'Key Legislative Developments on Migration in the European Union', *European Journal of Migration and Law*, vol. 7, no. 1, pp. 87–115.

Pesendorfer, D. 2006, 'Environmental Policy Under Pressure: Chemicals Policy Change Between Antagonistic Goals?', *Environmental Politics*, vol. 15, no. 1, pp. 95–114.

Peters, B. 2003, 'Legitimität – einige Bemerkungen zur Begriffsklärung', unpublished manuscript, Bremen.

Peters, B. 2004a, 'Public Discourse, Democracy, Identity and Legitimacy in National and Supranational Political Systems: What are the Questions?', presentation at the InIIS Colloquium Bremen.

Peters, B. 2004b, 'Interest Groups and European Governance: A Normative Perspective', in A. Warntjen and A. Wonka (eds), *Governance in Europe. The Role of Interest Groups*, Nomos, Baden-Baden, pp. 57–65.

Peters, B. 2005, 'Public Discourse, Identity and the Problem of Democratic Legitimacy', in E.O. Eriksen (ed.), *Making the European Polity: Reflexive Integration in the EU*, Routledge, Oxford, pp. 84–123.

Peterson, J. 1995, 'Playing the Transparency Game: Consultation and Policy-making in the European Commission', *Public Administration*, vol. 73, no. 3, pp. 473–92.

Platform of European Social NGOs 2001, 'Democracy, Governance and European NGOs. Building a Stronger Structured Civil Dialogue', Brussels.

Platzer, H.-W. 1998, 'Industrial Relations and European Integration – Patterns, Dynamics and Limits of Transnationalisation', in H.-W. Platzer and L. Wolfgang (eds), *European Union – European Industrial Relations? Global Challenges, National Developments and Transnational Dynamics*, Routledge, London, pp. 81–117.

Pollack, M.A. 2005, 'Theorizing the European Union: International Organization, Domestic Polity, or Experiment in New Governance?', *Annual Review of Political Science*, no. 8, pp. 357–98.

Powell, B. 2004, 'The Chain of Responsiveness', *Journal of Democracy*, vol. 15, no. 4, pp. 91–105.

Reutter, W. 1991, *Korporatismustheorien. Kritik, Vergleich, Perspektiven*, P.I.E.–Peter Lang, Frankfurt, Bern, New York, Paris.

Richter, E. 1994, Die Expansion der Herrschaft. Eine demokratietheoretische Studie, Leske & Budrich, Opladen.

Rittberger, B. 2006, '"No Integration Without Representation!" European Integration, Parliamentary Democracy, and Two Forgotten Communities', *Journal of European Public Policy*, vol. 13, no. 8, pp. 1211–29.

Rodenhoff, V. 2002, 'The Aarhus Convention and its Implications for the "Institutions" of the European Community', *Review of European Community and International Environmental Law*, vol. 11, no. 3, pp. 343–57.

Ronge, V. and S. Körber 1994, 'Die Europäisierung der Chemikalienkontrolle und ihre Folgen für die Verbandspolitik – aus deutscher Sicht', in V. Eichener and H. Voelzkow (eds), *Europäische Integration und verbandliche Interessenvermittlung*, Metropolis-Verlag, Marburg, pp. 321–48.

Rosamond, B. 2000, *Theories of European Integration*, Macmillan, Basingstoke.

Rosanvallon, P. 2006, *Democracy Past and Future*, Columbia University Press, New York.

Rossteutscher, S. 2000, 'Associative Democracy – Fashionable Slogan or Constructive Innovation?', in M. Saward (ed.), *Democratic Innovation. Deliberation, Representation and Association*, Routledge, London, pp. 172–83.

Rossteutscher, S. (ed.) 2005, *Democracy and the Role of Associations. Political, Organizational, and Social Contexts*, Routledge, London, New York.

Ruffer, G.B. (n.d.), 'Pushing the Limits of 'Liberal Communitarization'? Fundamental Rights and the Social Integration of Migrants in the EU', unpublished manuscript, Northwestern University.

Rustemeyer, R. 1992, *Praktisch-Methodische Schritte der Inhaltsanalyse. Eine Einführung Am Beispiel der Analyse von Interviewtexten*, Aschenforff, Münster.

Ruzza, C. 2004, *Europe and Civil Society. Movement Coalitions and European Governance*, Manchester University Press, Manchester, New York.

Ruzza, C. and V. Della Sala (eds) 2007, *Governance and Civil Society*, Manchester University Press, Manchester.

Sabel, C.F. and J. Zeitlin 2006, 'Learning from Difference: The New Architecture of Experimentalist Governance in the European Union', *paper presented at the CONNEX Seminar on 'Democracy, Rule of Law, and Soft Modes of Governance in the EU'*, Roskilde University.

Saward, M. 1998, *The Terms of Democracy*, Polity Press, Cambridge, Oxford.

Saward, M. (ed.) 2000, *Democratic Innovation. Deliberation, Representation and Association*, Routledge, London.

Sbragia, A. 1998, 'Environmental Policy: The "Push-Pull" of Policy-Making', in H. Wallace and W. Wallace (eds), *Policy-Making in the European Union*, 3rd edn, Oxford University Press, Oxford, pp. 235–55.

Sbragia, A. 2000, 'Environmental Policy. Economic Constraints and External Pressures', in H. Wallace and W. Wallace (eds), *Policy-Making in the European Union*, Oxford University Press, Oxford, pp. 293–316.

Scaff, L.A. 1975, 'Two concepts of Political Participation', *The Western Political Quarterly*, vol. 28, no. 3, pp. 447–62.

Scharpf, F.W. 1970, *Demokratietheorie zwischen Utopie und Anpassung*, Konstanzer Universitätsreden, Konstanz.

Scharpf, F.W. 1999, *Regieren in Europa. Effektiv und demokratisch?*, Campus, Frankfurt, New York.

Scharpf, F.W. 2002, 'Conceptualizing Democratic Accountability Beyond the State: The European Union', *paper presented at the Miliband Conference on Global Governance and Public Accountability*, London School of Economics and Political Science, 17–18 May.

Schmidt, M.G. 2000, *Demokratietheorien*, Leske & Budrich, Opladen.

Schmitter, P.C. 1983, 'Democratic Theory and Neocorporatist Practice', *Social Research*, vol. 50, no. 4, pp. 885–928.

Schmitter, P.C. 2000, *How to Democratize the European Union ... And Why Bother?*, Rowman & Littlefield, Lanham, Boulder, New York, Oxford.

Schmitter, P.C. 2002, 'Participation in Governance Arrangements: Is There Any Reason to Expect It Will Achieve "Sustainable and Innovative Policies in a Multi-Level Context"?', in J.R. Grote and B. Gbikpi (eds), *Participatory Governance. Political and Societal Implications*, Leske & Budrich, Opladen, pp. 51–69.

Scholte, J. A. 2002, 'Civil Society and Democracy in Global Governance', *Global Governance* vol. 8, no. 3, pp. 281–304.

Schonfeld, W.R. 1975, 'The Meaning of Democratic Participation', *World Politics*, vol. 28, no. 1, pp. 134–58.

Schultze, R.-O. 2002, 'Partizipation', in D. Nohlen and R.-O. Schultze (eds), *Lexikon der Politikwissenschaft. Theorien, Methoden, Begriffe*, vol. 1, C.H. Beck, München, pp. 647–9.

Schumpeter, J.A. 1947, *Capitalism, Socialism, and Democracy*, 2nd edn, Harper, New York, London.

Sen, A. 1999, 'Democracy as a Universal Value', *Journal of Democracy*, vol. 10, no. 3, pp. 3–17.

Sifft, S., M. Brüggemann, K. Kleinen von Königslöw, B. Peters and A. Wimmel 2007, 'Segmented Europeanization: Exploring the Legitimacy of the European Union from a Public Discourse Perspective', *Journal of Common Market Studies*, vol. 45, no. 1, pp. 127–55.

Skinner, Q. 1973, 'The Empirical Theorists of Democracy and Their Critics. A Plague on Both Their Houses', *Political Theory*, vol. 1, no. 3, pp. 287–306.

Smismans, S. 2002, 'Civil Society', *European Institutional Discourses, Cahiers Européens de Sciences Po*, vol. 2002, no. 4, Paris.

Smismans, S. 2003, 'European Civil Society: Shaped by Discourses and Institutional Interests', *European Law Journal*, vol. 9, no. 4, pp. 482–504.

Smismans, S. 2004, *Law, Legitimacy, and European Governance. Functional Participation in Social Regulation*, Oxford University Press, Oxford.

Smismans, S. 2005a, 'Europäische Institutionen und Zivilgesellschaft. Diskurse und Interessen', in M. Knodt and B. Finke (eds), *Europäische Zivilgesellschaft. Konzepte, Akteure, Strategien*, VS Verlag für Sozialwissenschaften, Wiesbaden, pp. 105-28.

Smismans, S. 2005b, 'How to be Fundamental with Soft Procedures? The Open Method of Coordination and Fundamental Social Rights', in G. De Búrca and B. De Witte (eds), *Social Rights in Europe*, Oxford University Press, Oxford.

Smismans, S. 2005c, 'Reflexive Law in Support of Directly Deliberative Polyarchy: Reflexive-Deliberative Polyarchy as a Normative Frame for the Open Method of Coordination', in O. de Schutter and S. Deakin (eds), *Social Rights and Market Forces: Is the Open Coordination of Employment and Social Policies the Future of Social Europe?*, Bruylant, Brussels.

Smismans, S. (ed.) 2006, *Civil Society and Legitimate European Governance*, Edward Elgar, Northampton, MA.

Smith, G. 2005, *Power Beyond the Ballot. 57 Democratic Innovations from Around the World*, The POWER Inquiry, London.

Steenbergen, M.R., A. Bächtiger, M. Spörndl and J. Steiner 2003, 'Measuring Political Deliberation: A Discourse Quality Index', *Comparative European Politics*, vol. 1, no. 1, pp. 211–33.

Steffek, J. 2003, 'The Legitimation of International Governance: A Discourse Approach', *European Journal of International Relations*, vol. 9, no. 2, pp. 249–75.

Steffek, J. and C. Kissling 2007, 'Conclusion – CSOs and the Democratization of

International Governance: Prospects and Problems', in J. Steffek, C. Kissling and P. Nanz (eds), *Civil Society Participation in European and Global Governance: A Cure for the Democratic Deficit?*, Palgrave, Houndmills.

Steffek, J., C. Kissling and P. Nanz (eds) 2007, *Civil Society Participation in European and Global Governance: A Cure for the Democratic Deficit?*, Palgrave, Houndmills.

Stokes, G. 2002, 'Democracy and Citizenship', in A. Carter and G. Stokes (eds), *Democratic Theory Today. Challenges for the 21st Century*, Polity Press, Cambridge, pp. 23–51.

Streeck, W. 1997, 'Industrial Citizenship Under Regime Competition: The Case of the European Works Councils', *Journal of European Public Policy*, vol. 4, no. 4, pp. 643–64.

Streeck, W. 2006, 'The Study of Organized Interests: Before "The Century" and After', in C. Crouch and W. Streeck (eds), *The Diversity of Democracy. Corporatism, Social Order and Political Conflict*, Edward Elgar, Cheltenham, Northampton, MA, pp. 3–45.

Streeck, W. and P.C. Schmitter 1994, 'From National Corporatism To Transnational Pluralism', in V. Eichener and H. Voelzkow (eds), *Europäische Integration und verbandliche Interessenvermittlung*, Metropolis-Verlag, Marburg, pp. 181–216.

Tansey, O. 2007, 'Process Tracing and Elite Interviewing: A Case for Non-probability Sampling', *PS: Political Science & Politics*, vol. 40, no. 4, pp. 765–72.

Teorell, J. 2006, 'Political Participation and Three Theories of Democracy: A Research Inventory and Agenda', *European Journal of Political Research*, no. 45, pp. 787–810.

Thompson, D. 2008, 'Deliberative Democratic Theory and Empirical Political Science', *Annual Review of Political Science*, vol. 11, pp. 497–520.

Urbinati, N. and M.E. Warren 2008, 'The Concept of Representation in Contemporary Democratic Theory', *Annual Review of Political Science*, vol. 11, pp. 387–412.

Verhoeven, A. 2000, 'The Right of Information: A Fundamental Right?', *lecture at EIPA (Maastricht), May 29, 2000*.

Vibert, F. 2007, *The Rise of the Unelected. Democracy and the New Separation of Powers*, Cambridge University Press, Cambridge.

Vitale, D. 2006, 'Between Deliberative and Participatory Democracy. A Contribution on Habermas', *Philosophy & Social Criticism*, vol. 32, no. 6, pp. 739–66.

Wallace, H. 2000, 'The Institutional Setting. Five Variations on a Theme', in H. Wallace and W. Wallace (eds), *Policy-Making in the European Union*, 4th edn, Oxford University Press, Oxford, pp. 3–37.

Wallace, H. and A.R. Young 1997, *Participation and Policy-Making in the European Union*, Clarendon Press, Oxford.

Warren, M.E. 2001, *Democracy and Association*, Princeton University Press, Princeton, Oxford.

Warren, M.E. 2002, 'What Can Democratic Participation Mean Today?', *Political Theory*, vol. 30, no. 5, pp. 677–701.

Wilson, F.L. 1983, 'Review: Interest Groups and Politics in Western Europe: The Neo-Corporatist Approach', *Comparative Politics*, vol. 16, no. 1, pp. 105–23.

Wolf, K.D. 2000, *Die Neue Staatsräson – Zwischenstaatliche Kooperation als Demokratieproblem der Weltgesellschaft*, Nomos, Baden-Baden.

Young, I.M. 2000, *Inclusion and Democracy*, Oxford University Press, Oxford, New York.

Zürn, M. 1998, *Regieren jenseits des Nationalstaates. Globalisierung und Denationalisierung als Chance*, Suhrkamp, Frankfurt a. M.

Zürn, M. 2000, 'Democratic Governance Beyond the Nation-State: The EU and Other International Institutions', *European Journal of International Relations*, vol. 6, no. 2, pp. 183–221.

Zürn, M. and J.T. Checkel 2005, 'Getting Socialized to Build Bridges: Constructivism and Rationalism, Europe and the Nation-State', *International Organization*, vol. 59, pp. 1045–79.